Acclaim for *INCOGNITO: An American Odyssey of Race and Self-Discovery*

2011 Finalist in the autobiography category for
The Next Generation Indie Book Awards

"Yours is such a riveting story that speaks to identity, family, the complexity of the racial divide, and the struggle to find a home in two cultures. Thank you for sharing it with us."
—*Sister Anita Baird, DHM, Archdiocese of Chicago, Office of Racial Justice*

"Incognito is the ultimate American story...this is one of those books that simply had to be written."
—*Dr. Larry Ross, Professor of Anthropology, Lincoln University*

"This is a book that will have people of all backgrounds talking for some time."
—*Cyrus Webb, Conversations Book Club Online*

"This stunning memoir will ask the reader to seriously reconsider the meaning of ethnic identity." —*Amazon.com top 50 reviewer*

"Having had the pleasure of enjoying Michael's play here at Elmhurst College, we were prepared for something special but the book exceeded our own high expectations. Michael writes with exactly the same passion that he performs with. The reader lives through the experience and emotionally participates in this stunning series of events."
—*Tony & Helga Noice, PhD's & Professors of Theater & Psychology, Elmhurst College*

Acclaim for Michael Fosberg's one-man play, *Incognito*

"Incognito has much to say about ethnic identity, the significance of race and ultimately what it means to be an American in the 21st century." —*Kansas City Star*

"Fosberg takes us on a fascinating journey of self-discovery... a profoundly American story." —*Chicago Sun-Times*

"A fascinating and gripping story!" —*NBC News Chicago*

"A marvelous piece of work!" —*NPR*

"Fosberg's justly acclaimed show is one of those rare solo pieces that manage to combine a sense of personal revelation with a palpable universal appeal." —*Chicago Tribune*

"Fosberg has clearly thought a lot about American life and his piece is full of insights about how we construct our personal identities and how, in an instant, one's sense of self can be altered forever. The fact that it is also, at times, hilarious, is just gravy." —*The Daily Herald*

"An extraordinary tale of race, identity, and family... a family journey through our nation's past and present." —*The Windy City Times*

"His journey becomes our journey, his astonishment at his lost heritage, ours." —*Chicago Reader*

"The story grabs hold and won't let go." —*Pioneer Press*

"We never know he's grabbed us till we weep." —*Daily Freeman, Woodstock, NY*

incognito

incognito

An American Odyssey of Race and Self-Discovery

MICHAEL SIDNEY FOSBERG

Incognito, Inc.

CHICAGO

Published by Incognito, Inc., Chicago, Illinois
(312) 563-1326
www.incognitotheplay.com

First edition published in 2011, second 2014, third 2018

Book and cover design by Tom Greensfelder
Illustrations by Lora Fosberg

ISBN: 978-0-615-41396-9
Printed in the United States of America

CONTENTS

I no longer want to be anything except what who I am. Who what am I? My answer: I am the sum total of everything that went before me, of all I have been seen done, of everything done-to-me. I am everyone everything whose being-in-the-world affected was affected by mine. I am anything that happens after I've gone which would not have happened if I had not come.

—Salman Rushdie, *Midnight's Children*

PACIFIC COAST HIGHWAY

Where the hell am I? Just a few minutes ago I was cruising north on Highway 1, the majestic shores of the Pacific Ocean on my left, the sun pouring through the sunroof, a mix of salty ocean smells and the musty odor of seaweed. As my truck hugged the coastal curves of one of the nation's most fabled roads, the vista of rolling green hills to the east contrasted sharply with dramatic jagged cliffs reaching down to the shoreline on the west.

I had left Los Angeles at 7:00 that morning, bound first for Berkeley and a visit with old friends. It was Friday, June 13, 1996. Maybe not an auspicious day to start, but something, some deep urging, propelled me forward on this journey anyway. I'd spent the past few weeks packing my belongings into a ten-by-ten-foot storage space, this precipitated by the announcement of my struggling actress fiancée that she wanted to put a hold on our wedding plans while she had a chance to "find her truth." The truth turned out to be that my wallet wasn't big enough for the Prada purse she had secretly charged to my credit card. Reeling from the sticker shock of a twelve-hundred-dollar handbag, I could hardly collect my thoughts, let alone her debt, before she was gone. So "my truth" was that she'd left, and I'd spent a small fortune vainly trying to keep her happy.

My therapist reminded me of the Chinese definition of crisis:

danger meets opportunity. My best friend countered with, "Hey, pal, she did you a big favor!" At least the "it could have been worse" cliché never sounded better. Once I got over the initial shock, I packed up the house, placed everything in storage and, on approaching the bewitching age of forty, I decided it was time for my long-delayed trip.

In theory, it was a great plan. In the days leading up to departure, I spoke of my journey with growing enthusiasm, hoping to convince myself of its importance, taking pleasure in the envious response it elicited in others. I sensed a longing in their eyes, a secret desire to see the country, but they were tethered by their own commitments and responsibilities. I, on the other hand, soon to turn 40, was free to roam, to explore, to adventure. And I was scared.

You see, I wasn't heading cross country simply to rejuvenate a broken heart. My mission was to drive West Coast to East Coast, stopping along the way to talk with each member of my family, to try to recapture a past I'd never known, a past shrouded in mystery. But here I was, navigating a construction detour off Highway 1 somewhere north of San Simeon and the Hearst Castle and now completely turned around, not knowing which way I was headed or how to get back to the main road. Lost trying to find myself. How appropriate.

Six years earlier I had embarked on the larger quest of which this cross-country trip was a part. That larger journey began some years earlier when I decided to search for a long-lost family member, my biological father. I had been raised by my mother and from the age of five, an adoptive father. The mysterious man who was my biological father was never spoken of, referred to, or acknowledged in any way. There were no pictures I knew of nor recollections on my part. He had disappeared suddenly from my life when I was only two years old. My mother had divorced him and remarried an old high school friend, and the biological father I had no memory of remained a mystery for all these years.

Who was he? Where could I find him? What did it matter, considering I was raised by my mother and a man I grew up calling "Dad," however uncomfortable the relationship had sometimes been? And why did I feel so strongly that someone who disappeared so long ago would be of any relevance to my situation today?

These were questions I was still asking myself six years later as I sped along what I thought would be a marked detour, anxiously trying to regain my bearings. With a road atlas crammed in my lap under the steering wheel, maps spread about the passenger seat, stereo blaring, I groped my way across the California terrain. I was always that guy people asked for directions, the traveler with great instincts. Yet with maps, directions, detour signs, a fiancée disappearing, a "new" father emerging, and few answers at my disposal, I was still lost attempting to find my way. There was something much deeper inside me indicating that this was not going to be a simple drive across the map, a rejuvenation of a broken heart, or a simple uncovering of a biological father. This would become a journey that would not only transform my sense of self but open a chapter on a deeply troubled American history of which I had barely scratched its surface.

THE VALLEY

Six years before I set off on my road trip odyssey, I had found myself living in a two-bedroom ranch-style home nestled among the foothills of the sun-baked, smog-filled San Fernando Valley. Tujunga is a small biker town just forty minutes from Hollywood when there's no traffic. It's known for being the home of both the Hells Angels and crank, a version of crack cocaine that had been spreading like wildfire in remote desert towns. If you had spent any time there, you'd immediately understand why. The main drag was littered with the finest in fast-food franchises scattered among mini malls featuring donut shops, auto supply stores, and beauty parlors with names like Magic Nails and Hair Affair. The Beverly Hills of what's dismissed as poor white trash.

I didn't go there for the waters or the scenery, I wasn't into crank, I've never been terribly fond of fast food or nail salons, and it certainly couldn't have been the Hells Angels. It was a woman that was the draw, which for me is always the more complicated position.

Jackie was a strange combination of Valley girl, sports enthusiast, biker chick wannabe, and office manager for an entertainment firm. We lived the Valley life along with her five-year-old daughter and coveted BMW sports car. I was splitting my time between being a miserable novice house painter and a struggling "under-five" actor, a soap opera

A humbling three-line acting part opposite Mark Harmon and Meg Ryan.

term for an actor who is more than an extra but has less than five lines of dialogue. It was a humbling position for someone with four years of training at a professional theater school and a strong acting background, a situation for which even the best theater schools could not prepare an actor. The old adage that there are no small parts, only small actors takes on a completely different meaning in Hollywood.

So there I was, trying to eke out a living, riding out what I thought should be my dreams: the house, the blonde, the kid, the car, the actor's life, the sunny skies. Never mind that the Valley, as it is simply and affectionately called, had the same significance in some circles as banishment to Siberia did to the Russian elite. The desolate feel of its former incarnation as a desert could not be masked by the glitz of strip malls, parched desert golf courses, and million-dollar stucco homes owned by nondescript television celebrities known for their ability to smile on cue.

As I sat gazing out over the smog-filled landscape one unemployed morning, pondering whether I could bear the 100 degree heat to chase a little white ball around a sun-singed course, my sister called. Lora Beth, or B, as we nicknamed her, was twenty-four and doing the struggling artist thing in the Windy City. Her doll-like voice peeped across the line.

"Are you sitting down?" She sounded upset, agitated.

"Yes," I assured her.

"Mom and Dad are getting a divorce," she announced with all the fanfare of an undertaker.

"What?"

"She's leaving him. She told me today."

"Leaving him? Maybe they just had an argument or something." But I had never seen or heard them argue. Nor had I ever seen them kiss, hug, exhibit affection, or, God forbid, expose any flesh. "Maybe Dad forgot their anniversary or—"

"Nope. I'm tellin' you, Mom decided she's over it."

"Over it?" Christ, what did that mean? "They've been married for more than twenty-five years. It can't be that simple."

"She won't say; she's not talking..." Her voice trailed off. Neither of us knew what to say either. For all our closeness, we wound up speechless. There were nine years and a few thousand miles between us, but at this moment we seemed light-years apart.

Three weeks later, I found myself in the drenching humidity of a Chicago summer, in the heat of family chaos, with little discussion of anything, let alone mention of the impending breakup. I had planned this visit a few months earlier, and it was just my luck that it happened to fall in the middle of a family crisis.

I waited patiently for either of my parents to approach the topic with me.

"Oh, Mikey, it's great to have you home, honey."

"Good to be home, Mom. How's everything?" I hoped tactfully to open the door to the topic despite my dread of discussing it.

"Everything's fine, honey. The house has really shaped up since you were last here," she said, referring to the dream home they had recently built for themselves in the swanky Chicago suburb of Lake Forest.

"I can see that. Very nice—"

I was about to press further but was overcome by a feeling of fear at broaching the topic. What was I so afraid of? I told myself I would be content to wait for them to bring up the subject. I was still waiting a week later, though my discontent had been boiling.

Just hours before I was to return to California, I found myself being driven by my mother through the streets of Waukegan, where I'd grown up. The faint smell of industrial waste from Lake Michigan's largest polluter filled the still air. We passed by the old park where I'd first learned to play tennis, the high school I attended, which looked like a World War II ammunition factory that had seen better days, the record store and head shop, Strawberry Fields, in which I'd had my first "magical mystery tour," and just down the street the crusty VFW hall where I smoked opium as a teenager at a rock 'n roll concert featuring a band called Hot Mama Silver and got so high that I couldn't find my way home. We drove by each of these landmarks in silence. I gazed out the window, recalling episodes from my childhood, while my mother drove us cautiously toward their home-soon-to-be-gone in Lake Forest, the 'burb of the 'burbs.

"Are you all right?" my mother finally inquired.

"Yes," I lied.

We passed one modern suburban home after another covered in aluminum siding made to look like wood, with their multi-car garages and manicured lawns sprinkled with occasional kids' toys. I checked my watch. It was just two hours before we had to leave for the airport. We pulled into the driveway, drove into the garage, and walked into the house as we had sat in the car, silent. I finally burst.

"So, Mom, what's this I hear about you and Dad getting a divorce?"

Stunned, she tried to reply, "I... I've... I've been meaning to talk to you about that..."

"When exactly did you think you'd be talking to me about it, on my way to the airport?"

"Well, honey, I don't know. There's really not much to say."

"Not much to say? I come all the way from California, spend a week with you, and on my last hour here you finally get around to talking, if you can call it that, and then you tell me, 'There isn't much to say!' What the fuck is that?"

I was losing control but felt there was no going back.

"Now, don't use that kind of language."

"This is exactly what's wrong with this family—we never talk."

"Nonsense."

"Nonsense? Then why is it that nobody seems to know what's going on?"

"That's not true!"

"Not true? That's bullshit."

"Don't talk to me that way."

"Fuck you, Mom! I can't believe you'd treat us this way."

"You don't talk to me like that. I'm your mother."

"Fuck you! I'll take a cab to the airport," I screamed as I bolted for the door.

I slammed the door behind me, the sun hitting my face as my feet hit the pavement. I sat down on the warm grass out front, numb and reeling. I was in shock over what I'd said and the way I'd spoken to my mother. But even more, I was deeply troubled by my own inability to speak the truth, to ask the questions that really needed answering.

Here I was, a grown man of thirty-three, shaking with anger as I sat on the lawn in front of the dream-turned-nightmare mega-home my parents had just built. There wasn't even a bedroom included for me. I'd been away at college when it was planned, my mother had said. The two large bedrooms upstairs had been built for my siblings as they navigated through high school, then into college.

I sat on the grass, feeling completely out of place in this environment. I had no connections here. No friends. No history. The house next door seemed bigger and more flawless than ours, the one next to that an even bigger monstrosity. Birds chirped, lawns were picture perfect, gardens bloomed unblemished; suburbia at its finest. But it wasn't my home.

I remember four different places we lived in over the course of my Waukegan childhood, but it's the last of these, where we moved when I was nine, that I always thought of as home. It was a funky brick duplex on the corner of Pacific Avenue and Hickory Street, and the first home my parents owned, or rather the bank did. We rented the other side of the duplex to a quiet family with a daughter my age. We didn't see much of them, though—it was if they didn't exist. Our house, quite modest by American standards, I later realized, seemed huge compared to our two previous places. There was a massive old oak tree out front, which made for more chores each fall when the leaves fell. But it also became a great source of entertainment, as my friends and I spent hours leaping into the enormous piles of leaves we made. In the house, the stuffy, dark, and sometimes dank unfinished basement was a constant source of fear

Our house on Pacific Avenue.

to my young mind. I can't remember a time I wasn't scared going down those echoing wooden stairs, whether it was to play—certainly not the "treat" it was meant to be—or to grab a board game from an old chest of drawers squeezed into a dark, musty corner. I'd turn on all the bare, hanging lightbulbs to give myself a sense of safety. There was a thick old green wooden door that separated our side of the basement from the neighbor's, and mysterious sounds from the other side fueled my sense of dread.

As with each of the family moves, there was a new neighborhood to get used to, along with new friends to make, a new school, and a new sibling. My brother Christopher had been born the previous year, and now there was a sister, Lora, nine years my junior, to get used to. It was a constantly shifting landscape. But I did eventually feel comfortable in the Pacific Avenue house, and that was some solace to someone who often felt he didn't quite fit in.

Our parents struggled financially in our early years. It wasn't until my brother and sister were in school and my mother rejoined the workforce as the owner/manager of a print shop that we started to inch up the ladder toward the image of what middle-class life should be.

Waukegan in those days was a tough, blue-collar town nestled on the western shores of Lake Michigan. Its industry regularly pumped toxic waste into the actively fished waters of the great lake. We ran and played on that lakefront, swam, fished, built castles in the sand. It was our own toxic public playground. Twenty years later, after the factories had closed and multimillion dollar lawsuits were settled, the town would have to deal with the mess left behind. We enjoyed few luxuries. Ours was essentially a working-class family. Vacations were scarce, extracurricular activities infrequent, and dining out a rarity. My parents scrimped and saved wherever they could. I never felt as if we had to go without, but it also seemed they raised us to get by with less. We were a lights-out-after-you-leave-the-room kind of family. Items were bought and paid for with cash. Sears Roebuck was the preferred shopping spot.

Christopher and I shared a room, and for a short time the small spare room was turned into a nursery for our new sister. My parents' frugality eventually made an addition to the house affordable. The tiny den became a more spacious family room; upstairs, the dilapidated screened porch was turned into separate bedrooms for my brother and me along with a doubling of Lora's space. Even with these additions it was still tight in the house; the kitchen could barely hold three, and our dining room was strictly a five-person affair.

My mother began to develop the decorator within her, and artwork began to appear on walls and tables. As my mother found her design mojo, themes began to take shape. Furnishings we never had before began to appear: a couch with brightly colored upholstery, chairs for the living room, full flowing drapes my mother had sewn, a steel-and-glass coffee table my dad had crafted (a table I still associate with several trips to the emergency room when my brother cracked his head on it while roughhousing). There were framed prints on the walls, a Paul Klee reproduction (destroyed somehow in a teenage spitball incident), crafts my mother had created, new candleholders for the tables, magazine racks filled with *Time* magazine, and tablecloths my mother had embroidered.

To all appearances, we were now living the American dream. We had the two-car garage (albeit one for the neighbors who rented the other side of our duplex), the three kids, family portraits, steaks for dinner, smiles all around.

Though there was a large age gap between myself and my siblings— I was eight years older than Christopher, nine years older than Lora— on the surface we seemed like a normal, happy, working-class family living in the suburbs of Chicago. We ate family dinners together like most and stuck close to our relatives in those years. Holidays were usually split between families, one at my mother's parents, another at my father's. Cousins were plentiful on both sides, and grandparents figured actively in our lives. And yet for me, there seemed always something unspoken. Something so subtle, so undetected that for the most part it only played itself out in my mind.

Was it the fact that this family—the exception being my mother—was not my full blood? Could I even comprehend what that meant between the ages of five and seventeen, and if we were to all appearances a regular, normal family, did it matter? Was the difference in age between me and my siblings a gulf too wide? I imagine that knowing I had been adopted by my Waukegan father had something to do with feeling I was an outsider compared to my two siblings. The strong psychological effect—both conscious and subconscious—that not knowing one birth parent, or both, can have on a person is difficult to describe to people who've grown up with both biological parents. There's little awareness of how it might affect someone. Such disbelief or incomprehension of adopted peoples' plight is compounded by an inability of many of those adopted, especially at a very young age, to put words to their feeling of absence. The doubt is magnified by the look on many faces when the subject arises of "What's wrong with you? You've got two parents, what's your problem?" This look, or sometimes even spoken comment, only sharpens the feelings of alienation and disconnect for me and I suppose countless others.

There's a picture of my family, from Christmas, I think, in which we are sitting huddled together on our extra long, creamy smooth modern leather sofa—one of our household's few extravagances. I was probably fifteen or sixteen at the time. Enormous grins are plastered across our faces as we bunched together for the pose. There is my mother on the far left, her dark hair cut short, with a grin like her father's. My father, with blond hair that's beginning to grey on the sides, wearing his traditional striped shirt, exhibits the biggest grin of all. Next is my brother with his shaggy blond mane and identical grin to his father's, and Lora with a slightly darker, longer shag, clutching a Snoopy doll. I sit on the outside right with the same picturesque smile, leaning in as if trying to make a connection with Lora, my

The Fosbergs.

family. My hand is grasping her arm, my head touching hers. My curly dark hair is a bit wild and big, round glasses sit squarely on my face. Certainly the outside figures in this picture seem related, but the inside people are of another planet. My mother seems comfortable on her outside edge, while I appear to be groping, holding on, trying to find a way to fit into this picture.

I didn't speak to my mother for almost six months after my blowup the day I left for the airport. She tried calling a few weeks after the incident.

"Michael? Can we talk?"

"I don't think so, Mom. I just think it would be better if we didn't talk for awhile. I need a little time to sort some things out."

"How much time?"

"I just can't talk to you right now." I hung up.

I suppose I blamed my mother for everything: the failure of this marriage, the failure of her first marriage to my biological father, her difficulty communicating with her children, the breakup of our family, and on and on. She was the "face" of our family, the spokesperson, as it were. Yet she was also the one who *never* spoke about feelings, or problems or issues, and for that too I laid the blame squarely on her.

Was she miserable in her present relationship? Had she been miserable in her first marriage? That hadn't occurred to me. I had never even bothered to ask her in all these years what had happened to my biological father. Nor had she ever volunteered anything about this man whose image lay buried deep in her memory vaults.

But now, just as I was about to lose Dad no. 2 and had even a remote possibility of someday acquiring a Dad no. 3, questions came flooding in about Dad no. 1. Who was he? What happened? What was he like? Where was he now? Was he a good father? Where did we live? Why did my mother and I leave? And why hadn't she told me anything?

I now found my own relationship with my girlfriend Jackie mirroring that of my parents. Like my mother, I could not find it in me to talk about problems in our relationship, and our life together abruptly came to an end. I left the woman, the kid, the car, and the house in the Valley and moved to a small, rent-controlled studio apartment in the beach-side community of Santa Monica.

I reclined on a futon stuffed in one corner of the room. An oversized bright red painting of a muscular female Russian weight lifter with a neck the size of a telephone pole and the words "Steroids for Stella" etched in bold yellow at the bottom of the canvas stared down at me. A black-and-white photograph taken by a former neighbor of an approaching storm somewhere in the depths of the Grand Canyon hung above the pint-sized closet crammed with clothes and paraphernalia. Four wooden hand-carved masks from some place in Mexico that I can never remember sat atop a polished 1950s bureau. An old poster from a production of Noel Coward's *Private Lives* with Elizabeth Taylor frantically embracing Richard Burton peeked at me from the far corner of the kitchenette. A 1940s sign from the elevated stop outside Wrigley Field that read "Chicago Cubs Playing Baseball Today" hung above the doorway leading outside. Afternoon light streaming in gave the appearance of another room or perhaps even a whole wing to my tiny domain.

The rich smell of avocados crept in from the tree that shaded the courtyard. I stepped out onto the tiny flagstone porch. Once outside, the scent of avocados was entwined with the seaweed-and-salt breezes from the sea. It was a relief to have escaped the culture of dirt bikes and amphetamines, the 45-minute drives to town, and the gourmet platter of fast-food chains. But I felt empty, and it wasn't just the breakup with Jackie. It went far deeper than that.

THE STARVING ARMENIANS

My earliest memories of childhood go back to the man who family members called Papa Charlie, Garabed Pilibosian, my mother's father, an Armenian immigrant. He and my grandmother Rachel took in my mother and me from the time I was two until my mother remarried when I was around the age of five. We all lived in their old three-bedroom Tudor revival house in central Waukegan.

Next to the mayor of Waukegan at the time, Robert Sabonjian, my grandfather was probably the most popular Armenian in a town full of them. The Armenians had settled into this industrial working-class town of 60,000 approximately 50 miles north of Chicago, as well as further north into Wisconsin near the towns of Racine and Kenosha. There were hundreds of Armenian family clusters—Hoogasians, Hagopians, Emersians, Bedrosians, Paprigians, Goshgarians, Nahabedians, and Pilibosians—in the region then, and it seemed as though my grandfather knew them all.

Living with us too was my mother's chubby, nebbishy, and much younger sister, my aunt Diane, or Dee, with whom I shared a bedroom. She became a kind of big sister to me and, later, my sitter.

But the main attraction in my world all through my childhood and well into young adulthood, was my adoring grandfather Garabed. His wrinkled olive skin, bald head with matted gray hair on the sides, black-framed glasses, along with his penchant for sharp clothing (creamy gabardine shirts, double-pleated pants, and porkpie hats were specialties) gave him an aura almost of a gigolo. His zest for life was unmatched. He'd stride into a room, decked to the nines, with a crescent-moon grin, and women's heads would turn.

His wife was a different sort. A specialist in mismatched clothing for her frail frame, with a full head of gray atop a wrinkled face, she never

Aunt Dee and me.

liked to go anywhere. She rarely smiled, complained constantly, cleaned house excessively, and nagged Garabed. She came off mostly as a grump, but somehow a loveable one.

"Garabed, stop buying clothes. You have enough clothes," she'd bray at him in her shrill voice. He'd bellow that deep belly laugh of his and shake his head as if to say, *You can't stop me.*

My grandparents ran Karcher Cleaners, a small dry cleaning and tailoring shop in what was then a thriving section of downtown. The store faced onto the street on the ground floor of Waukegan's tallest building, the five-story Karcher Hotel. The lobby was suffused with the dark mustiness of its heavy leather furnishings. A dimly lit chrome-and-glass cigarette vending machine was stashed in a corner like some seedy old bum. The 1940s-style hotel restaurant came complete with soda jerk and corner booths.

My grandparents cleaned, pressed, and altered all the clothes themselves. There was a tiny waiting area in front with three chairs and an end table, and behind the counter hung rows of plastic-encased garments.

Rachel and Garabed.

The complicated and imposing pressing, cleaning, and sewing machinery was off to one side, humming, whistling, and sighing, tended by the embossed hands of my grandfather. I loved to go there as a kid, watching how my grandpa cleaned and pressed each piece with such care and attention. There was an art to the way he pressed crisp new pleats to the waist of a freshly cleaned pair of slacks or restored a languid dress to its unwithered form. The steam and heat were overwhelming. Sweat bled out of my grandfather's pores as he methodically worked through a stack of clothes, all the while smiling and singing the songs of his homeland, with a slight bounce in his step and a gleam in his eye. I sat in the chrome-and-leather chairs in the waiting area watching him or gazing at pictures in *Life* magazines. My grandmother attended to the needs of the customers as they came and went, while my grandfather, dressed in a drenched white tank top and gabardine slacks, traded jokes with customers from behind a veil of steam.

Before my mother remarried, my grandfather was "the man" to me, a role he played throughout my life up until the time of his death. He shared many vital secrets of life that have stuck with me. His secrets always centered around having fun and invariably entailed some sort of contest, such as the ever popular, yet scarcely known outside my family, Easter egg battle. We would each select a dyed egg based on the sound it made when we tapped the pointed end on our front teeth. The deeper the sound, the more solid the egg, and the better for battle. We would each hold our eggs in our hands, while one of us would tap the other's egg, point to point. The egg that cracked was the loser and this person would go back to the basket and continue to test eggs for a heartier combatant. To this day when I walk by a basket of dyed eggs, I grab one and tap it on my front teeth to test its strength for battle.

Another whimsical pastime was the hot pepper war. Grandpa had a rather extensive garden in his backyard, and his favorite plants were hot peppers. He would bring in handfuls when they were in season, and we would struggle to see who could eat the most and the hottest.

"Tsakis [a term that means roughly 'Dear One'], you eat three, I eat three, OK?"

"No, Grandpa," I'd tell him. "I'll eat four, you can eat three."

"Ha!" he'd laugh at me. "You eat one, then we see."

I'd eat one, maybe two, and be panting for relief, racing to the sink and drinking directly from the faucet as my grandfather would laugh and roll his eyes while downing his third.

"No cheating, Tsakis," he'd call out. "No water, keep eating," he would torment me good-naturedly as he buckled over with laughter.

And speaking of cheating, no real life lesson would be complete without a course in "how to cheat at golf." These lessons came much later but were equally important. He would take me to the local municipal course, and because I idolized him, I watched him like a hawk—his every move, every swing, which clubs he used, how he stood, even how he wore his hat slightly cocked to one side and tilted back.

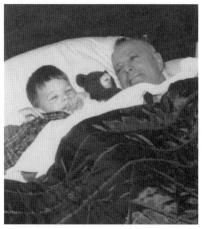

Me and Grandpa Charlie.

"Grandpa," I'd call out from across the narrow fifth-hole fairway as I stood some one hundred fifty or more yards from the hole, "Which club should I use here?"

He'd calculate the distance in his head and shout back, "Use the five iron. Put it next to the cup."

I'd flail away at the ball, eventually getting it on the green a few strokes later. At a distance I could see his face go red and a trail of Armenian obscenities spewing from his mouth as he'd hack away at his ball buried in the rough.

Finally both of us on the green, ready to putt out, I'd ask him how many strokes he'd taken to that point: "Grandpa, what do you lie?"

"Three, Tsakis, three. One, two, three," he calculated as he pointed across the fairway, mentally retracing his strokes.

I had just watched him hit his tee shot into a fairway bunker, his bunker shot back into the woods, from the woods he laid up to the center of the fairway, then hit a solid iron approach onto the green. That made four in my world, an everyday three in his.

In my book, Garabed could do no wrong. He was a sharp dresser, played cool games with me, and made his devotion to the Armenian church where he was the deacon a ceremonious affair. He used to pace the aisles during Sunday service in his flowing robes embroidered in white satin, swinging a silver incense burner back and forth. The smell of frankincense would fill the parish hall while smoke billowed from that incense pot as he chanted in a songlike Armenian, the congregation moaning in response.

One of the Armenian community's most memorable events was the hugely popular and wonderfully wacky picnic held each August and sponsored by the St. George Armenian Church. This was the one time of year when all the local Armenians would gather together to drink, dance, and feast. Like many others, I eagerly anticipated the picnic, despite the awkwardness of being brought out to be introduced to strange new relatives each time.

"Tsakis," my grandfather would call, "This is your aunt Anoush," he might say. "Come over here, give her a hug."

I would blush and drag my feet over to a usually large, olive-skinned, garlic-smelling woman with matted hair who generally spoke little English but would grab my face and press it in her round pudgy hands as she slobbered a big wet one on my cheek.

"Good boy, Tsakis," she'd chuckle, as she waddled off in search of another unsuspecting related victim.

These obligatory introductions aside, I reveled in the sights, sounds, and smells of these affairs. The air was filled with the delicious smokiness of the skewered lamb shish kabob mixed with traces of buttery rice pilaf, the aroma of freshly baked loaves of pocket bread, and the hint of rich, sweet wine. Children ran like wild animals set free; the elder women, faces like road maps, huddled in groups laughing and gossiping in rapid-fire Armenian; the men embraced, clutching cigars, drinking wine, and playing backgammon. Garabed—like a captain, running the whole show—strutted about in a taupe porkpie hat, gabardine shirt, and cotton knit slacks, kissing the women and dancing to the haphazardly assembled band, bottle of wine in hand. He would lead the snake dance around the tent, weaving through the onlookers, open hand raised in the air, feet kicking, steppin' out to the beat of the oud, an Armenian lute.

"*Gini kuses?* [Do you want some wine?]" he would shout out. He would give each of us grandchildren a taste of the bittersweet deep red Armenian concoction, and as each of us swallowed the heavy liquid and made faces like prunes he'd belt out a hearty laugh. The festive crowd of now partially intoxicated dancers, musicians, and merry onlookers, teased him on, clapping and snapping their fingers. "*Badreh*, Garabed, *badreh!*" Dance, Garabed, dance.

By the end of a day of this ethnic frivolity, completely satiated, stuffed to the gills with kabobs, replete with slobbering kisses, and weary from drink, dance, and merriment, I had to be literally dragged home. Tears trickling down my checks, I would grab for my grandfather's hand, and he would wrap his heavy arms around me hugging me tightly.

"Go home, Tsakis. You go home now. I see you tomorrow. Gimme *bacho*. Good boy. Go. Here, take this with you."

I would give him a tear-soaked kiss as he handed me an aluminum-covered plate piled high with rice and shish kabob. I would savor the tastes for the entire next week.

Food was a copious event in my upbringing, and my family would quite often congregate at my grandparents' house for magnificent savory meals prepared by the Julia Child of our Armenian culinary quarter, my grandmother. It eventually turned into a substantial feast, with myself, my parents, and my young brother and sister, along with my mother's older sister, her husband, their four boys, and of course my aunt Diane.

Grandma would be in the kitchen ordering around her "girls," who had no choice but to assist, while the men would watch sports, play cards, or engage in a rousing round of backgammon on Grandpa's beautiful, ancient, handmade, inlaid, dark wood board. As the aromas from the kitchen crept into the family room, our salivary glands would swell with anticipation. Delicate cheese and meat pastries covered with cardamom and sesame, a soup of fragrant peppery broth and extra-lean meatballs stuffed with nuts and garlic, lemon-saturated grape leaves rolled around a meat/nut/rice combination, sumptuous flaky breads, a steak tartare–like dish, and our favorite, a kind of Armenian pizza, a pungent spicy ground lamb on crisp dough. And that was just for starters!

As a boy growing up in an Armenian family, the irony of these feasts was that we were repeatedly told all about the starving Armenians. It was "starving Armenians" this and "starving Armenians" that, with little detail beyond the fact that they as a people had had little to eat growing up in the old country. "They" were those who survived the

Turkish genocide of nearly two-thirds of the Armenian populace in 1914–1915. The term stuck, and we'd constantly refer to ourselves as the starving Armenians. There was nothing starving about us now, however, except the way we gobbled our food as if it were the last meal on earth.

Once we all crowded up to the table, arms started flailing, plates were flung, and food was devoured. We'd all help clear the table, and then occasionally there would be what I can only call an Armenian rumble. Rachel might say something to Garabed. He would respond, then she would get a little cross with him. Before you knew it, they would be going at each other in get-down-trash-talking Armenian. Rachel's hot temper would meet head-on with Garabed's cool, sharp retorts. Her eyes would become blood red and she would spew out words faster and faster. Garabed's white wispy eyebrows would stiffen as he shook his head and returned fire.

"I told you not to plant any more hot peppers."

"Godsood Ches-sedare?" he'd ask with a laugh.

"You'll never change."

He'd laugh at her truthful remark.

"Shad gahos-esed," she'd drill him.

"Ganeeg me sants sedared."

"Dune mist et bes gahos-esed."

I kept waiting for the subtitles to roll. After a few minutes the tone of their conversation would come back down, and they'd start speaking English again, Grandpa laughing and smiling, Grandma with the perpetual scowl on her stony face.

The evening would end the same way all family dinners in Armenian households end. As we prepared to leave, my grandmother would load us up with plate after plate of leftover food. This, as any Armenian will tell you, is the way it always is. You go to your mother's or grandmother's for whatever reason, but especially for a dinner, and you never leave empty-handed.

I loved both of my maternal grandparents and found the traditions, rituals, and love the community offered comforting. I felt accepted as well as a part of the wonderful cast of characters within their community. I hung my hat only on the Armenians' hook during my childhood and knew nothing of my birth father's heritage.

THE ACCIDENTAL FATHER

I was four years old, and it was late one crisp fall afternoon. My mother and I were cruising down Glen Flora Avenue in her green 1960 Ford Fairlane. Waukegan at the time was a mix of small-town Americana five-and-dime's, soda jerks, barber shops, family-run clothing stores, industrial-looking schools, clean parks, and gritty-looking working-class suburban homes, at least near where we lived. I could barely see above the dashboard as I sat in the stiff plastic seat next to my mother. I had on a light, plaid, wool-lined jacket. We stopped behind a car making a left-hand turn. Suddenly we felt a forceful impact from the rear, and our car went careening forward, smashing into the car attempting to make the left turn. I was thrown back against the seat, then head first into the dashboard. This was long before the days of mandatory seat belts and air bags.

My mother pulled over to the side of the road in front of an abandoned National Guard building with its gargoyles and gothic facade crumbling behind the barbed wire fencing that surrounded it. I had fallen to the floor of the car under the dash. Half dazed I looked up at my mother, checking her face to see if I was all right. There was a look of terror. When I went to touch my face I felt blood gushing from my nose. I began to cry. A tall, blond-haired man with bright white teeth and a lean face appeared on my mother's side of the car.

"Are you all right?" he inquired.

"Yes, yes, I think so," my mother answered tentatively. She glanced up at him and a look of recognition came over her face. "Johnny? John Fosberg? It's me, Adrienne Pilibosian. Waukegan High School, class of '53."

"Adrienne! Are you sure you're all right?"

He gazed inside and saw me still on the floor. He reached across my mother and extended a clean white handkerchief toward me.

"Here, take this, son," he said gently.

I was too scared to move or even respond to this strange grown-up, so my mother took the handkerchief and wiped my face and chin. Then, squeezing the cloth into my hand, she set my hand against my nose to halt the flow of blood.

"Thank you," she said, turning back to him with a look of relief and gratitude. "I'd like you to meet my son, John. This is my Mikey."

He smiled a big toothy grin that reminded me of Andy from *Mayberry R.F.D.*

"Hello there, Mike. My name's John Fosberg."

I managed a disquieted "hi" from under his now-bloody handkerchief.

"I think you're gonna be OK. You just got a little banged up, that's all," he tried to convince me.

"Thanks, Johnny," my mom said.

"Listen, would you like me to escort you home?"

"No, thanks. We'll be all right, I think."

I sat quietly while they talked, watching from the floor below the dash.

At least, that's how I remember the meeting. My mother tells me it wasn't quite so dramatic; in fact, she says it never happened that way. She tells me the accident in question happened much later and that John couldn't possibly have been at the scene. Who are you going to believe, the memory of a four-year-old kid or your sixty-year-old mother? Either way, less than a year later, my mother married that blue-eyed blond-haired gentleman named John Fosberg, and I was no longer the only man in my mother's life.

I vividly remember the wedding, sitting in a pew by myself away from most of the family and friends. I couldn't keep still during the service. I sat, I stood, I crawled along the floor under the pews. Nor was I much better at the reception. I ran around the room from table to table, crawling under people, standing on top of chairs, shouting for attention. Meanwhile, my mother performed the typical rites: cutting cake, posing for pictures, and dancing with her new husband, completely enamored of her "new" man.

John Kenneth Fosberg.

I don't think it occurred to me at the time that I may have had a dad prior to this one. I was too young to formulate consciously that kind of picture or to know what questions to ask about the circumstances of my birth. Nor did I wonder how our lives would now change. I was too busy wreaking havoc and trying to draw attention.

After the wedding, we moved into the apartment building next door to my grandparents. My new father never seemed to be at home, though, as work apparently demanded a great deal of his time. Outwardly, nothing really appeared all that different to me as I eagerly raced across the driveway to assist my grandfather in his garden. As I saw it, there was one great advantage to this move: I now had my very own room. It was two years after my parent's wedding when I officially became my new father's son. The adoption papers came through and my name was changed from Woods to Fosberg, matching that of my mother's new married name.

Yet the loss of attention from my mother began to play itself out in uncomfortable ways which first became apparent as I began stealing money from my mother's purse. I used to go into her pocketbook while she was busy in another room and take small change—nickels, dimes, quarters, maybe a dollar when I was brave. One day I got bold and went for a ten. I bought armloads of candy with the money and doled it out to all the kids in the neighborhood—bubble gum, jujubes, Necco Wafers, Pez, Tootsie Rolls, Jolly Ranchers, Red Hots, candy corn, O'Henry bars. I was the most well liked kid on the block. At least it was some consolation for what I had lost in my mother's greater attentions to my new father.

I don't know what made me think my parents wouldn't notice the money was gone. When they came home from work, it didn't take long for them to figure it out. I think they laughed out loud at the sight of chocolate-stained neighborhood kids running around our yard, pockets bursting with candy. I was severely spanked by my new father, the old bare-hand-on-the-buttocks variety, and banished to my room, red bottomed and teary eyed. This only reinforced my burgeoning jealousy of the man who commanded my mother's new affections.

Johnny and me.

I don't remember what it was like not having a father before him. I'm not sure I really knew how I felt once I suddenly had one. I remember after the initial shock wore off and the jealousy seemed securely tucked away, the idea of having a dad seemed pretty cool, and the sense of distance I felt began to dissipate. Like any relationship, I suppose it was a process of feeling each other out, getting used to the idea of being around one another and trying to enjoy shared experiences. Even if I wasn't quite sure what it all meant, or how it was supposed to feel, I did have a dad now. He took me places occasionally—to baseball games, a few car races, the motorcycle track, places my mother would never dream of going. He tried to interest me in the things that interested him. If he had been there from an earlier time, I might have developed a natural curiosity about these activities, much as I did with my grandfather's interests, but instead I felt they were in a way being foisted upon me. It was a subtle difference, but an emotionally important one.

For example, when I was seven my father tried to introduce me to fishing on the lake with Buzzy. My father's best and oldest fishing pal, Buzzy, was a man who lived to fish. He wore a floppy camouflage hat overfilled with fly lures, worms, and fake silver and blue minnows studded with sharp dangling hooks. The owner of at least a dozen fishing rods, he told fish stories that were actually true. This was a guy that fish feared. I was always fascinated by the multitude of fishing paraphernalia he could dig up. They were like dangerous prehistoric toys, with a sci-fi twist.

It was a Saturday morning at 5 a.m. when my dad woke me quietly, dragging my limp, half-comatose body out of bed. I threw on some old clothes, and we made our way to the lake. Once there, I was suited up in an overstuffed bright orange life jacket, and we climbed into the aluminum craft well stocked with the latest in bait. We motored to "the spot" under darkness, then cast our lines for hours in search of the perfect catch. Buzzy concocted the proper lures to entice the fish du jour using live worms and minnows, whatever the occasion merited.

Looks like there's no way out of this!

By the end of the morning I reeked of an otherworldly concoction that only a true fisherman can appreciate.

Though my father took me out like this many times, I seldom caught anything. With little action on the end of my line, and the usual overpowering urge to go to the bathroom once out in the middle of the lake, I could see my fishing days were numbered. Besides, at age seven, the last thing I wanted to do was to sit still in a small motorboat for hours on end, throwing some line repeatedly over the side with little results.

"Dad?"

"Do you have a bite?"

"No, Dad."

"You sure?"

"Yeah."

"What is it then?" His eyes still fixed on his pole and the gentle bobbing of the boat.

"I gotta pee."

"What?"

"I said I gotta pee."

"Well..." he contemplated as he thought he felt a pull on his line. "You're gonna have to wait."

"I can't, Dad."

"What do you mean you can't?"

"I've been waiting for the last hour."

"This is the first I've heard of it."

"I can't hold it any longer."

"Didn't I tell you to go before we left?"

"I did."

"Well, you'll just have to wait a while longer."

"But Dad..."

"Look, we can't drive to shore every time you have to go to the bathroom. We're trying to fish here. You've gotta have patience."

Patience was one thing I did not have. I was too hyper and too athletic to be cooped up in a boat for any length of time. I had a form of ADD known as ADFD—attention de-*fish*-ient disorder. He was never able to hook me on fishing. I just wasn't the type.

It was obviously one of my father's great loves, and I'm sure he shared this pastime hoping to make some sort of connection between us. But I possessed an energy that was more like my mother's: an active interest in exploring, a curiosity for the arts, a developing sense of play and team sports. Plus, I was afraid not only of the water—I never learned to swim well—but of the very fish we were trying to catch. I hated grabbing those squirming beasts. Although worms and minnows seemed manageable, I was scared of most anything else alive—from insects, mice, and snakes to full-grown fish.

I came to loathe those aquatic expeditions and pined as I got older for the courts or fields where ball was played. I don't ever remember thinking how my dad might perceive this, but I wished he would stop dragging me out on the lake. This fishing/round ball disconnect remained an unspoken, perhaps even unrecognized disappointment for us both.

When we moved into the duplex on Pacific Street when I was nine, my father began working even longer hours than he had before and seemed to have no time to play the games or sports I was interested in or to read together. But he continued to try and interest me in fishing, along with woodworking and other trades at which he excelled.

My father was attracted to tools and working with his hands. He assembled a workshop full of power tools in the basement, which he used to build and remodel things in our house. I was intimidated by the tools, and combined with my unfounded fear of the basement, this became another passion of my father's that I didn't share.

I liked to play sports, and games, and ride bikes. I wanted to run in the park, explore the woods, shoot hoops, play tennis, try golf. None of these were really a part of his vocabulary. When he did have free time, he would sleep, read Time magazine, or watch the news. He was not the athletic type.

I spent hours alone outdoors in the yard throwing a tennis ball off the side of the chimney, simulating entire baseball games. I marked out the strike zone with chalk on the house, made up my teams, and pitched complete games with determined animation. It was always the same two teams, the Cubs versus the Mets, and I was always Ferguson Jenkins, star pitcher for the Chicago Cubs. The great Ernie Banks was at first, Glenn Beckert at second, Don Kessinger at short, and Ron Santo at third. I'd run through all nine innings, then quote the great Ernie Banks, "It's a great day, let's play two!" and do it all over again, Cubs winning every time.

Gradually I moved to the driveway, where, at my constant urging, my father put up a basketball hoop. It was the homemade variety, made in his shop and painted white. It wasn't the professional quality you'd find in stores, not terribly sturdy or the most beautiful hoop you'd ever seen, but it did the trick just the same. I spent afternoons on the driveway trying to perfect my best "white men can't jump" version of the Chicago Bulls. In those days they always faced the glorious New York Knicks, a team I had somehow embraced. The unstoppable combination of Bill Bradley and Dave DeBusschere at forward—two white guys who could score, and sometimes jump—gave an innocent, young, skinny, white kid dreams of basketball stardom. I learned to dribble and shoot, fake and drive from watching their every move, perfecting my play by myself day after day.

In high school I was one of two white kids on Waukegan's freshman team, but I was relegated to the pine for lack of speed and an inconsistent jump shot. I began to gravitate to the theater, inspired to get started in part by a friend of my mother's, a former drama teacher and English professor. I worked on every play my high school put on from the time I was a freshman until I graduated. I played El Gallo in *The Fantasticks*, Fagin in *Oliver*, the chaplain in *Mother Courage*, the professor in *The Lesson*, an odd assortment of adult roles that no teenager should have the misfortune of playing. However, I was bitten by the stage bug, and once I got my first taste, I plunged forward, foot firmly on the accelerator. And I not only relished my roles but also became a lightning rod for controversy and change.

One evening during a rehearsal of *The Fantasticks* the director/teacher was staging a scene that required a white actor playing the role titled "the boy" to kiss a black actress playing the role titled "the girl." (The musical's plot is the allegorical story of two children who grow up next door to each other; when their fathers erect a wall between their houses in an attempt to ensure their children will fall in love, the children discover the plot, go out into the world renouncing their love and families, only to return, realizing they were truly meant to be together.)

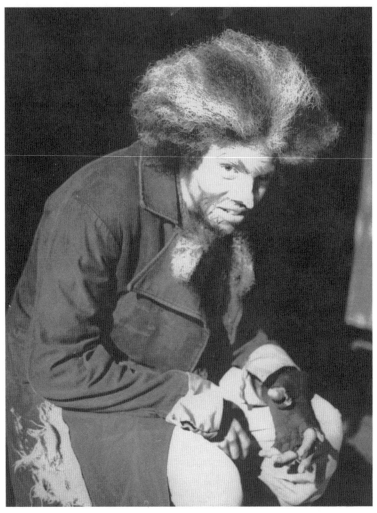

Me as the character Fagin in the musical Oliver. *That is my real hair with sprayed streaks!*

The director became uncomfortable with the kiss for some strange reason, and I stepped forward insisting they kiss—it was the love scene after all and a simple kiss was required to make it believable! After much consternation and delay, the director finally caved in, the actors kissed, and we moved on.

My parents attended all of my performances, though my father slept through most of them, probably dreaming about his Black & Decker power tools or his Sears Craftsman ratchet set. It never occurred to me how much courage it must take to stand on a large stage with hundreds of people watching you from the audience. I just plunged ahead, loving the attention it afforded me. An odd fact considering that in so many other realms I was an especially timid kid: afraid of the water, of insects and fish, afraid to play spin-the-bottle, afraid to speak in class. Put me up on a stage, however, and I felt I was in my element.

My mother had instilled in me a passion for the arts. She took us to museums, theater, opera, movies, whatever she could squeeze in between working, being a housewife, and a mother. We saw Renoir at the Art Institute, *One Flew Over the Cuckoo's Nest* at Drury Lane Theatre, *Swan Lake* at the opera house, and the Chicago Symphony Orchestra at Ravinia Festival. I developed a love for movies and listening to music. Aunt Dee would play for me her early Beatles albums along with the Rolling Stones and Paul Revere & the Raiders. I'd eventually gravitate toward The Jackson Five, Marvin Gaye, The Supremes, and, of course, James Brown. My father showed no interest in movies and seemed to hate music. If my mother played old Harry Belafonte albums, when he came in, he would walk over to the stereo and turn it off without even taking the needle off the record.

My father and I could never seem to find common ground. Chris, though, followed in his footsteps and spoke the same language. Like our father, he was not the athletic type and lived to tinker with things. He could repair practically anything electronic. He also loved to fish and the two of them would go on fishing trips together. I guess it never really dawned on me how odd it was that my brother and my father enjoyed many common interests when I shared so little with the man we both called dad. I just accepted ours as a normal father-son relationship—normal being not connected. Not that I even knew what normal implied, or for that matter what a father-son relationship amounted to or was supposed to look like. I certainly wasn't aware in those years how my relationship with my father colored so many of my teenage hungers and choices. It didn't then seem strange that I should find a part of what was missing between my father and me in the upside of what was even then extremely risky behavior. I didn't go out looking for this specifically, but when I first experienced alcohol and drugs, I knew I had found something significant, something that might just give me courage and lead to the sense of acceptance I sorely lacked.

It shouldn't be a surprise that studies done over the years by various social scientists indicate that teenagers who have poor relationships with their fathers in two-parent households (or in homes with no father present) are at much greater risk for smoking, drinking, and illegal drug use. It was not a surprise to me anyway when I later heard about them. The bigger questions are: What happens to these disenfranchised kids once they discover such paths? How often do the effects of an uninformed, rash, and perhaps desperate decision of a perplexed, misunderstood teenager stay with him the rest of his life? And would someone like me, if I had had a different relationship with my father, have taken another road? I'd like to hope so, but I have few regrets.

I suppose it could be argued that most kids will experiment with drugs and alcohol when they hit a certain age. Peer pressure, curiosity, a desire to fit in, all combine to give a young person the courage, or maybe better put, an excuse to try a drink or use a drug. In my case, at least, I craved acceptance; like everyone, I wanted to fit in somewhere, to feel wanted, a need that was not being met in the awkward relationship with my dad. I wouldn't say it was from lack of effort on his part. He tried. We both tried. I certainly can't blame my youthful indiscretions on our inability to find common ground together. It wasn't his fault I was uncomfortable; it was my situation to overcome. However, once I discovered activities that could make me feel like a part of a group, I adapted quickly. The theater did this for me, sports also to some degree, and now, a new kind of bond.

Everyone's first time is memorable in some way. If my first drinks were administered by the grace of my grandfather as a joke at an Armenian get-together at an age far too young to have meaning or significance, my first encounter with drugs was something more magical, an initiation of sorts.

During the summers of my high school years, my parents had dear friends who owned a cottage on a lake just north of us in a small Wisconsin town called Winneconne. The tiny town had gained some notoriety years earlier when the state inadvertently left its name off the official Wisconsin map. In retaliation, the town fathers voted to secede from the state. They printed their own currency and established their own state constitution in a half-serious effort to bring notice to their geographic plight.

With the prospect of house-sitting for their friends one hot summer weekend, my parents had invited another family to join us. To my great fortune this family included two beautiful high school girls who just happened to be every Waukegan High School boy's dream. These girls were notorious for their long dark hair, tall slender figures, and boy-melting smiles. It took me days to just get over the fear, not to mention the joy, once I discovered my delicious fate.

Me between the Smittle girls, with my brother and sister in front.

So there I was lakeside with two of the most beautiful creatures I could have imagined. Kim was a member of my junior class at school, and her younger sister,

Roz, was two classes below. On a lazy Saturday afternoon, we three sat on the edge of the pier, our feet dangling in the warm, still waters of Lake Winnebago. Me, my wild, uncombable hair, tall and thin and scrawny in my swim trunks. The girls had perfectly tanned, smooth, silky skin and looked shapely in their bikinis. We sat gazing into the reflective waters as our parents lounged up shore, mixing martinis or whatever their summer drink du jour happened to be.

"Can we go out on the lake?" Kim asked as she gently flipped a dollop of water my way with the ring-clad toes of her right foot.

"Sure," I answered, quickly sizing up the opportunity with a modicum of anxiety. "There's that huge rubber raft," I said as I pointed toward the boat house. "We could take that out." I dreaded my deficient swimming skills.

"Great. Roz?" Kim called out to her younger sister who was making a lame effort to gauge the water's temperature by cautiously sticking her left leg deeper into the abyss from the pier above the cool waters. "Jump in!" she shouted as she pushed Roz into the brink.

"Not funny," Roz yelled, flinging water at her sister.

I moved toward the raft as the two splashed water back and forth, screaming with rival sisterly glee. "Gimme a hand here, Kim, and we'll drag this thing to shore and launch it." Kim pulled herself away from battle for the moment and bounded toward me laughing.

"Aye, aye, Cap'n," she joked as she grabbed a side of the raft. Roz, now fully drenched, made her way toward shore and took hold of the boat as we slid it down the shoreline. Kim moved back to the pier and dove under the now-floating raft. I carefully made my way through the muck of the lake toward the boat. Kim shot up from under the boat, spraying her sister with water. The battle resumed as I grabbed the raft and hopped in, sliding onto the water bed–like bottom. "Aaaah," I sighed while stretching out along the undulating, cool bottom of the raft. Suddenly water spurted above the sides, splashing down upon me. "Hey! Knock it off! No water in the boat!"

"What, 'fraid yer gonna melt?" Kim poked her head above the side, quickly hopping, sliding, and crashing down into the raft.

"Hey, gimme a hand!" Kim and I grabbed her arms as Roz jumped up and we pulled her aboard. We lay there on our backs, rocking gently as the sun beat down on us and the raft drifted slowly across the lake. Kim rose and looked out over the side toward shore, checking to see if anyone was watching.

"Roz, did you bring matches?"

"Yeah."

"Great." Kim looked over at my languid body undulating from the movement in the boat. "Hey, Mike, you wanna get high?"

"Yeah, sure," I said, as if it was something as common as drinking water. It was my finest acting yet. I lay there in the bright sun, looking up at these two beautiful girls and watched as they each pulled a small plastic baggy from their bikini bottoms. Kim retrieved what looked like a short, white, hand-rolled stick while Roz produced matches. I could feel my heart pounding against the water in the bottom of the boat. Roz leaned over toward Kim and ignited the small white stick as she inhaled, sucking in the smoke then holding her breath as she passed it to her sister. Roz followed suit as the boat bobbed and buckled from their movements.

I knew what was next, where it was headed, what was expected, and now sort of how to do it. Nervously, but taking great care to hide my naïveté, I snatched the burning stick from Roz, pursed my lips, and carefully inhaled the smoky tonic, trying not to cough or show my fear. Then, as if I'd done this ritual just that morning, I handed the joint back to Kim, holding my fear and inhalation deep inside my lungs. I watched as Kim released her first toke and prepared for more, then gently let my breath escape with relief at having survived my initiation without being detected.

"You like?" Roz said as she took the burning ember from her sister.

I nodded. I liked that I felt accepted, that I was here on this lake with two of the most beautiful girls I could imagine, feeling giddy, laughing, and having a good time. I felt connected with drugs, and to girls, and with being alive.

———————

My father had little time to prepare himself when I finally announced my senior year that I wanted to go to college for acting. "Look, don't put all your eggs in one basket," he said. One of his more famous and now wholly true wisdoms. "You need to get a well-rounded education. What happens if things don't work out as an actor? What are you gonna fall back on?"

What I heard was, "You're not going to make it." By this point we spoke completely different languages. He spoke common sense, I heard negativity. I spoke of a love for the arts, he heard nonsense.

I couldn't much blame him. After all, he worked long hours in a factory where he designed and made hydraulic fittings for large industrial equipment and machinery. He went to work five days a week, 8 a.m. to 6 p.m., in a starched white shirt with a narrow collar, a skinny tie, pressed pants, polished black leather shoes, a loaded pen holder in his shirt pocket, and a silver aluminum lunch box packed neatly by my mother.

I went to auditions, learned lines, and was known, on occasion, to prance around a stage in tights. How could I have possibly expected him to understand me? We had different views of life, of work. Yet for all our differences, he instilled in me a sense of passion for what you love, a sense of commitment. He was a worker among workers, an honest and decent man. He didn't need to tell me that, he showed me every day he went to work and came home exhausted. The very things I found so irritating about him, I realized much later, were the greatest gifts he gave me: work hard, have integrity, be honest, save money. He was a good provider, put us through the schools of our choice (albeit, not always by his choice!), and was always there to pick up the pieces should we ever fall apart. I may never have had what one would consider a close relationship with him, we fought on several occasions and he was known to have gone to my mother and thrown up his hands exclaiming, "You deal with him! I don't know how to get through to the kid!" Yet what father didn't have problems with his son? He gave me what he could, which in retrospect was solid footing. The rest I had to learn on my own.

His father, Theodore, was a well-respected member of the Waukegan community, a vice president at the local bank, a straight-up churchgoing guy who took his son fishing, taught him how to work with his hands, and encouraged the value of hard work. Compared to my father's relationship with me, his father's relationship with him seemed relaxed and easy. His mother, Ruth, was a devout Christian whose family came from Sweden and struggled through the Great Depression like many other working-class immigrants. The hardships she had endured bespoke the experience of many families coming to the New World. Her mother died when she was seven, forcing her father into painful choices for survival. He gave up his two youngest to other families for adoption, while Ruth stayed with the three remaining siblings as they took charge of household chores while their father worked long hours on the railroad. Being thrust into an adult role early on with no electricity, no running water, and no indoor plumbing defined her generation's sacrifices to reach for the American dream.

Ted and Ruth Fosberg.

While growing up we spent a considerable amount of time at my father's parents, but there was nothing overtly Swedish about their household or community, unlike my maternal grandparents saturated in Armenian culture. Other than the occasional meal of Swedish potato sausage—which I detested—there were no household clues as to their heritage, no cultural immersion nor outward celebrations at which we would meet new non-English-speaking relatives. And for as much as they instantly made me feel a part of their family, I never felt part of a community like that of the Armenians. I did, however, love going over to their house and diving into the cabinet they kept filled with an assortment of candies. They were sweet on their grandchildren, and I found myself loving them back with an ease somehow missed between my father (their son) and me.

Did the awkwardness of my relationship with my father have anything to do with the fact I was adopted? I think so, but I couldn't say for certain; I had no experience on the other side to weigh it against. Would my experience have been different if I had been raised by my biological father? Undoubtedly. But I would have to find him to discover what had been lost.

ON THE ROAD

With thoughts of my grandparents and the mystery of my natural father swirling in my head, I found myself back on the road, now heading east. I had left Berkeley early on Monday morning after having spent a beautiful mid-June weekend in the Bay Area. The weather had been exceptional—warm summer breezes, hot sun, cool clear nights. People's Park, the infamous hippie/radical rallying place during the sixties, was packed with vagrants, the homeless, misplaced youth, nineties hippies, drug dealers, and leftover radicals from glory days gone by. Half a block away, Telegraph Avenue was swarming with tourists and hawkers pacing in front of the tie-dyed head shops and Grateful Dead record stores, the smell of incense and patchouli heavy in the air.

I'd stayed the weekend with friends, a mixed-race couple with a beautiful six-year-old daughter the color of a mocha latte. I smiled and watched them as they meshed as a family, taking turns with their daughter, helping her draw, listening attentively as she sang children's songs complete from memory. I left with both a sense of wholeness and a pervasive sense of loss, a childhood missed.

I headed toward Salt Lake City on I-80, radar detector on and stereo going full blast. My mind wandered and tormented me with thoughts of the fiancée foresworn, and the ex before her, and the ex before that.

I sang, I cried, I laughed, I talked to myself. I went around a revolving carousal of CDs, pressing the skip button whenever any kind of love song started in. The unending gray pavement and monotonous driving routine began to feed my mind's frenzy.

It was somewhere between the white flatness of the Great Salt Lake and the sprouting hills of Provo that my mind started in on the questions about self: How did I wind up at the age of thirty-nine trekking across the country following yet another breakup? Had my struggles in love been connected to my troubled father situation? Whatever had I hoped to discover on this journey? The doubts and self-critiques were unrelenting. Relief came only when I pulled in for the night at the McDonald's of layovers, a Motel 6. There's the comfort of familiarity, at least, in the two-story buildings, u-shaped in configuration and sporting aqua-colored doors, windows with blinds closed, and a parking lot of license plates representing practically every state in the Union. Normally I steer clear of hotel chains and fast-food restaurants, but when it comes to sleep and cleanliness, I am not a camping type. I had packed no sleeping bag for the rough outdoors, no tent to erect in the wilderness. I was going strictly commercial, and that meant sleeping in what I considered America's finest cheap motel chain.

After a dinner experiment at an Indian restaurant in downtown Provo, I returned to the safe if antiseptic confines of my motel room to plot my strategy for the next day's journey. It would be on to Capitol Reef and the red cliffs Utah is so famous for. A hike in the mountains might quiet the chatter in my head before I made the leap into family history.

As I began to unpack a bag, searching for an elusive toothbrush, I found an audiotape version of Jack Kerouac's *On the Road* stuffed between an old pair of socks and my underwear. I'd forgotten I had picked it up along with an audio copy of John Steinbeck's *Travels with Charley* while examining the shelves of some of Berkeley's best bookstores woven among the head shops along Telegraph Avenue. I sat on the edge of the bed in a pair of old ripped up shorts and a Miles Davis T-shirt, staring at the fuzzy black-and-white photo of two young men leaning against a car on the cover. Kerouac and friend? It was hard to tell. I plunked the first cassette into my never-travel-without-it boom box. David Carradine was the reader.

"I first met Dean not long after my wife and I split up. I had just gotten over a serious illness that I won't bother to talk about, except that it had something to do with the miserably weary split-up and my feeling that everything was dead."

I was half listening to Kerouac's words, half thinking about my own journey. Here I was, alone in a cheap motel on the outskirts of Provo, Utah, the wound of my recent breakup still fresh and oozing, the breakup of my parents in the background. Certainly Kerouac had no idea of the discoveries he would make on the road, nor had I any idea of what I would find. I had a vague itinerary for penetrating family silence, but no idea of what I would unearth.

What could I possibly hope would come of all these visits I had charted across America? How absurd and pretentious to think you can "discover" who you are! Who and what you are is not an object you discover, I somehow was realizing, but rather a state of being.

I was on the road, like Kerouac, trying to get at least some answers to far simpler, more concrete questions than the larger existential one of how I fit into a larger scheme of the world. When did my biological parents marry? How was I conceived? Where did we live? Who were my grandparents on my natural father's side? What light, if any, could those first few years shed on why I felt the way I did, somehow so out of place in the world? I felt small and helpless, ridiculous for even making this attempt. Again I heard Kerouac's words as they pushed their way through my thoughts. Jack (also the book's narrator) was speaking to his friend Dean Moriarty:

Hell, man, I know very well you didn't come to me only to want to become a writer, and after all what do I really know about it except you've got to stick to it with the energy of a benny addict.

And he said,

Yes, of course, I know exactly what you mean and in fact all those problems have occurred to me, but the thing that I want is the realization of those factors that should one depend on Schopenhauer's dichotomy for any inwardly realized…

and so in that way, things I understood not a bit and he himself didn't.

LOSING MYSELF

No one who tries drugs or experiments with alcohol in their teen years sets out to become an addict. It's not a goal. You're simply focused on having fun, breaking rules, impressing friends, or trying something slightly risqué but not life-destructive. You've heard some harrowing stories, leafed through a brochure, or been forced to sit through a class expounding on the evils of substance abuse. There are giggles, smirks, denials, incredulity at the outrageous claims that one drink, one joint, could lead to a demented life of heroin addiction and failure. Few heed these warnings, and few end up in the gutter as depicted in these cartoon-like scenarios. Nevertheless, addictions do happen, and they certainly start somewhere, with something.

During my last years of high school and into college, my parents became the enemy. Not unexpected behavior for a young male of my age, but in my case I think resentment over never quite feeling a true fit with my family played a role as well. Besides, they really just pissed me off. This was especially true of my father. He was the cowboy, I was the Indian. He could never get a handle on the acting thing, and once I discovered late in my last years of high school that drugs and drinking could make me feel part of a rebellious clan, he didn't know which end was up or where to turn for help.

My mother's approach was slightly more laid back. Although she was supportive of my theatrical endeavors, it was still her lot in life to worry, a tradition passed on by her hand-wringing mother and countless generations of mothers before her.

"You know, Michael," she told me one day while discussing the growing use of drugs among high school teens. "I'll never search your chest of drawers or your desk; I don't want to know what's in there," she assured me as if granting a false sense of freedom. "It's just none of my business." It was a proclamation befitting failure, but on whose part it wasn't clear at the time.

Two years later, when I was deep in my high school experimental drug binge, she confronted me as I stepped in the door one evening. In her hands lay a familiar looking plastic baggie containing a small amount of a brown leafy substance.

"I found this in your dresser," she said with a pained look on her face. "This has to stop. I don't want you doing heroin!"

How we got from pot to heroin I'll never know. It was the inevitable jump most uninformed parents make, crazed hysteria wrapped in melodrama. I don't think I even knew what heroin was at the time. No matter, I would be doing it soon, according to my mother's theory.

One Saturday morning while I was sleeping off a hangover, the door to my room was flung open and an object hurled on my bed, smacking my feet.

"I believe this is yours," came the grim voice of my father. "No more car. No going out on weekends. You're grounded, young man!" He slammed the door shut before I was even aware of what had just happened. Apparently the night before I had been out with the fellas, and I hadn't searched the car well enough. A stray, full can of Old Milwaukee beer now lay at the foot of my bed nestled between my guilty feet.

Once I had discovered that euphoric feeling of assurance and acceptance alcohol and drugs afforded me, I embraced these substances as a means to connect with my peers. Since my imagined conquest of the two high school beauties out on the lake on a lazy summer afternoon, I had found a way to feel liked, one of the group. At least that's what it felt like at the time. It didn't occur to me that these mind-altering substances were building illusions more than any kind of long-term acceptance. But drinking and drugs were also about having fun in the moment, and I had a lot of fun.

I marched off to college at the University of Minnesota where I headed down two separate paths simultaneously. The first, and most important, was learning more about the crafts of acting, writing, and directing. The second, which gradually overtook the first in importance, was descending by degrees into drug and alcohol addiction.

Freshman year in the obligatory dormitory was a virtual smorgasbord of drugs and drink as us new recruits sowed parent-free oats and dabbled in whatever we fancied. The drug revolution of the sixties had come and gone, but its traces lingered in the group I quickly became associated with. There were two roommates from Texas next door who would bring back shopping bags full of peyote buttons from home every holiday break, dole them out to drooling, unseasoned drug wannabes, and watch as each of us passed out from the powerful effects. There was my roommate's girlfriend, who we affectionately dubbed "Mushroom Maggie" for her bountiful crops of hallucinogenic mushrooms creatively integrated into home-cooked meals. And, finally, there was the gang of hippie leftovers who'd smoke hash under glass and dash off to the notorious Minneapolis capital of sleaze, Moby Dick's, a bar in which happy hour was served up with the catchy phrase "All drinks are doubles" and dispensed at the ridiculously low price of forty cents a pop.

I partied, did homework, attended most of my classes, and dreamed of great accomplishments beyond school, like most my peers. We went to keggers, used fake IDs to get into bars, tailgated at games, and attended alcohol conglomerate-sponsored events complete with near-naked girls and drinking games, and plenty of drunk coeds. But this was merely Triple-A ball, a preparation for the big leagues back in Chicago.

Me and my college roommate... not quite "in focus"!

I didn't drink or use every day, and I didn't go from smoking a joint with my two high school fantasy dream girls to kickin' a can in a gutter somewhere looking for my next fix. But over the years the groundwork was laid, and my tolerance level increased.

Living in Chicago after graduation and struggling to establish myself as an actor, I also went through a revolving door of girlfriends. Unable to commit to a relationship with anyone or anything, I bounced from stage to stage, relationship to relationship, job to job, one apartment after the next. I sought comfort from whomever I was with at the time. I could not find it within myself.

At some point in my mid-twenties I was introduced to a cocaine dealer who suggested I could buy some, sell a little, and keep a portion for my own use. With a producer friend I entered into what we thought would be a little cottage business. Although I never smoked crack and never tried heroin, the cocaine selling and using, as Richard Pryor once said, "Got too good to ya," and I eventually found myself consuming more than I sold.

As clients would come by to purchase inventory, a request was usually made to sample the merchandise prior to sale. I'd always oblige and join in on the "free" samples as if I were buying myself. A half dozen or so customers on a nightly basis soon produced a healthy addiction. Before I knew it, I also was drinking large quantities of alcohol and then trying to counteract the high with Nyquil, a cheap and disgusting approach to try and come down from a high.

Soon I began to use in the afternoons. First it was five o'clock, then it became four, then three, and so on. Before long I'd start when I woke up, usually around ten or eleven o'clock. I'd swear I would wait until after noon, only to give in to the thirst I had acquired. I was out of control.

My girlfriend Erin lost tolerance for the late nights and bleary-eyed mornings. I would hide drugs everywhere so as not to arouse her suspicion. I'd wander off to the bathroom repeatedly or step into our walk-in closet pretending to look for something, anything, while I would secretly snort up. Erin began to detect it in my eyes and my behavior, and she'd threaten to inform my parents. I'd relent and swear I'd quit, only to begin again in secret a few days later.

Not only did I try to disguise my escalating affliction from family and friends, but I began to hide myself. I went from being the life of the party to isolating myself in the caverns of my secluded coach house, paranoia now working overtime. What had originally given me hope, acceptance, and likeability had now driven me into a dark world of isolation, depression, and despair. I escaped any sense of accountability by entering another state of consciousness (or unconsciousness, as the case may be), one of drugged-out drunkenness and a feeling I began to identify as love, which came disguised as sex. What I thought was love was really desire, lust, an aching for acceptance. I wanted to be loved and accepted by anyone, someone, everyone.

Somehow, even in my fog, I managed to maintain fairly decent, albeit shallow, family ties. I was mostly making a living as an actor in plays, occasional writer, freelance acting teacher, and producer of random theater, which made my mother and father happy and proud that their son was making a living doing his art. As a family we still did holidays together, celebrated birthdays, bought gifts, and exchanged cards. For the most part they attended all the crazy plays I managed to become involved in, plays my dad sometimes slept through, but no one could blame him. I had ventured far beyond the mainstream commercial fare most playgoers are likely to sample and was dabbling in experimental work that required patience from even the most seasoned theater subscriber. Plays in which babies were stoned to death, plays that made no sense, and plays in which I appeared naked.

Over time my addictions crept into my work too. Whereas I had once sworn never to appear on stage under the influence, I soon found myself jacked-up and paranoid backstage.

During one particular performance of *Frank's Wild Years*—the show in which I finally earned my union card from the Actor's Equity Association, the stage actors' union—I experienced a moment of startling clarity. Written by and starring Tom Waits, the wildly independent musician, troubadour, and poet, this sold-out show was an

As the character Jimmy Porter in the play Look Back in Anger.

oddball alternative rock/roots musical in which a down-on-his-luck musician enters a warped dream state while trying to make sense of his sordid past.

During a surrealistic street scene I played the role of a hermaphrodite dressed in fishnet stockings, five-inch pumps, a silk black lace teddy, topped with a frizzed-out wig. As half man/half woman, I stumbled my way across stage to the sounds of the band and an actor addressing the crowd as a carnival barker, while others posed as all manner of freaks stalking the stage. As I stood on the edge of the stage gyrating, barking at the audience in a raspy Harvey Fierstein voice, I caught sight of myself, the reflection of my figure in the glasses of a person seated in the front row. I suddenly felt a chill come over me. As high as I was on coke smoothed over with a few drinks, I couldn't get past the frightening idea that this was me. I was twenty-seven years old, standing in front of hundreds of people in a ridiculous outfit—an outfit for a character obviously conflicted about who and what he/she was—and higher than a kite.

That moment of self-recognition may have triggered my spiral toward the bottom of anguish. The week following the show's close, I plied myself with everything I could get my hands on in an effort to douse the flames of my discontent. Late one night while lying in bed with unsuspecting Erin, I felt my chest seize up and my breath get tight. I shifted position in an effort to catch a breath, but the pain deepened. I felt I might be experiencing a heart attack. As the pains in my chest became more intense, panic set in. I lay there, crippled with spasms rolling through my chest, feeling unable to breathe, get up, or speak. I wanted to wake Erin and plead for her help, but I was too afraid this was the end. I lay writhing and scared, hoping beyond all hope that I could weather this attack and be given yet one more chance. I pleaded with God, a God that had little shape or form for me, to help me get beyond what was surely death's doorway. Curled up in a ball, rocking gently, begging for one more opportunity to wake up,

I thought of that moment I experienced on stage and realized the depths to which I had fallen.

After what felt like several hours of pain, fear, and paranoia, the painful waves subsided, and I was able to breath easily once again. But the impression was lasting. I vowed I would never go back there. I lay on my side in the early morning hours and as the sun rose, folded my hands, thanking God for sparing me, according me one more day.

"How'd you sleep?" Erin asked when she stirred.

Worried there might be something lurking behind her simple inquiry, I responded matter-of-factly, "Great. And, you?"

"Good. I'll make us some breakfast," she said as she threw on her robe and headed for the kitchen. "Eggs all right?" she called back.

"Sure, fine, great." I stared up through the skylight above our bed as rays of the morning sun hit my face. It was a blessing, I told myself, seeds sown for a big change.

The change came in two parts. Part one was a trip to California to purchase a car from Erin's parents and drive back to Chicago. It was just the break I needed to clear my head and my body from the downward spiral cocaine had taken me on. I gritted my teeth, pulled up the old boot straps, swore off all forms of alcohol and drugs and, down payment in hand, made my way to southern California.

Part two was a warped extension of part one in which I was so smitten by the LA weather, the beaches, and the Hollywood swagger that I decided to stay, not return with the car, and break off yet another relationship. As an actor I saw opportunity and had great hopes for a fatter paycheck. As an addict now sobered, I discovered a way to flee my past, set a healthier course, renew my hope for self, and start afresh as an actor. Although now sober and making small inroads into the glitz machine known as Hollywood, I was clutching the steering wheel for dear life hoping to navigate through yet another botched affair.

A REVELATION

My parent's impending divorce may have broken our family, but my outburst cursing my mother set off a nuclear explosion. I'd crossed the sacred respect-for-your-parents line and ventured down the dark alley of disrespect, alone and brooding. I wanted to take back my words, but I couldn't. I was angry, confused, and disconsolate. I was now living in my tiny Santa Monica apartment where I'd moved when I broke up with Jackie, five years after giving up Chicago for Hollywood, and knew it was just a matter of time before the phone started ringing.

"Michael, it's me, Christopher."

"Hey, Chris, what's up? How are things with you?"

"Good, good. Listen, I wanted to talk to you about Mom and Dad."

"What's to talk about?" I stubbornly refused to give up my anger.

"Well, Mom says you're not speaking to her."

"I've got nothing to say," I stonewalled.

"Look, I can't say I blame you for being hurt, but we've got to help them get through this somehow," he reasoned sensibly.

"Christopher, you really think she deserves our help after what she's done?" The problem was, *she* hadn't done anything. *They* had agreed to a divorce, and I had blamed my mother. How I arrived at this distinction was still a puzzle. How I went from never being able to establish a solid bond with my father to blaming my mother for what I saw as the destruction of our family, a family to which I'd never felt wholly connected—was yet a mystery unrevealed.

Next up to bat on the telephone was my father.

"Michael, I really think you're being unreasonable with your mother," he approached diplomatically.

"Dad, I don't know what's gone on with the two of you, and it's probably none of my business, but I don't think it's fair of her to just drop the ball and run."

"Well, your mother and I have sought out counseling in an effort to try to find common ground. Unfortunately we just weren't able to resolve our issues in a way that would allow us to continue married." His normal pragmatic tone and manner hid the pain I knew he felt. I wanted to support his reasoning but was far too attached to my inexplicable anger.

During my childhood I never felt particularly connected to my father or fully part of the family, yet here I was, desperately wanting to save them, us, our family unit. How ironic. Yet my efforts to resurrect that which seemed to have no chance of rebirth were to pout like a child and run from the problem in a huff.

I barricaded myself in my tiny one-room dwelling, took no more calls, and began to write what you might call a manifesto on my life and goals. My moods were dark, my friendships strained. At times I felt on the verge of self-destruction. As winter approached I found myself isolated, unstable, and frequently unemployed. The revolving carousel of agent representation and auditions for bit parts was losing its charm. House painting took greater precedence in my work routine, and I found myself sleepwalking from job to job, simply trying to do what it took to pay my rent and feed and clothe myself.

At some point it dawned on me that I had but two friends who actually continued to take my calls, one a charismatic New Jersey-raised, Italian-bred actor on the rise, the other a funky eccentric blonde female bartender to whom that actor had introduced me. The three of us had met at a raucous bachelor party in the bar where she worked, during which the rowdy drunken crowd watched the groom—whom neither of us knew—have sex with an unidentified stripper. It was a shocking event, and yet it wasn't so much the disgusting festivities that bonded us. It was more that not one of the three of us was drinking that night.

What I discovered later that night was that these two rather hip yet completely sober people were members of a group dedicated to turning their lives around through abstinence from mind-altering substances. It was not long after our meeting that I found my way, with their help, into the rooms of Alcoholics Anonymous.

At first it was odd to be attending a meeting for drunks and druggies. Sure, I'd been drunk and high most of my waking hours before I ventured out to sunny California, but I had a hard time calling myself an addict when I'd been clean for almost two years. I'd quit, I reasoned. I'd made a vow after my near-death experience that I would never go back there again. I'd stopped drinking all forms of alcohol and took no drugs whatsoever, even eliminating coffee. I was clean and healthy again, basking in all the warmth, sun, and outdoor activities Southern California had to offer. Yet I began to see the creep of isolation that had been so debilitating while in Chicago. The fear, the distance from family, and what I perceived as shyness were preventing me from any means of self-discovery, not to mention significant work in my chosen field. After all, how can one claim to be an actor and be afraid to talk to people? After hours of discussions with people who had stories not unlike mine, I began to realize that, although I had quit using several years earlier, my alcoholism lay untreated and I continued to behave in a manner consistent with alcoholics. My moody ups and downs, the emotional rollercoaster to which I had subjected my friends and family, the inability to accept life on life's terms, were from this perspective all roots of addictive behavior. Alcohol and drugs were not so much my problem, in other words, as was my approach to life. I had used substances to try to ease my pain and suffering, or "dis-ease" as many in these meetings referred to it. And maybe, just maybe the dis-ease I felt, even if I could not clearly pinpoint its exact source, had much to do with the loss and absence of my biological father at such an early age.

In frequenting meetings, I began to find the welcoming hand of fellow addicts a relief. In Los Angeles there were hundreds of meetings each day at points all across the city where people shared their stories, offered help and support, openly wept, and encouraged involvement and participation in everyone's recovery. It was virtual love fest meets group therapy meets social network meets bitch session. Where once I had found courage and acceptance in substances I abused, I now found these qualities in those very sober people who had similar quests of their own.

SID

The winter of 1991 in Los Angeles was as wet as they come. Heavy rains came down with such force that the water would rebound off the hard summer-baked surfaces. I felt trapped in my crate of an apartment as I watched the heavy rains blur the existence of the outdoors. I'd now alienated myself from my family, especially my mother, and taken up with a British blonde named Jo.

Oddly enough, she was still married and living with her husband and their son in the last holdover of hippiedom, Topanga Canyon. This sprawling canyon stretching from the beach to the San Fernando Valley had the highest concentration of tie-dyed clothing next to San Francisco's famous Haight Street. Jo and her family had recently relocated from Woodstock, New York, the East Coast version of West Coast free-love, and had one of those be-who-you-are, sleep-with-who-you-want type of relationships. How I got entangled in this free-love sandwich is still a bit of a mystery considering my wholesome upbringing. I guess I just couldn't resist her British charms.

There was in fact very little that was British about her except her accent, a few provincial English colloquialisms such as "Strike me pink," "Bob's your uncle," and the classic "Bugger off!" and an occasional craving for that disgusting spread that looks like crude oil, Marmite. A reconstructed nose on a head of platinum and auburn dyed locks in combination with a couple of sizable chest acquisitions made her blend right in with the Southern California Baywatch mystique. I fell for those curvaceous reconstructed parts, and we began sleeping together, then working together in what would eventually become an artistic partnership. She started bringing her seven-year-old son over, and he'd sleep on the little bit of floor space at the foot of my bed. Eventually she moved in, and I found myself sharing a box that was hardly big enough for one with both of them.

As Jo and I got closer, I began to share details of the foolish tirade I'd unleashed on my mother, the estrangement I felt from her, and something of my background.

"It's naut about your mutha, you know," Jo admonished me.

"What are you talking about?"

"Your anger. It doesn't directly have anything to do with her. She's just the catalyst."

"What catalyst? What are you talking about?"

"It's your fatha."

"He's not the one who wanted the divorce."

"No, stupid, naut him. Your real dad—your biological, or whatevah you want to call it, bloody fatha."

"What?"

"Do you know who he is?"

"No."

"Have you evah asked your mum?"

"Sort of."

"What 'sort of'?"

"Well, I know his name, and she told me once that I looked like him."

"Anythin' else?"

"Not really."

"Sounds to me as if you need to talk to her."

She had a point. I hadn't spoken to my mother in nearly six months. Why had I said such awful things to her? Certainly I was angry, but was my anger as misplaced as Jo had inferred? Why did I condemn her for making choices she needed to make? Why hadn't I ever pressed her for more details about my first two years? What was I afraid of? Was I afraid of rocking what family foundation I did have, or did I fear an answer to my questions?

"You know," she continued, "I nevah had the opportunity you've got."

"What opportunity is that?" I asked, confused by her optimism.

"Well, for awl you know, yo'r fatha is still alive, out there somewhere, perhaps hoping you'll find him someday. My fatha died when I was three years old."

"How did he die?"

"He used t' have a liddle w'rkshop in the back of the Tudor manor we lived in. He loved t' tinker with things... you know... fix things, w'rk with his hands. I'd sit for hours and watch while he'd fix this or that, or carve things from pieces of wood he found. One day, he was attempting to repair a broken vacuum sweeper and hadn't botha'ed to unplug it—he accidentally electrocuted himself. I walked in t' find him lying on the fleur with his tongue hanging from his mouth. Before I knew what was happening, I was carried off by nuns only to return four days layta without a dad."

"Jesus… that's tragic."

"I've always wondered what it would have been like to have grown up with me dad. I'll nevah have an opportunity to see him again, but you may possibly have that chance."

Did I? I'd never even imagined what it might have been like to have grown up with my biological father. Knowing so little, how could I? Now I felt almost obligated to search for him so I could put her story to rest, allow her to live vicariously through my own experience. It also somehow felt easier to consider seeking out my biological father knowing she was behind me, encouraging me.

Finally I called my now newly divorced mother.

"Mom, it's me."

"Hello, Mikey."

She was still referring to me as if I were a small child! I thought I could hear something in her breath as she answered, perhaps hesitation or fear. Or was it me?

"I'm glad you called," she added.

"Listen, Mom, I'm sorry for what I said. I'm sorry I hurt you." I forced the words, forced myself through the lingering anger and fear. "I'm sorry I haven't spoken to you in so long. I... I... I have some questions I need answered." Nervously forging forward, I completely neglected to inquire about her newly divorced emotional frame of mind.

She cleared her throat and said slowly, "All right. I'll give you all the answers I can."

I gathered courage. "I need to know about my father—my biological dad."

"What do you want to know? I'll tell you whatever you need to know," she volunteered quickly. I had expected resistance, but her answer was swift and to the point. "Who was he? Where did you meet him? When did you marry? What happened? What was...."

"Hang on, hang on," she interrupted. "Let me get to these questions first. I've told you his name was John Sidney Woods." It was true, she had.

"I met him at school out east when I transferred from the University of Illinois to Boston University. He was a handsome man, beautiful. I fell in love"—I could hear her struggling, not sure if she should continue—"and then got pregnant."

"Was I a mistake?" I thought aloud.

"Mikey, don't use that term, honey. That's not right. Maybe you weren't exactly planned, but you were never a mistake. Anyway, we were very young and scared, Sid and I. Sid, that's what everybody called your father."

This was the first time I'd heard my mother refer to him by that name. It suddenly became clear that my name, Michael Sidney, was a tribute to my father. My whole life I had been embarrassed by it. I thought it sounded silly. I never used the name, refusing even to sign a middle initial. Strangely, I had never made the connection.

"Sid and I were just kids. There was no reliable birth control back then. We had no money, no means to support a child."

"I suppose an abortion was out of the question back then?"

"You've got to remember, honey, this was 1957. I didn't know any-place where I could get an abortion. There was no legal abortion. I didn't even know anyplace where I could get an illegal abortion. I mean, those are dark alley kinds of things. I didn't know anyplace where I could do that. I had no idea. I don't think Sid did either." Silence. Then she continued in a solemn, somewhat guilty tone, "I remember trying quinine tablets when I first discovered I was pregnant. Someone had told me that taking them could induce abortion. Sid went out and got some from somebody somewhere. Hot baths and quinine. Of course that didn't work. When you're young, you're very fertile. If you're not healthy, then it works, but I was always healthy. So I decided to go away, to leave town. I really had no plan. I didn't know what I was doing. I hoped that he would want to marry me, but he didn't say that. So I decided that I had to go away, do something. I certainly could not go home. I was nineteen years old, twenty by the time you were born. I had a friend who had gone out to Los Angeles, so I scraped together all the money I could from my part-time job and bought a one-way ticket to California."

"Did you call your parents and tell them what was going on?"

"Nobody ever called anybody long distance those days. Unless you were wealthy, you wrote letters. People wrote letters. I think I wrote them a letter once I got out to California and told them I'd quit school and was visiting my friend, and that I didn't know how long I was going to be out there—a total lie."

"Weren't they worried about you?"

"My parents and I did not have the greatest relationship. We weren't on the best of terms. You know your grandfather was an Armenian immigrant who survived the Turkish slaughter of his country. He witnessed the massacre of his village and the death of his parents. He was made a slave to a Turkish family until the political situation in Turkey changed, bringing the genocide to a halt. He then escaped to an orphanage for Armenian refugees in Syria, then made it to France, and finally to America on a false passport. His life was tough, which made him strict and unforgiving. I was always getting into trouble because I didn't fit the mold like my older sister. We were constantly at odds with one another."

"So, what happened when you got out there?"

"I got a job doing telephone solicitation. By this time I was getting kind of big. You could not work if you were pregnant, they wouldn't hire you. So what was I going to do? I couldn't make any money. I was selling encyclopedias over the phone, or some stupid thing like that. It wasn't working out, so my friend introduced me to this woman, Mrs. Layden, who ended up placing me as a daytime companion with an elderly lady. I tried it for three or four days and I couldn't stand it. It was the saddest thing that I… I just couldn't do it. Then she put me with this wealthy family, a doctor and his wife and kids. It was a horrible experience. They had no furniture and they didn't treat their kids well and they treated me like I was some kind of non-person."

The stories were flowing now. It was my first real glimpse of her past. Her words came easier as the questions leapt from my mouth.

"Did you keep in touch with Sid?"

"I kept writing him and he asked me to come back to Boston as soon as you were born. I went back and we got married and lived in the area known as Roxbury, a very poor neighborhood. We lived in an old house bordering the projects near the Fenway Park and the museum. I used to walk you there in your stroller. We would pass the dry cleaners on the way and the lady from the shop would come out and talk to us. Your father had about three jobs trying to make things work. We

One month.

didn't have any money. We had no furniture to speak of, never really went anywhere, and I never knew if we were going to have enough food from day to day. I was so scared those first years. Just terribly scared."

"What about your parents? Didn't you tell them about your child? Couldn't they help you?"

"I wrote my parents when I got back to Boston with you, and my father wanted nothing to do with me. They disowned me."

"You mean, they wouldn't talk to you?"

"I remember while we were living in Boston, my grandfather died and I had to go home for the funeral. When I got home, my father didn't say a word to me. None of our relatives knew anything about the fact that I had a child. No one was told, and it was made very clear that was not to change."

Mom and me.

I suddenly had this picture of a young, extremely frightened, twenty-year-old mother with few resources struggling to get by with no help from her parents—how alone in the world she must have felt. Then it occurred to me how her insurmountable fear had become my fear as a young child. Those profoundly important first two years of my life were fraught with fear and instability.

No wonder I had such difficulties confronting the hazards in my life. "What was my father like?" I asked timidly.

"Your father was a good man. He loved you very much. He was a good father to you. He used to play with you and take pictures of you. He was quite the photographer."

"Do you have any pictures?" I asked.

"I must have one or two somewhere. I'll look for them."

"So what happened? Why did we leave?"

She hesitated. I heard her move, shifting in her seat. She swallowed loudly. "I don't know, I guess things just fell apart," she explained. "We were so poor, there was so much pressure on us, and we were just kids. Finally, after almost two years of this, my parents sent my oldest sister and her husband out to check up on us and report back. When my mother heard about our situation, she came out to visit and

In the park.

begged me to come home. I knew I couldn't live like that any longer so I packed us up and we went back to live with your grandparents in Waukegan."

"What happened to my father?" I asked.

"He called a few

times but there wasn't much we could do. It was so difficult. We got a divorce and later, after I married John Fosberg, Sid agreed to allow Johnnie to adopt you. He called once more when you were about eight or nine years old. You answered the phone and when he asked for me, you gave me the phone. He just called to see how we were

doing. I've never spoken to him again."

I answered the phone? I spoke to my father? I tried desperately to pull up images, snapshots of my past. I tried to picture all of us together. What did it look like? As I tried to process all of it, I realized what I had to do.

"Mom, I'm going to try to find him," I blurted out.

She shot back, "What? Why do you want to do that? You have a father, John Fosberg. He raised you. He is your father."

"Yes, he is my father. He did raise me, I understand that," I said. "Look, I don't know how to explain this. It's as if I were a large jigsaw puzzle and there is one piece missing. I don't even know if it is a significant piece or not, but I know I need to find it to complete the picture."

How do you explain something that's missing? And how do you even know it's missing if you don't ever remember having it?

"If there's any way I can help, let me know," she offered almost in a whisper.

"You said you spoke to him when I was eight years old?"

"Yes?"

"Do you remember where he was living at the time?"

She paused. I shifted in my seat. She cleared her throat.

"Well, I think he lived in the Detroit area at the time. I'm not sure, but I think that is what I remember him saying."

We said our good-byes and I could still feel my mother's uneasiness mixed with a trace of relief... or was it mine?

REALLY.

A COUPLE OF THINGS MY MOTHER NEVER TOLD ME

A week went by as I weighed the new information my mother had given me and where it might lead. I knew I wanted to find my birth father, but I was at a loss as to how exactly I was going to do it. Jo's story about the death of her father and my conversation with my mother gave newfound immediacy to my intention. But the anxiety that was stirred up made the walls of my already tiny apartment seem to close in around me even more. It was time to take a walk to the beach.

As I meandered, the questions returned: How would I find him? Is he still alive? Should I hire a private detective? How could I pay for that? Aren't there agencies to help people find their parents? Where should I begin?

I wandered aimlessly through the maze of shops and restaurants of Santa Monica's downtown. As I passed a delicatessen I noticed a young boy, no older than five, sharing a lunch with his father at the counter and stopped to watch. The boy was the spitting image of his father, a short bowl cut of dark hair covered a small round face holding his tiny smile. He chewed eagerly as his father fed him half of a corned beef on rye. Mustard, bread, and beef bits dripped down the front of his napkin-protected body. They moved and reacted with ease and familiarity. The father smiled as he took his napkin and wiped the boy's mustard-stained cheeks. I wanted my bowl cut, my corned beef on rye. I wanted to see someone who looked just like me. Most of all, I wanted the relationship.

I hurried across the street and passed by the Santa Monica Public Library. I stopped for a moment. *What are the chances that after twenty-five years, my father could still live in the Detroit area?* I asked myself. I retraced my steps and went into the library.

"Do you shelve phone books of other cities?" I inquired of the young librarian.

"All major U.S. metropolitan areas and most outlying counties. You'll find those around the corner in the back of the reference section."

I was soon staring at the spine of the Metro Detroit white pages. I slowly removed it from the shelf, found a spot at a nearby table, and headed for the W's. The listings for Woods started:

JOHN S. WOODS	17610 Fairway Dr.	(313) 345-5391
JOHN WOODS	3547 Tilman Avenue	(313) 895-3126

Then five more listings of JOHN WOODS with corresponding addresses and phone numbers. Then a JOHNNIE, and a JOHNNY.

I stared down at the page. I was completely unaware of anything around me—time, place, people. I retrieved a pen and paper from my pocket and quickly scribbled down the names and phone numbers, then neatly replaced the directory and swiftly made my way for the exit.

I raced back the nine blocks to my apartment. Once inside, I paced the three steps across and three steps back of my cubicle, finally placed the piece of paper with the names and numbers on my desk and sat down. I gripped the receiver but could not pick it up. What if I find him? What would I say? What if he didn't want to speak to me? How would I react? Was it fair of me to impose myself on a man who'd been absent most of my life? What if he has a family and this creates an embarrassing situation? What if none of the names on this list are my father? What will I do next? What if it all turns out to be nothing and I never find him? Do I really even want to do this? Why go to all the trouble? What on earth could I possibly learn?

It was mid-afternoon, and Detroit was three hours ahead. I needed to make my move. What would I say to someone should they answer? Obviously I'm looking for a John Sidney Woods, but how many men could have that same name and what would help me determine if he were my father? I'd ask him if he lived in Boston in 1957. Was that enough? How about if he had been married to a woman named Adrienne Pilibosian? An affirmative answer to that question would certainly confirm my fate.

Finally I grabbed the phone and punched in the top phone number on the list, my heart pounding. I heard the phone ring twice, then a click. "Hello?" The voice was deep, low, resonant. Startled, I held on, unsure if I should hang up or continue. What were the three questions again?

"I... I'm... I'm looking for a John Sidney Woods?" I said tentatively.

"You're speaking with him," came the voice back on the other end. *Could it be?* I thought. "Did you live in the Boston area in 1957?"

"Yes I did," he answered.

I slowly formed the next sentence, almost stuttering to get it out.

"W-w-w-were you m-m-m-married to a... w... w-w-w-woman by the name of Adrienne P-p-p-p-pilibosian?"

He paused for a moment. It felt like an hour.

"Yes, I was."

My dad. First try. First time. Thirty years later. "My name is Michael Fosberg, and I'm your son!" I blurted out.

I felt like the wind had been knocked out of me. My whole body was shaking. I didn't even hear what he said next. I suddenly remembered horror stories from friends—or was it television reality shows?—of children locating their parents after many years apart, and the parents spurning them.

I blurted out, "Look, it's all right if you don't want to talk to me. I just wanted to find out how you were... and let you know that I was all right."

"No... my God, son... How are you? Where are you?" he said unexpectedly.

Son?! He called me "son"! I savored the word as I searched for a way to answer his simple, yet almost overwhelming questions.

"I'm... I'm fine... I'm... I'm good... I live in Los Angeles, well, Santa Monica actually, not far from the beach."

"Nice place?" he asked innocently.

As I glanced around my cramped quarters, it suddenly looked incredibly foreign to me, an unfamiliar setting filled with familiar things. The voice on the other end of the phone was somehow so close to mine. It's rich, thick quality penetrated my memory. It felt like a warm, soothing, vocal embrace.

"It's small," I said, "but quaint and comfortable."

"What have you been doing with yourself, son?" he inquired.

"Well..." I stumbled as I quickly realized I hadn't thought through how to address him. I started again, "Well... J... Joh... Si... S... D... D... Dad..." I set it out there clumsily. After all, I had just met the guy, and only over the phone, but he is my father, how else should I address him? "It's been a good life so far," I finally said, sounding as if my life were somehow almost over.

"Did you get a good education?" he asked me.

"I think so. I graduated from Waukegan High School, then went on to college at the University of Minnesota in Minneapolis, graduating with a bachelors in fine arts."

"Which arts?"

"Acting, directing."

"So are you acting or directing?"

"Well, let's just say I'm still looking for that proverbial 'break' in show business."

"Well, if you love what you do, son, don't ever give up on it. And your mother, how is she?"

"She's pretty good, I guess."

"What do you mean, 'you guess'?"

"Well," I began reluctantly, "she just got a divorce, and we're not exactly on the best of terms right now."

"Just remember, son, she's the only mother you've got. Don't be too hard on her."

I was eager to shift the conversation from a discussion about what I now realized was my beguiling mother. "So, how about you, what has your life been like?"

"Well..." he began, "I've been working for Ford Motor Company the last twenty years as a purchasing agent. Before that I was with Chrysler Corporation for fifteen years. I've been married to a woman named Sue, and we have... no children."

Thirty-five years wrapped up into a couple of brief descriptions. He continued, "You know, son, there are a couple of things you need to know that I'm sure your mother never told you."

What on earth could he possibly be talking about? I wondered.

"What's that?" I asked.

"Well, first of all, I want you to know that no matter what you were told, or what you thought happened, I have always loved you and thought about you a lot."

I did not move. I could not breathe. Had I heard that correctly? Was this the absent fatherly love I'd sought out for these past many years? For the first time my father, my birth dad, my biological procreator, my blood, my pop, told me that he loved me.

"There's one other thing that I'm sure your mother never told you."

"What's that?" I managed to squeeze out between the tears now making their way slowly down my cheeks. There was a slight pause. I tried to regain my composure as he cleared his throat.

"I'm African American," he said.

My body went numb. I felt light-headed and my legs began to give way. I braced myself against the bureau with my left hand as I continued to hold the phone with my right. I suddenly felt very warm. My eyes darted around searching for something, a clue, a map, some help.

"Your grandparents are Roy and Lois Woods, descendants of the Woods and Robinson families of Columbia and Jefferson City, Missouri, and have been living for the past forty years in Virginia Beach, Virginia."

I sat down slowly on the bed in stunned silence, trying to breathe without trembling. My throat was dry and choked. I struggled to respond, but all I could say was, "Wow." There was no movement, no shifting, no shuffling feet, just the silence of the phone connection. He cleared his throat again, relieving me of yet more breath. *Oh no, what next?* I thought.

"Are you all right?"

"Yes... yes... I'm fine... I'm great..." stumbling rapidly, "you're right, she never bothered to mention that."

"Your grandfather was the chairman of the science and engineering departments at Norfolk State University and the science building is named after him. There are unconfirmed stories in the family that his great-grandfather, Al Woods, was first cousin to John Brown. Your great-great-grandfather was a member of the 54th regiment of the colored infantry during the Civil War. Your grandmother's father was Charles 'Lefty' Robinson, once an all-star pitcher with the Negro Leagues. Your grandmother has four siblings, all still alive and well."

I couldn't seem to formulate words, let alone sentences. I'd suddenly inherited a rich family history dating back to slavery. I went from growing up in a white middle-class family to being a black man, in the blink of an eye. Why hadn't my mother told me?

My father continued, "Your grandmother is approaching eighty but still cooks and busies herself around the house and with the church. Your grandfather is a step behind her at 79, holds various honors

The original paper on which I copied the Detroit listings, with notes about information my father shared with me during the phone call.

throughout the community, and teaches Sunday school every week."

I strained to try to put an image together. What do they look like? What does he look like? Do I look like him?

And as if somehow answering my thoughts, he slowly offered, "I am very light skinned and have been told I could almost pass for white, but like most black families, there are all sorts of shades in our blood. I'll put together a couple of pictures and send them your way and maybe you could do the same?"

We exchanged addresses, and I promised to send some photos.

"I'll write you a letter and try to fill in more of the blanks," I promised.

"I'll dig up some photos," he said, "but I'm not much of a letter writer."

"Say, listen... D-d-d-dad." There it was again, that "D" word. "You do want to keep in touch, don't you?"

"Absolutely, son. I've been hoping you'd get in touch at some point in your life. I was just never sure when it would be. I half expected you years ago when you were in your twenties. We have lots to talk about and plenty of time to do it."

We hung up the phone. Damn! I felt so alive at that moment, so invigorated, so at *peace*. Damn! How amazing was it that the first call I made turned out to be the one? I wanted to call everyone I knew. I wanted to scream out, I FOUND MY DAD! I thought about when I was twelve years old, lying awake late at night in the top bunk above my fast-asleep brother, and how I would stare at the ceiling and whisper aloud, *I wish I were black... I wish I were black...* Why would I utter those words—a crazy thought for a young white boy—unless deep down I thought I was? Perhaps those first few years around my father, his family and relatives, made a subconscious lasting impression that was only now becoming clear. After all those years of thinking I'd been switched at birth!

I looked down at my arms, my body—I am, damn it, I am! All my life I couldn't figure out what was wrong with me when there was really nothing wrong with me at all.

I'M BLACK, GODDAMN IT. I'M BLACK!

"I ALWAYS THOUGHT YOU
WERE BLACK!"

In the excitement of that first moment of discovery, I felt on top of the world. I had uncovered the long-missing piece, unearthed the other half of my genetic roots, and I felt a childlike joy and relief in finding my biological father, my dad, my African-American heritage.

But how I would I explain all this, and identify myself, to those who knew me as white? What attitudes would I encounter? What repercussions might I face?

My mind was on overload, tossing up a smorgasbord of emotions, information, and reconsiderations. Then I started in on the "what ifs" and "if onlys."

If only I'd known before I filled out applications for college!

What if Jo had gotten pregnant before I'd learned about my father, and the child had been born with dark skin? "Who the hell have you been sleeping with, Jo?" I might have screamed with rage and misplaced jealousy. "No one! I swear the child is yours!" she'd respond with total truth and innocence.

Hell, what if Jo were to be secretly dismayed by my new racial categorization?

"I'm black," I told her not hours after I'd spoken to him.

"What?" exclaimed my British bombshell, dubbed thus for both her blonde mane and her penchant for verbal explosiveness.

"I found my father, and it turns out he's black."

"Bloody hell! You cawn't be serious?"

"I spoke to him not more than an hour ago. He lives in Detroit. His parents, my grandparents, are still alive and living in Virginia." An enormous smile spread across her face, and she flung her body at me and wrapped me in her long slender arms.

"What happened? What'd he say?" she asked.

I went through the details of that first conversation as she stroked my hair and kissed me gently on the forehead. Her closeness made me feel sheltered, and her incredulity that my mother had never said anything I found comforting.

"No wonder you're so angry with her!" she sided.

It took about a week, but eventually the anger boiled over, as Jo had predicted it would. I couldn't believe my mother had kept this secret from me for all these years. Anger at not having been told, a sense of betrayal for her having essentially lied to me by concealing the truth, and the hurt I felt at being abandoned all came together in my mind in what I attributed to a perfect storm of deception on my mother's part. Yet perhaps it wasn't so much about what she hadn't told me as about what I had never bothered to ask. I guess I'd always presumed my biological father was white. I couldn't fathom that not only had I not been told, but that my mother had been with a black man. It's not something you think about necessarily when, as a white person, you set out to discover your roots. I guess one assumes from appearance what one is.

Even after a comment she'd made when I was still in elementary school that my father had some Indian blood, I was still convinced he'd been essentially white. I'm "white," my mom's "white," therefore my biological father's got to be "white"… right? We had been given an assignment to explore our family roots. You know, the "my dad's Irish, and my mom's Italian" kind of thing. When I pressed my mother, the only detail I could pry from her lips was that she thought my father had said he had some American Indian blood—Cherokee—she seemed to recall. I had held tight to this piece of information, tentative though it seemed, carrying it throughout my teen years like a devout Christian would wear a cross. It never felt solid somehow, but I wore it nonetheless, as if this were my connection to my paternal past. At one point, when applying for colleges, I decided to take advantage of this once-mentioned racial anecdote, checking the American Indian box on several applications.

I still couldn't quite believe that my mother would withhold half of my racial identity from me, that she would deceive me. I just didn't want to believe it. She was my mother. She wouldn't do anything to hurt or betray her baby, would she? Mothers don't do that. *Maybe she didn't know he was black,* I kept telling myself. *He said he was light skinned, maybe she just never figured it out.* I struggled to convince myself. We were too close when I was growing up for her not to tell me this.

She could not have known, I insisted to myself. *My mother would not lie to me.* I was her firstborn, the child out of wedlock, the one she risked so much to protect.

Yet no matter how hard I tried, I could not convince myself. I became obsessed with my anger. I threw objects across the room. I shouted and swore.

"How the fuck could she have done this to me! So what if she's my mother, does she think she can play God as well? This is my life—that's evidently not important to her. Thirty years of deceit!"

I had to call her, but what would I say? *You betrayed me, Mom, so fuck you.... I hate you, Mom, so leave me alone.... How could you, Mom?...* Click.

Just as I reached to make the call, the phone rang. I slowly picked up the receiver, certain that it was my mother, as if some psychic warning had gone out to her.

"Hello?" I strained to control my voice and keep my anger in check.

"Foz, it's me, Tommy."

"Tommy?" I had been so convinced it was my mother that his name and energetic voice didn't register.

"Hey, buddy, it's been a while. I was just calling to see how you been doin'."

Tommy was an old friend, a happy-go-lucky actor-director type living in Hollywood—ironically originally from Detroit—to whom I hadn't spoken for years. "Well, buddy, you'll never believe what has happened to me..." I began. I gave him a condensed version of "Finding My Father," or, "A Black Man in a White Man's Body."

"I always thought you were black," he said quite matter-of-factly.

How he came to this conclusion was beyond me. But his response was the first in a series of similar reactions among many of my friends. The theme was consistent: *We thought you were black all along.* How did they think they knew? What did they see? Was it that I owned practically every James Brown record ever recorded? Or could it have been that I could recite every word of every Richard Pryor album, complete with characterizations, dialects, and facial expressions? Or perhaps it was those wild outfits I wore in high school: platform shoes, multicolored rayon shirts, wide purple corduroy pants, topped off with my kinky afro and a wide-brimmed hat? Or better still, it may have been, as one friend put it, "Foz, you were cooler than cool. Anybody dat cool we knew had to have been of another race."

I also remembered the par-

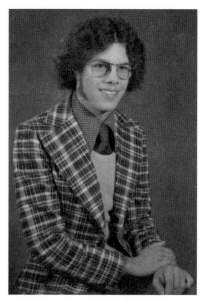

Waukegan Township High School, graduation 1975, age 17.

That's me on the left attending a college costume party.

ents of a high school girlfriend who, upon meeting me one summer, with
my wild afro and dark tan, pulled their daughter aside and asked her a
bit too loudly, "Nancy, exactly what nationality is that boy?" And maybe
it wasn't simply my 'fro that had gotten me cast as a mulatto in my first
professional show out of college, for which they cornrowed my hair.
Only I, it seemed, couldn't see this possibility of my biracial self.

"That's great, Foz!" Tommy continued. "Are you gonna meet him?"

"Well, sure, I hope so, but not for a while, I guess."

"So what's troubling you?"

"I'm angry, Tommy. I am *pissed off.*" I laid out what I felt, with
emphasis, now embracing Jo's creed. "I can't believe my mother never
told me! She lied to me, Tommy, betrayed me, and I don't know what
the hell to say to her."

But Tommy saw it another way. He said, "No, Foz—don't you see?
This is an *opportunity.* You have an opportunity to absolve your mother

of her shame. Imagine what it was like for her—she was given this shame by her parents, Armenian immigrants, and has held on to it your entire life. You can help her to let it go, help her release her guilt and shame."

There it was. Simple, thoughtful, and to the point. I'd never heard anything quite so beautiful, let alone sensible. What must it have been like for her, a nineteen-year-old first-generation Armenian girl away at college in Boston in 1957, falling in love with a black man, disowned by her family when they find out she's carrying his child, then forced to leave the man she loved by pressures greater than she even understood. Finally, she returned home to a mostly hostile family environment and was forced to raise her child as a single mother.

This was the answer I'd been searching for. All my anger, all the hurt and betrayal spinning around in my head, suddenly stopped. *This isn't about you*, I thought. *It's about what she'd had to go through to raise you.* The enormity of this gesture was still sinking in as Tommy and I said our good-byes.

I sat collecting my thoughts as I tried to put what Tommy had said, and the fresh realization about my mother's early predicament, into perspective. My head was swimming with thoughts about her, about us, about my father, my family, my race. So many things had happened so quickly. I was still searching for a way to wrap my arms around my new sense of self, my new identity.

———————

"Get the fuck outta here!" Unlike my childhood friends, my sponsor—the person who helps an alcoholic through the program's twelve steps—was incredulous.

"I know," I said, happy to talk with someone as surprised as I was. "Can you believe it?" It still had not fully registered deep within me.

"Damn, Foz, I always knew you had it in ya!"

I shared my revelatory tale at AA meetings, discovering it had a power to uplift a room full of addicts trying to sort through the messes that we called our lives. Sometimes just hearing others' triumphs—and often embarrassments—can put one's own life into perspective. And I found an opportunity for forgiveness in the telling and retelling of the story. And yet at first I was still unable to offer that most precious and difficult of gifts—forgiveness—to my mother herself. When I actually picked up the phone to call her, a voice in me still insisted that she didn't know of my father's black heritage. She couldn't have. The little boy in me still couldn't believe that his mommy had not been truthful.

"Hello, Mom?"

"Michael?" Her voice sounded weak. "Are you all right?"

"Yeah, Mom."

"Everything's OK?"

"Yeah, sure," I said. There was nervousness in her questions as if she knew why I had called. I took a deep breath and formed the words slowly, carefully. "I found my father." There was a pause. It seemed like a long pause, although it might have been only seconds. Then came a flurry of words, her nervousness firing rapidly through the phone line.

"You did? That's great. That's great. That's what you wanted. You're happy. Are you happy? Are you sure? That's what you wanted. You found your father. That's what you wanted. Wasn't it? Are you all right?"

"Yes," I said.

"That's good. That's good. I'm glad."

I had been was so preoccupied with the silly notion that she couldn't have known he was black, that she would not have held this secret for all these many years, that I couldn't resist posing the question, slowly, awkwardly. "So, Mom, did you... *know*... he is"—how else could I put it?—"black?"

She laughed, a genuine laugh, nervous, and yet slightly relieved. "Yes."

"So, what was that Cherokee Indian thing you told me while I was growing up?" More nervous laughter followed by stammering as she searched for words. "I thought he told me his family had Indian blood. He was awfully light skinned, you know. There must have been some type of light blood in his family. I didn't know what to tell you, Michael. I didn't want you growing up confused or ashamed. I didn't want you to grow up resenting me—or yourself for that matter. I sought advice from a therapist, and we decided that it was best not to tell you right away, to wait until you got older. As you got older it became harder to tell you. I was afraid you might reject me, be angry with me, resent me. I didn't want to lose you. I'm sorry Michael. I didn't—"

"You don't have to apologize," I interrupted. Release her from her guilt, Tommy had said. "You did what you thought was right," I continued. "You did the best you knew how, and that's OK with me. I found my father, and I still love you."

She made a choking sound as she struggled to get out the words: "Do you? Are you... do you mean that? Are you sure?"

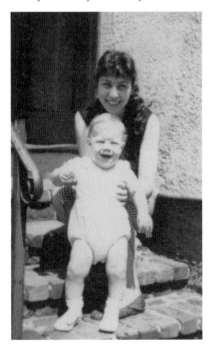

"Yes, Mom," I reassured her. "Everything is all right. I still love you."

I heard her deep intake of breath, and then a sigh. We said our good-byes. I set the phone down gently in its cradle.

The next day while I was out working, my mother left a message on my answering machine.

"Michael... hi, I... uh... I wanted to thank you for what you said yesterday. I mean, if you really mean it? I can't begin to tell you what that meant to me. I'm, well, let's just say I'm relieved and happy you found your father. He's a good man. Thank you, honey. I'll talk to you soon. I love you. Bye."

I stood above my answering machine and listened to the quality of my mother's voice, the lightness, the release. I felt such a sense of fullness, of empathy. I thought of the call from Tommy—an innocent call from an old friend had made this all possible.

IF THE SHOE FITS

The phone was ringing. It was 6 a.m. Pacific time, nearly two weeks since I had first spoken to my biological father. A "hello" barely audible and semiconscious crept out of my mouth as I grabbed the receiver.

"Hey, shuga, how ya doin'?" asked the southern drawl from the unidentifiable female at the other end of the phone line. Had I heard it correctly, or was I just dreaming?

"You still got dem big feets?" she continued as I tried to make sense of what I was hearing. The sun had not yet risen, and my mind was as murky as the room was dim. But there was something familiar about that voice. "Shuga, you there?"

"Yes," I answered, suddenly alert.

"Where the hell you bin? We bin expectin' you ten years ago!"

My dream sleep state had given way to realization. "Granny?" I hazarded meekly.

"Yeah, shuga, it's me. How the hell are ya?"

"I'm great now," I answered. "I feel like I'm finally home."

"You shore are. Our door has always bin open fo' ya. I always thought that if there was any warmth in Adi, 'n da warmth that was in John Sidney, there had ta be warmth in you. I jus' had da feeling dat there was enough warmth 'n closeness dat one day there would be a knock at 'r door an' you gon' be standin' an' wantin' to know is this the residence of the parents of John Sidney Woods."

"Well, knock, knock, I'm home! Tell me, how the heck are you?"

"I got no reason ta complain... wouldn't do me no good no how. Once in a while I get a visit from Artha. Other den dat I'm not bad fo' an old lady."

"Who's Arthur?" I ask

"Oh you know, he come creepin' 'round in my hands—arthritis."

My seventy-nine-year-old, southern Virginia, African-American grandmother, Lois E. Woods. Her energy and joy of life came tumbling through the receiver, infectious and lovable. I conjured up a picture in my mind of a big woman, with a big smile, and warm embracing hug. "Can you send me some photographs of you and grandpa?"

"Well shore, shuga. I got plen'y a photographs of all of us. Lemme look through what I got 'n I'll send some yo' way."

We exchanged addresses and phone numbers. I would like to see her soon, I said, thinking about all the time I'd missed out on.

"Don't you worry, shuga, we gonna get together soon, all a us, you, John Sid, Poppa 'n me. There's gonna be plenty a time fo' dat."

I hung up the phone. I was wide awake now, sitting straight up in bed, with a feeling of warmth about me I'd never experienced.

About a week and a half later, I returned home one day to find on the doorstep a small package with a Virginia Beach return address. I unlocked the door, threw off my coat, and sat on the bed, staring at the package clutched in my hands. I sat transfixed by the return address, that of my newfound grandparents. I shook the box for a clue to what was inside, but nothing moved within. Finally I opened the box and exposed its contents: an envelope of photos and a small object done up in tissue. I carefully unwrapped it. I sat motionless as I stared at the item in front of me.

In my hands lay a small, white leather Stride Rite shoe with faded laces; a baby shoe, perfectly intact. A few wrinkles of wear, a crease across the toes, the tongue broken in, laces loose and brownish from age, the soles slightly worn. I held my forgotten past in my hands and wept like the child that wore that shoe, thirty-two years ago, the child that was separated from the shoe as he was from his father, his father's family, his father's heritage.

I sat there paralyzed, without sense of time or place, in the darkening room, surrounded by swirling imaginings of a childhood foregone. Finally, I set the

Me, Granny, and Sid.

shoe aside and picked up the envelope of photos. I opened it carefully and was immediately presented with an image of a small, chubby, blond-haired child in the arms of a beautiful black woman with a young, light-skinned black man standing beside her. The woman wore a clean, white, pressed dress and matching white accessories of earrings, bracelet, and purse. The child looked happily at the camera while the woman, and the proud smiling man with hands on his hips, gazed at him lovingly. The child's arm rested comfortably on the woman's shoulder as his legs dangled under her arms, with a pair of brand new white leather shoes on his feet.

On the back, handwritten, were the words:

Aug. 1958
Tavern Rd.
Proud grandmom

A childhood lost, now found.

THE "N" WORD

arge family dinners hosted by my Armenian grandparents filled my Waukegan childhood. These centered around mouth-watering delicacies and often featured traditional televised holiday sporting events, an assortment of board games (backgammon was the headliner), or an occasional venture into the drawer packed with photographs of distant relatives we'd yet to meet or, in some cases, never would. Faded, black-and-white photographs showing poor Armenian families posing in their Sunday best—dark clothes, dark faces, short smiles, distinctly Eastern European—or portraits of stern, wrinkled faces led us on journeys deep into family history.

The dinners were usually rousing, noisy affairs, with seven kids and seven adults vying for attention. Of the group, my Uncle Al, the husband of my mother's older

Garabed's sister, Elizabeth, with husband and children, Louise, Hagop and Ashad.

Dead-end kids at a park in Waukegan. My mother's uncle, Arthur Bedrosian, is the small boy center.

sister, was typically the loudest, most opinionated, and at times most obnoxious. It seemed no one could or would stand up to his "beefs." His bravado was displayed in such a passive-aggressive fashion that it was difficult to push back, let alone take his words seriously. Of medium height and build, with dark, habitually askew hair, he was known for his craving of Necco Wafers and for the tobacco pipe he occasionally smoked. He would first clear the stem with a white pipestem cleaner and then pack the bowl with the care and precision of a watch repairman. The great puffs of smoke would billow above him as we'd choke on the sickly sweet smell of his chosen tobacco. It was a fascinating ritual that I never tired of watching.

From the time we were little, he'd confront us repeatedly about our future ambitions—the most dreaded of our conversations with him.

"Well, Michael, what do you plan to do with your life?"

"I'm not real sure, Uncle Al. I thought maybe I would get through junior high school before I made any kind of decisions," I managed with my slight teenage wit.

"You gotta have a plan. Do you have a plan?"

"No."

"Are you planning on acting or what?"

"I guess so."

"Well, what's it gonna be?"

"I like to act," I tell him.

"Tough job. I'd consider something else if I were you. How about writing? Can you write?"

"I really don't know."

"Well, son, let me tell you something," he'd always begin, as if his were the only advice on the planet worth anything, "you've got to make some choices here. Get with the program."

"What program would that be?" I'd ask innocently.

"You know—pick a field, follow a path, get some training."

"But I'm still in the eighth grade."

"Never too late to start. Never too early."

By the time he was done with me, I felt like a blundering idiot, this for a kid who was barely fourteen years old.

He was a fairly successful self-made architect who, with his two brothers, had inherited a sizable construction firm from their father. They went on to build the company into a thriving contracting business in Waukegan and the surrounding communities. They would eventually hand it over to their sons, my cousins, who unlike me apparently already had their destiny well planned for them.

The three oldest of his four sons had very high opinions of their own entitlement as they competed for who would be seated next to their father at the head of the table. The youngest was mischievous, but quieter, sort of an adorable runt of the litter. We all exchanged verbal banter, got into trouble together, and tried as best we could to maintain some sort of equal footing in our respective familial standings. However, the deck was stacked against my brother, sister, and me since we were raised in a much more modest environment, our blue-collar working-class ethic versus their upper-middle-class affluence.

The gulf was most apparent during those elaborate family dinners.

The first three sons would slovenly grab choice bits of food, proceed to inhale their overflowing plates of Armenian ambrosia, and then smack us down with loud opinions as we'd make feeble attempts to stand our ground. My uncle and his family not only out grossed us, they out boasted us as well.

"Frank Lloyd Wright was just an average guy," my uncle would declare as we prepared ourselves for forthcoming opinions from his well of pet theorems and architectural expertise. "Not terribly talented, just lucky, if you ask me."

His wife, my mother's older sister, always sat quietly, seemingly unaffected by her husband's forceful opinions. She was a brilliant doctor, a talented gardener, and an artistic weaver, yet she never attempted to rein in her husband. She'd smile and laugh, but rarely challenged.

One evening when I was in my early teens, the dinnertime discourse suddenly took an unusual turn. My uncle, talking about his employees, mentioned something about a particular handyman I'd seen around their shop, a black man.

"If he wasn't so lazy, he'd get a lot more accomplished. That's the problem with those niggers, they're too damn lazy. They're never gonna get ahead."

Pain shot through me. I'd never heard this word uttered by anyone in my family. There were some titters of laughter from the boys. I bowed my head as if in shame. No one said a word to him. He carried on as if it was our everyday dinner table language.

"Sometimes I feel like I'm being taken advantage of. I mean he's a good man and all, but you'd think those niggers would get with the program, you know?"

There was that "program" again. Was I like them, unable to get my program together, therefore lazy and unmotivated?

His boys continued to smack their lips as they devoured their food, occasionally piping in with groans of agreement. I looked around the table, hoping someone would speak up, but everyone kept eating and talking with no mention of his transgression. I felt disgusted, yet too weak—not to mention too young—to stand up to him.

I can't remember anybody telling me explicitly it was wrong to use that word, but I knew it was bad and always felt ashamed whenever I heard it, which was surprisingly seldom. It was especially shocking to hear it from the lips of someone I knew so well.

A few months later, Uncle Al threw out the term again, and this time one of his sons jumped in with "Yeah, those niggers can't be trusted. They lie all the time."

Again, no one at dinner protested either the use of the term or the character stereotyping. My parents never took us aside, either, to talk the issue through. We just kept on eating our dinners, conversing, and playing our board games as if nothing was happening.

One day I decided I could no longer take the badgering about my career path and the belittling of people to whom Uncle Al felt superior. At first I told myself I would no longer go to family dinners. I'd stay home and feign illness. However, how could I give up those mouthwatering meals my grandmother slaved over? So I decided to arm myself with similar ammunition. I resolved that if my uncle used the N word again, I would stand and call him a kike and see how he liked it.

I gathered my courage for the next dinner, carefully going over in my head how I would counterattack if necessary. I repeated over and over, *Don't let him bully you.*

But once at the table, face to face, I lost my courage and was relegated to my usual position of near internal combustion masked by exterior passivity.

"So, Michael—this acting thing, is this what you plan to do with your life, or is it just a passing fancy? You know, let me tell you something... you really should consider taking up something a little more stable. Something with a future."

"I'll keep that in mind," I'd answer meekly.

I don't remember him using the N word again, and I never did call him a kike. Looking back on it now, I realize I would have been lowering myself to his level had I carried out my plan. Hate for hate, an eye for an eye, was that any way to deal with racial intolerance? But as an angry teen, I didn't know how to confront his racism. Or was it really racism? Maybe it was more classism? Besides, what did I know about the anti-Semitism he may have experienced growing up in a predominantly Christian working-class town? His father had been a pillar of the community and had offered assistance to minority groups in the past. Why, then, did his son, my uncle, harbor such prejudices? Surely, he didn't learn them at home. Or did he?

The matter became especially poignant, as well as confusing to me, when I discovered much later that my uncle was one of the very few people who not only knew that my biological father was a black man but had actually met him. He and my aunt made up that first search party my grandmother sent out to Boston when my mother and I lived struggling in the projects of Roxbury. He certainly was not thinking about my racial background—although I was completely unaware of the mix of my own identity at the time—when he chose to use the N word during dinners. Or was he?

OUT OF THE CLOSET

Having opened the door on my new racial identity, I began to tell friends and family members about it. I didn't know what to expect, but the personal excitement of my discovery, more than the implications of my shifting racial status, drove me to share my truth. I plunged forward with an enthusiasm that overwhelmed the caution I should have heeded, not realizing that each revelation might require delicate discussion. *Whom to tell? And how should I go about it?* I gave little thought to these sensitive questions.

Within my family, I was probably closest to my sister at the time, she of the squeaky voice. She was a visual artist and shared an aesthetic interest. Nine years younger than me, during our youth she looked up to me as her big brother, and my performance endeavors, habit of collecting odd and unusual things, appreciation for artwork, popularity at school, and wild sense of style became an example for her to follow as a budding artiste. As she grew older and more sophisticated in her artistic temperament, she visited me in Chicago and came to many of the crazier more avant-garde plays I performed in.

As excited as I was to share my news with her, there was something nagging me. In spite of my feelings of estrangement, we grew up in a fairly cohesive white working-class family, and now suddenly I'd discovered a new and different father. How would the introduction of a new family, my new family, affect our relationship? Would she feel threatened by my discovery? How could I expect her to understand what I'd felt most my life but never been able to express: the absence of a sense of true connection, the deep childhood loss, the buried inner confusion? Both she and my brother were aware I'd had another father, however, as had been the case with me, there was no discussion among any members of my family about this taboo topic. More important now, how would she react when she heard that my father was of a different race?

"B, it's Michael. I've got something to tell you."

"Yeah? What's that, homey?" The name she chose to call me dripped with unsuspecting irony.

"Well," I said, then hesitated. "You know how I've never known who my birth dad is, my biological father?"

"Yeah, I guess. We never really talked about it."

"Sure, I know, but..." pausing again, my uncertainty now grabbing at my stomach, "well, I've always wondered."

"Did you ever ask Mom?"

"No, no, I didn't."

"Why?"

"I guess I was scared."

"Scared of what?"

"I don't know, the truth? Upsetting Mom maybe? I really don't know."

"So?"

"Well, I asked her."

"You did? Why now?"

"Just seemed like the right time, Mom and Dad getting a divorce and all."

"And?"

"And she gave me a few answers. Nothing too specific; just enough to put a few pieces together and then track him down." I hesitated a minute. "I found him."

"Really? Your father? Well huh, what d'ya know?" She sounded wary.

I tried to revive the call, and my pleasure. "Yep, I found my dad!" A word that instantly felt awkward as it passed my lips. I thought, *Jesus, have I made a big mistake sharing this with her?*

"Wow," she muttered. "How was that?"

"Great," I continued. "It was great. Turns out all this time, the reason mom kept it a secret, was... well... Let's just say I guess she had her reasons."

"How's that?" she replied cautiously.

"He's black."

"What?" she asked, incredulously.

"African American."

"You're, you're... kidding me, right?"

"Nope."

She laughed awkwardly, looking for a way to lighten the moment. "Damn, my brother's a brother." We laughed and talked of speaking more soon.

I couldn't help wondering after we'd hung up if she'd been more baffled by the uncovering of her brother's new race or the interjection of the discovery of a new father. I never actually thought about how my siblings might feel about my wanting to look for my birth father. Would they feel it a threat to the family we had together? Would they see it as a slap in the face? Might they think I would turn my back on them?

It hadn't occurred to me previously that my news might stir up buried feelings my sister might have not only about our family but also about race and identity. Had she ever thought much about what it might mean that we were only half siblings? Did it matter? Perhaps another topic never approached for fear of rocking the family boat. What kind of attitudes about race, blacks and whites, had she developed over her life, and how might those affect her feelings toward me, and her mother, in light of my news? In our, at times, deeply felt conversations about life, art, and their relation, I don't recall ever discussing race, so I had little sense of how she would respond over time.

And what about her blood brother, Chris? They were much closer than I was with either of them. They shared not only a bond of the same mother and father, but being only a year apart in age they had essentially grown up together, played and fought together, shared secrets and friends together, whereas I had already graduated from high school and left home when they were still in grade school.

Had she and her brother ever discussed our family dynamic? And if so, had they ever considered the possibility that my biological father was of a different race? I'd assumed he was white, so I imagine they did as well. More important, did a shift in my racial identity even matter particularly to them? It's not as if I had changed color overnight or had become a militant black Muslim. How would Chris react to my news, I wondered. Although we once shared a room, we were far from the closest of brothers. We never really had similar interests and geographically he was the most distant of our Waukegan family: he now lived in London.

When I called Chris, he responded much as Lora had. There was the incredulous, "You're kidding me!" Then there was the same hesitation in his voice, the same wariness. Perhaps he too was resentful I had brought this out into the open with our family or felt I was being a bit selfish in my quest to find my birth father, without considering its effects on our Waukegan family. "Did you tell Dad?" he inquired, perhaps hoping I wouldn't, and that this inconvenient discovery might just go away somehow.

Our mutual father, Chris's biological father, would present the most difficult challenge for me. He was the man who had raised me since the age of five, the man I grew up with, the decent, honest man who'd shown me some of the ropes in life. Whether he was present for me or not, whether or not we had much in common in our activities and interests, he was the central man in my conscious memory, save my Grandfather Garabed. I loved my dad, and he me. How do I tell my dad that I'd found my birth father? And what had he known about his former wife's former life?

——————

It took me a few days to finally gather the courage to call him. I eventually felt compelled to make the call for fear he'd hear first from someone else in the family. I knew he'd be logical, because that was his take on life. I used to refer to him with friends teasingly as Mr. Spock from the Star Trek series. What had I to fear but logic and reasoning? After my parents' divorce, their house was sold, and he now lived a quiet bachelor's existence ninety minutes north of Chicago, beyond the manicured lawns and multiple car garages of Lake Forest.

"Hey, Dad, it's me, Michael."

"Hello, son, how ya doin'? What do I owe this call to?"

"Just calling to see how you're doing."

"Well that's awfully nice." He took the bait. "How's things your way?"

"Pretty good," I told him calmly, trying to contain my apprehension. "How's things out in the boonies? How's the new place?"

"It's all right. You know, same shit, different place." He rarely swore, and I found this unobtrusive slip quite out of context. There was a silence as we searched for ways to connect.

"You gettin' along all right?"

"Sure, sure, just fine," he said, as I waited to see if he might tell me more.

"You lonely at all?"

"I'm fine, son. Why do you ask?"

"No reason really. Just... you know, making sure you're OK."

It was a typical conversation for us, devoid of emotional life. Too scared to open up or too manly to know how.

"So Dad, I have a little something I need to tell you," I said uneasily.

"What's that, son?"

"Well... you know how I was born with a different father?"

"When I met your mother she said it was a package deal. It was you and her together. I accepted those terms."

"I know, Dad, and you've always provided for me. It's just that I always wondered who my birth father was. You know, who my biological dad was. I mean, who knows, I might look like him, or we may have the same voice… you know?"

"Sure," he said understandably. "I think that's probably pretty natural."

"Well…" I continued, "… I found him."

"You did? That's great." It sounded like he meant it. "Well at least I hope it is. Was it?"

"Yes, it has been," I said, slightly relieved by his apparent openness.

"Where'd you find him?"

"He's in Detroit. We've talked a few times. But I think there is something you should know."

"He's all right, and you're all right, aren't you?"

"Yes, Dad. Listen… my father… he's African American."

"Jesus Christ." There was an excruciatingly long silence. "Your mother never told me this." His mood had shifted.

"I kind of suspected she hadn't."

"She should have told me," he lashed out. "I should have been informed."

"You're right, Dad. You had a right to know. But would it have made a difference?"

He stopped, realizing the weight of the question. His anger subsided for the moment. He collected himself.

"No, you're right. It shouldn't have mattered. It didn't matter who your father was. In fact, to tell you the truth, I didn't really even want to know. It was really none of my business. I just felt… well… your mother, she was never really good at letting me—us—know things."

"We all seem to have a little of that, I think. Wouldn't you agree?"

"You're probably right about that too." He sounded resigned.

Suddenly the reality of having two fathers hit me. It was bad enough they were both named John. What would I call them? How would I respond when asked by one about the other? And then it hit me—how lucky can I get? Two dads, who both love and care about me. What more could I ask for? Awkward to be sure, but certainly not unmanageable.

I continued to tell people I knew about my family discovery. A strange thing took place when I told African Americans I'd been close to. With my new knowledge conveyed, they all claimed to have suspected some black heritage years prior to the discovery. One black couple I'd known for a long time went so far as to say, "Welcome home, we knew you had to be one of us." I laughed, too embarrassed or confused to question the source of their confidential information. It had been as if they had kept a secret from me and, once I found out, were just nodding their heads in agreement. "Uh huh, yes honey, we know." When I pressed an old friend who had a similar reaction for what clues he noticed, maybe the ever so slightly mocha color of my skin, he replied, "It's the way you carry yourself. The way you walk into a room. The way you talk. Your style, your dress, it's a thang, man."

Freshman year in college.

"What do you mean, 'a thang'?" I asked.

"A thang, man. You got it. How else can I explain it? You walk into a room and you got it. I can feel it. You can't see it or describe it. You know what I'm talkin' about."

Did I know? The truth was, whenever I met people of color, I'd always felt some sort of unspoken connection. I'd see black people in stores or restaurants or out in the streets, we'd make eye contact and nod our heads as if to acknowledge indirectly a kind of undeclared bond. Was there some kind of memory trace from infancy? Or secret black radar I was unaware of that could detect—for blacks—just who was black? Was there a blackdar?

UNDERCOVER FATHER

After several months of sharing my one-room dwelling with Jo and her terribly perplexed son, we decided it was time to pool our resources and rent a home. Relying on what little I had hiding in the corners of my checkbook and the aid of her inheritance-laden, free-love, soon-to-be-ex-husband, we rented a ramshackle two-bedroom bungalow in Venice, California, just blocks from the beach. Unlike the predominately stucco Southern Californian homes, this was a charming little wooden house on a "walk street"—essentially a sidewalk with houses lined up on either side.

Jo and her husband having finally agreed on divorce terms, we were at last feeling free to be a legitimate couple with some sense of normalcy to our relationship, her son splitting his time between our house and his father's. Having more room also allowed us to set up shop and start an art business out of the tiny, rundown garage pinned behind our house.

Jo was what is called a faux painter, a decorative artist. She painted walls and ceilings in people's homes with rags, brushes, and an odd assortment of tools in an effort to make things look old and pretty. I'd had a little experience in this field, having graduated from struggling house painter to working on a crew of faux-finishers and scenic artists in a valiant effort to make money between the infrequent acting gigs. We decided to join forces in the business of making rich people's multimillion-dollar homes look old. The amount of money the wealthy were willing to lay out to make new things look fashionably decrepit was astounding.

John Sidney Woods.

It was the middle of summer, approximately five and a half months since I made the call that turned my world as I knew it on end. I'd stayed in touch with my paternal grandparents, exchanging phone calls every few weeks or so. My father in Detroit meanwhile had become mysteriously ill. He couldn't eat and suffered from debilitating stomach cramps and sharp pains. When I called, he seemed to be in extreme pain—or else faking it with the skill of a pro. Something was terribly wrong, and I felt completely helpless as I attempted to develop a relationship with a man I now awkwardly called Dad.

"Dad, how're you feeling today?"

"Pretty much the same."

"What does that mean? What is the same?"

"Just can't seem to keep any food down. I'll tell ya, this sure is one hell of a diet."

"So what do the doctors say?"

"Going in for more tests next week."

"Next week? You could starve by then!"

"Don't worry, son, I've eaten enough over the last twenty years to accumulate a little extra baggage. That oughta last me at least a couple weeks."

"I'm serious, why can't they see you any sooner?"

"You know how doctors work, son. It's just like Hollywood—hurry up 'n wait! Don't worry, I'm gonna be all right. They're checking everything, making sure your old man's gonna be all right." There was an awkward silence, as if he was listening for something. I heard some commotion in the background, a rustle of papers. Then he said, "Look, I can't talk now, I gotta run."

"Are you OK?" I ask, presuming he was in pain.

"Yeah, sure, I just can't stay on the line." He paused.

"Well, OK. I guess I'll talk to you soon." I was clumsily trying to stall for more "dad time" and was secretly hoping he could hear the dejection in my voice.

"Look, it's just not safe."

"What? What are you talking about, safe?"

"I'll explain it all later. Listen, let me call you next time."

Safe? What did that mean? This was not at all the word I expected or wanted to hear. "Dad, are you all right?"

"Sure, I'm fine. Well, I'll be fine. Look, I'll call you soon and explain everything. Don't worry."

Don't worry? Classic, the way it unintentionally increases worry. It sounded like a warning. What's not "safe," I wondered? Was it me? The questions raced by faster than I thought it possible to think. I had little choice, though, but to take him at his word and await the next call.

———

More weeks went by, and work was slow. I tried not to create mental movies about my father's situation but without much success. Jo and I were busy creating old art in people's homes but barely making enough to get by. We were active in what we referred to as the "powder room circuit": sponge-painting the guest bathrooms of the wealthy with no taste. Powder rooms were a safe place for those who were too cheap to hire a decorator to experiment without having to make a bold, or better yet, a subtle design choice for the rooms they actually lived in. We went from powder room to guest bath, each one slightly more ostentatious than the last. I hated smooshing paint behind toilets of the rich and pseudo-famous, even if they were paying us more than their hired help. We were the hired help that spoke the same language. We were the pretentious bragging to their friends, "Oh, I've hired some lovely artistes to decorate our boudoir."

But all I could think about was that last phone conversation with my dad. I wondered about his health. I wondered about his life. I wondered what the hell was going on.

I finally decided to take matters into my own hands. Since things sounded strained at home, I thought I might catch my dad at work. I dialed the number he'd given me for his office, and a strangely high-pitched voice answered the phone.

"Hello?"

"Uh, hi," I managed with unsure difficulty. "I'm looking for John Woods."

There was a long pause.

"I'm afraid he no longer works here."

"Excuse me?" I wasn't quite sure I'd heard the answer correctly.

"He doesn't work here."

"Oh." I tried to collect my thoughts. Perhaps I'd dialed the wrong number. "Do you know where I might find him?"

"I'm afraid I can't help you."

Can't help me, or won't, guessing from the terse response. I tried to press further, but the chilly voice presented a wall of unresponsiveness.

"Good luck," the voice finally offered, and then hung up.

How did they know I wasn't a client or a business associate? I might have been calling to confirm a contract or business deal. I may have wanted to discuss an ongoing transaction. What the hell was going on? I impulsively dialed him at home.

A raspy female voice answered, throwing me off guard. Once again I found myself backpedaling.

"Hi. I'm, uh, I'm looking for John Woods."

"Is this Michael?"

"Yes," I answered, unprepared for this new voice, and the fact that she knew me.

"Hello, Michael, this is Sue. I'm Johnny's wife."

I felt clumsy, uncertain how to respond. I apparently took too long.

"You're looking for John."

"Yes," I managed, still trying to find my voice.

"He can't talk just now." She sounded cold, matter-of-fact.

"Oh."

"He asked me to tell you that he'll call you back when he can."

Did he really tell her that? Why did she sound so cold? "Is he OK?"

"Yes, he just can't talk right now." I heard a click.

And like that, she was gone. You'd think she'd want to talk a bit more, get to know me, ask a few questions, perhaps welcome me to the family. And why hadn't I been ready to jump in with more? And what of my father? Maybe he was indisposed, in the bathroom, sick, eating, outside the house, with a guest—there were a million different possibilities, but it was too late to confirm any of them.

Her tone of voice, not to mention her abrupt hanging up, wouldn't leave me, though. Something seemed terribly wrong, but I couldn't tell what it was. I wasn't sure how—or if—I fit into his life at this point, and it didn't feel right of me to push where I might not be wanted.

He's my father, but what exactly did that mean for us? He did not raise me; he hadn't really been a part of my life. I hadn't a clue how he'd felt all these years. Suddenly, twenty-five years later I show up "knocking on his door." He wanted to stay in touch, he said, but how do we begin to establish a relationship after so much time has passed?

Is it possible to re-create or reestablish a father-son bond after so many years? And for that matter, what exactly does a father-son bond look and feel like?

The next morning the phone rang early.

"Michael, it's me, your father. You awake?"

"Yeah, sure," I lied as I attempted to clear my throat, wipe my eyes, and gain some sort of consciousness.

"Listen, I can't talk long. I'm on a pay phone."

"A pay phone?"

"It's not safe for me to talk at home. There's a situation, see… I think the phone might be bugged."

My dad, the spy. I had visions of espionage and the underworld. The Detroit mafia. The government listening in, watching his every move. Or perhaps he was involved in some sort of international intrigue? Then I thought, what the hell is he talking about? He told me he worked for Ford Motor Company. Maybe that was a front. On a more basic level, was he in trouble? Or more pressing, was I?

"Bugged?"

"I'm in a situation. There's an investigation. The FBI. I can't go into it right now. But everything is gonna be OK. I just need to be careful. I want us to be careful."

"OK," I struggled to say. Not knowing what to add, I repeated myself, "OK." My speechlessness was becoming a pattern.

"Listen, I want to give you a number where you can reach me."

"Sure." *A cell phone*, I thought. *No, can't be, they're traceable. A hideaway? A safe house?*

"You got a pencil?"

"Yeah. Go ahead, shoot." Was that a poor choice of words?

"You can reach me on Tuesdays and Sundays at (313) 559-7745. There's a woman there, her name is Wendy. She knows about you."

"Who is she, a friend of yours?" I inquire cautiously, not knowing if he could, or would, really tell me.

"Yes. Look, I'll explain it all to you when I have more time. I've gotta run. You take care, ya hear me?"

"Yeah, OK, Dad. I'll talk to you soon."

"I love you, son."

And for an instant, the foreboding of danger faded as I grasped his last sentence with the part of my heart that so longed to hear those four words. I stumbled as I tried to return the feeling. "I love you, too," I said quickly. "Goodbye."

The late afternoon sun cast shadows across the postage-stamp yard as I sat on the front steps of our tiny bungalow. What the hell was going on? How did finding my father turn into something so mysteriously complicated and furtive? Who was this Wendy, and what did she know?

A HOLDING PATTERN

An earlier than expected heat wave had brought throngs to LA's beaches the summer of 1992. People strolled by our tiny walk-street bungalow wending their way to the shore while I sat hunched over my desk, trying to nurture our fledgling "powder-room circuit" business into a legitimate full-blown decorating contender. I stared out the sun-streaked windows, secretly wishing I could surf. Alas, this kid from Chicago could barely swim.

As I tried to drum up leads for our faux-finishing business, Jo finger-painted samples of wild new finishes out back in the garage. She applied soft yellows, slight beige, faded greens, brushed, smooshed, ragged, rolled, and spotted—all manner of colors and techniques in order to win over the tastes of the rich. For me, the cold-call sales pitch was becoming an improvisational challenge for my dormant acting chops. I had flashbacks of working a disastrous phone sales job straight out of college, when all I could think about was acting. I lasted but two hours with my weak-pitched banter, attempting to peddle something I couldn't muster the authenticity to advertise. I now found myself dialing architects and designers daily, pretending I was a faux artist. The irony was thick.

It was about a week into that steamy July when I got a call from my long-lost family again, but it wasn't the call I had expected.

"Hey, shuga, it's yo' granny."

The southern drawl lingered across the phone line. "Hi, Granny, how're you doing?"

"Not bad fo' 'n ol' lady." Obviously this was one of her catch-phrases. "Now listen, shuga, you don't pay Sue no mind. You hear?"

"What? What are you talking about?" Caught off guard, I wasn't quite sure I had heard her correctly. "Sue? Dad's wife Sue?"

"Dat's da one. You gon be gettin' a letta any day now, 'n don' you pay it no mind. Yo' Daddy didn't have nuttin' to do wit it."

"She wrote me a letter?"

"Dat's right 'n she jus tryin' ta upset you, dat's all. Don't you pay her no attenshun. You know how we feel 'bout cha. We bin waitin' a long time fo' ya ta come 'round. We don't need her goin' off upsettin' every-than'."

What next? Sue, the FBI, a bugged phone line, my dad's mysterious illness, a mysterious woman named Wendy—what did it all mean? I wondered if my grandmother knew about all these other mysteries, but I was afraid to ask. She was terribly upset, and I figured it'd all become clear somehow. Still unsure of exactly how I fit into my father's life, the last thing I wanted to do was mention something I shouldn't. I wasn't sure what was and wasn't known and to whom. Taking a cautious yet thoroughly confused approach, I said my goodbyes and promised to phone her soon.

A few days later the letter arrived amidst a typical pile of bills and junk mail. It was handwritten, in a left leaning script, clean and straight across the page.

"Dear Michael," it began,

> Johnny and I are in our twenty-seventh year of marriage. I knew of you prior to our marriage but had been assured you were no longer a part of his life. You were no longer a part of his life because your mother decided she couldn't handle the black/white issue (as you now know).

I stopped. What did she know about my mother? What had my father told her? What black/white issue was she referring to? Nobody had said anything to me about any kind of racial intolerance, prejudice, or racism on my mother's part. What was she presuming I knew? It went on:

> He fought for you through the legal system. Unfortunately he did not have financial resources equal to your mother's, but he exhausted what he had, and at the time it was considerable. The rest is history! You were adopted and reared as white....

Had I any choice in the matter? Did she resent me because of a decision I didn't make? Born "black," reared "white." I had "passed," without knowing the truth of my existence. But I was now being told that not only had I passed, but I was resented for it.

> Johnny is delighted to know of your background, ambitions, and dreams; however, he was equally as shocked to hear from you as you were to reach him on the first phone call. He called his parents immediately. It took some time for him to share this with me. He wasn't certain what my reaction would be. When he did tell me I was so pleased for both of you. That was an honest sincere reaction.

> It wasn't until some time had passed that I began to fully process the implications of it all. It would require of me something in my heart, I knew I did not want. So I inquired of him whether he would like to establish a relationship with you. He thought he would. On the other hand, he wasn't sure what kind of relationship was possible because of racial barriers, lapsed time, cultural differences, etc. I assured him that all could be overcome if it was something both of you wanted. With that I knew I had to come to terms with this. Well, I think I have. I have decided your mother deprived him of you for 32 years when he finally signed those adoption papers, it would be inhumane of me to do it a second time. I have been a part of his life for 27 years. Now it's your turn.

My turn? What exactly did she mean?

As you can see, I have not mastered the principle of "unconditional love" and I am not proud of myself. Actually, I am rather
ashamed. But I do know that I love him too much to keep you from
him again. I also know that I have not found it in my heart to welcome you. You see, I am as guilty as your mother and her family.

This letter is difficult for me to write. It forces me to take a long
hard look at myself, and I don't very much like what I see. However, it lets me know I am not the person I would like to be and
I have a lot of work to do. Not your problem!

Keep well, Sue

I sat down on the floor, warm midday sunlight streaking in through
the front windows, and stared at Sue's letter. I felt slightly dizzy, drown-
ing in new information yet not quite able to make sense of it all. After
all these years I finally find my father and he appears to be willing to
develop a relationship, but there seems to be another huge obstacle in
my path—his wife! What exactly was she implying by the phrase "my
turn"? I wondered if she knew about the FBI interest. And if so, did
she know that I knew? Although what exactly did I know other than
just that the FBI was involved in some way? Hell, I didn't know if my
dad was working for them or hiding from them! And who was Wendy?
Did Sue know her?

The reference to the enormity of "racial barriers and cultural differences" was difficult for me to wrap my head around, too. If you
don't grow up black, do you know what it means to be black, live black,
walk, talk, eat, and socialize black? And certainly there is not one
definitive experience of such an upbringing. But what does it mean to
me to be black? To her? To my father? How different might my life
have been had I been raised black? What cultural differences exactly
did she have in mind?

The man who raised me couldn't teach me those things, what it is
like to "be" black. He was raised in a Swedish-American household and
experienced white culture from his parents' point of view. He taught me

the cultural mores of his parents—a sense of well-mannered quiet reserve, a respect for elders, authority, and family, a sense of ethics and integrity. My Armenian mother also nurtured me in a white culture, although one with different traditions. But what did I know about the differences between white and black cultures in some generic sense and how it might affect what I'd hoped would be a relationship with my newly discovered black father?

Within the white environment in which I'd been raised, I was taught always to accept people for the content of their character, not the color of their skin, though it was acknowledged that the color of skin dictated a great deal as to how one is viewed or received. I instantly became so aware of my whiteness and blackness—or lack thereof. If I look white, am I therefore white?

How did Sue really view me? Was it as a child who "passed" as white? Or was I more of a black man who was hiding? And what was to happen now?

It may have been a mistake, but I quickly hurried off a response, hoping to capture the distress I felt in her implied "you or me" argument, as well as claim something of my biracial birthright and, I hoped, overcome her hesitancy to accept me.

Dear Sue,

This certainly is a strange predicament we find ourselves in and it took a lot of thought and courage for you to express your feelings with me.

Let me begin by saying that I know just a little about the history of my mother's relationship to John and the problems she may or may not have encountered with the black/white issue. I know that her parents adamantly opposed the relationship, but I don't really know much about how my mother felt. At this point expressing her feelings has not been one of her strong points. She has however brought me up, God bless her, with no racial barriers, prejudices, or color distinctions....

My intention was not to cause you any discomfort by reconnecting with my father. I do not expect you to welcome me with open arms. I do hope however that we can gradually get to know one another and build some sort of relationship as I hope will happen with my father. I realize you feel no connection to me. I hope we can begin to find a place where we can connect. Should you feel as though you cannot begin to do this, I will respect your feelings and try to work within your boundaries on my relationship with my father.

Looking at oneself is never an easy task. I want you to know that by sharing that part of yourself with me, you have helped me take a look at myself. I thank you.

Ten days later, I received a letter back from her. It was written on festive notepaper with a string of colorful balloons running along the left edge.

Dear Michael,

Thank you for such a prompt response. I appreciate your kind words and recognize a sweet spirit in you. But why doesn't that surprise me?

Then, like a schoolgirl, she drew a smiley face between this and the next sentence.

On the other hand, some of your words let me know I had not communicated clearly. I will attempt to do so now.

Clearly, the balloons were not a sign of truce.

First off, let me apologize if in any way I offended you when I spoke of your mother. That was not my intent. It was done only to explain Johnny's position and then only as it pertained to you. Never would you need to defend your mother, her family, or yourself to me!!

Johnny told me he shared with you that he is the target of an FBI investigation. That is indeed the truth. Our lives have become one long endless day of stress that never comes to closure. It is the most unsettling, frightening, and anxious experience of our lives. But through it all we have each other and we know one day it will all be over and we will still have each other. When one or both of us becomes anxious or fearful, one comforts the other and makes it better. We gain strength from each other and we manage to rise above. There is nothing that life can bring us that we can't handle with God's help. We will smile again!

You see, the FBI investigation does not compare to the challenge you bring to our lives. What you, your mother, and her family represent are Johnny's past. I want it to remain there—in the past. Johnny and I are each other's present and, we thought, future. We "signed on" for life. There is no room in my present or future for his past. For me, Mr. Fosberg is your dad, your father. You are his son; not my husband's. I wiped the plate clean when I accepted Johnny's marriage proposal because he made it safe for me to do that. So in order for you to re-enter his life, I must exit. You are so right! What a horrible predicament!

I am putting your relationship on hold until the investigation is over and Johnny begins to heal. I will not leave him to go it alone. I am both his emotional and financial support system and will be until he can soar alone. (As he would for me!) When the marriage has been dissolved (separated), one of us, preferably Johnny, will notify you. At that time you will have clear access to establish your relationship. Until that time I can only express my sorrow for putting you on hold. The one comfort I have in all of this is in knowing that God never closes one door without opening another. I clearly don't know what the future holds for me but I do know that things will be okay. I have learned it's not so much what happens in our lives but rather how we handle it.

Pain is inevitable but misery is a choice. The measure of my life is how I give it away. I am praying for guidance, wisdom, harmony, and inner peace for all of us.

Take care, Sue

P.S. I, too, am sorry for any discomfort I may cause you.

This is what my grandmother had warned me about. In my haste to make nice and woo her favor, I got sucked into Sue's drama, and she had now staked her claim, or threatened to pull up her stakes and leave my father without support. My paternal grandparents, my father, my long-lost family all tied up in confusing, conflicting relationships. After thirty-odd years the journey to find my father had come to another impasse. Sue was essentially putting me on hold until further notice. Could she do that?

Yet now I was more baffled than ever as to the nature of the FBI investigation. What had my father done and why was he being so secretive? Was she a part of this investigation? Did she somehow have a hand in whatever was being examined?

And what about Wendy? Was it time to call the number my father had given me?

I sat motionless, again staring across the makeshift office in our bungalow. I felt trapped in what seemed a never-ending maze, each corner I turned leading to an apparent dead end, each dead end to a secret door, each door to a new long and dark hallway leading to another dead end.

ANOTHER BROTHER

August in Los Angeles was hotter than ever as I struggled to make sense of my growing family/father mystery and continued to push decorative samples to Beverly Hills designers with signature one-name monikers: rag-finishes, floated brush, Italian plaster, gold leaf, murals, and all manner of paint techniques, a cornucopia of styles and colors. I slowly traded my paint-splattered jeans for a more respectable outfit as I attempted to generate more income for our flailing mom-and-pop operation. We thought we had the goods in our assortment of painted finishes, just not the jobs. I grew obsessed by the hunt for bigger, higher profile jobs and the money we needed to survive.

I knew very little about starting a business, yet plunged forward, faking—faux?—what I could get by with and learning the rest on the fly. What I lacked in business acumen I tried to make up for in determination. Being broke and desperate while cohabiting with a still officially married woman in a beaten-up beach bungalow did not top my list of fun things to do. We had to succeed. There was no other option.

I kept a checklist of things to do on a legal pad attached to a clipboard on my desk. As I crossed out accomplished goals—the best part of keeping a list—I continued to add new chores and the list kept growing. When I reached the bottom of a page, I transferred the yet-to-be-completed tasks to a new page and started all over again. The assignment "call Wendy" continued to move from the top of one page to the top of the next. The lists came and went over the ensuing weeks, but the "call Wendy" item was never checked off. I felt paralyzed, secretly hoping the phone would ring and the caller would be my father, saving me the possible agony of taking this next step.

Day after day I phoned designers and architects whom I'd never met, pitching them our wares and the opportunity to meet for a show 'n tell. Why was it easier to call a complete stranger than to pick up the phone and dial my dad? I'd cross off one task, record another, then stare out the window searching for the courage to make the one essential call I truly needed to make.

"What're yor knickers awl in a twist about?" I turned to find Jo, now perched above me, her blonde mane, midriff and shorts completely splattered in paint.

"What? Nothing."

"Bloody hell you're not. "

"Really, it's nothing. Just adding to the list," I said as I held up the clipboard.

"You look like Guy Fawkes with his hand caught in a barrel."

"Guy Fawkes?"

"November 5th? Remember I tol' you? British Independence?" I stare back blankly, and she continues, "Neva mind. I finished the Waldo sample." Another of the famous Beverly Hills one-name decorators.

"Waldo?" I enquire, my mind elsewhere.

"Waldo, for Liz, Liz Taylor!"

"Right! How's it look?"

"Fucking brilliant. She'll be licking the walls of that bloody powder room they'll be so delicious."

"Great," I tell her, "I'll run the sample down to the big fella," — Waldo, the flamer — "and see if I can get him to sign off on it."

"Perfect, darling. But first, tell me what you were doing."

I stumble slightly as I attempt to stand, avoiding the question. We hug, and she reeks of chemicals and sweat, but I kiss her anyway, careful not to soil my clothes. She pinches my ass sarcastically, and I blush before I speak. "I'm anxious," I tell her. "Don't know what to do about the crazy thing with my father."

"Why don't you phone 'im?" she says with a conciliatory British tone.

"It's Wednesday," I say. "He said Tuesdays and Sundays."

And before I knew it, Sunday was nearly upon us; another full week had gone by. Jo continued to paint samples out back in our garage/makeshift studio while I cold-called myself into a frenzy attempting to scare up more work from the rich and famous. Waldo loved the sample, but Liz was too busy to pay us any attention; the job was shelved. The five-page confidentiality agreement we were forced to sign before entering her house now seemed like a grand illusion. At the end of the week another one-name celebrity decorator passed on an inquiry regarding a soap opera king and producer who'd just bought a ten-million-dollar remodel in the heart of Beverly Hills and wanted the entire house glazed. The prospect of glazing thousands of square feet of wall space for months on end brought dollar signs to my eyes and visions of a couch, a few chairs, maybe even a proper dining room table.

It was finally Sunday, a day of rest for normal folks but not for those afflicted with self-employment. On this most typical of Los Angeles beach days, in the heat of the summer with the cool beach breezes drifting slowly across our postage-stamp lawn, Jo was busy once again in the garage preparing a sample, faint strains of the ever-booming boom box filtering a mix of funkinatia and soulastic tunes through the house. I was typing "exciting" introduction letters to various local, high-profile architectural firms. The phone rang. "Real Illusions," I answered with businesslike cheer, forgetting it was a non-businesslike day. There was silence, then I caught myself. "Hello? This is Michael."

"Michael?"

"Yes?" My breath slowed. The deeply rich tone was unmistakably like mine.

"It's your dad."

"Dad? How are you?" I struggled to hide both my excitement and fear.

"I'm fine, son, fine. Feeling a little better, but still not out from under it yet." I was unclear as to whether he was referring to his health or his case with the FBI. "Can you talk?" he added. Was I the one, I thought, or he who was in trouble with the Feds?

"Sure, Dad, I can talk. How 'bout you? Is this a good time?"

"Listen, I want to explain a few things for you."

"Sure, that'd be great."

"Where can I start?" wondering aloud and perhaps seeking my lead.

"How about with the FBI?" I say timidly.

As he clears his throat, I stare at the bougainvillea clustered against our front porch windows. The brilliant colors blur as I shift my concentration when he starts in.

"A while back," he begins, "I was trying to do business with a couple of brothers attempting to secure a contract for some printing from Ford." I thought at first he might be referring to siblings, but by his inflection I realized he meant African-American men. It seemed slightly odd, I thought, that he—a man approaching sixty who had been raised in what I sensed was a highly educated household—would use this kind of slang. "As I told you, I was a purchasing agent for Ford Motor Company, and my job was to dole out the contracts for print jobs."

"Printing jobs?" I inquired. "What type of printing jobs?"

"The whole nine yards," he offered. "Everything from brochures, to spec sheets, year-end reports, and shareholder crap. I dealt with it all, every kind of press and process out there; letterpress, monotype, offset, even some digital. You name it, I've done it."

"So what did these brothers want from you?" I stumbled over the word, attempting to sound as if I were down with him.

"Well, these cats had just taken over a medium-sized operation that had been slidin' on the edge of bankruptcy. They were lookin' to revive the business and get it back on solid footing. Quiet as it's kept they had also been under investigation for bank fraud and money laundering, so when they walked into my office, I had no idea they were wired. FBI musta thought it was Christmas when they heard me ask for 50 Gs collateral."

Bankruptcy? Bank fraud? Money laundering? Wired? Collateral? "Cats"? So much for my international spy theory, this was just plain old bribery, or graft. My new old man was asking for kickbacks and got pinched. An egregious act, but one, I'd been learning in my short time as an independent businessman, fairly common among those who wanted to get ahead.

"What happened?" I finally asked.

"Got fired, and now under investigation. Feds are a bunch of motherfuckers, think they got my house bugged, layin' to try 'n trip me up, think they might catch me double-dippin' again or something. I was just trying to help a brother get a leg up. Not too often black business gets a sniff of any automotive contracts. Brothers were bad from the get-go. I shoulda known better than to trust them two. They're lucky I didn't take them down—just get my Glock and ring them out."

I was so thrown by his language, it wasn't easy to process his story. I had visions of gangbangers and hos, do-rags and semi-automatics, rims and Benjamins, and there was my dad, a graying, slightly overweight, sixty-year-old professional dressed in suit and tie, flashing gang symbols and poppin' gats. Here was a man, my father, who at times sounded as if he were a business man from Ford Motor Company and at others like a slick street thug from the corners of downtown Detroit.

"I've got an attorney workin' on the case, thinks he can get me off. There's a couple of federal judges that handle these cases, and the lawyer thinks if we get lucky with the right judge, he'll be lenient. In the meantime I have to lay low and be careful with my home phone. Can't talk there; I don't want them to think you're involved in any way."

I went from trying to decipher gang slang to worrying about being an accessory to a crime. What about Sue, how much could she have known? And my grandparents, were they in on the real story? "So where are you calling from?" I carefully asked.

"Like I told you, I am at the home of a woman named Wendy. We've known each other for a long time. A Jewish gal I know from work. Been together maybe twenty years. Are you sittin' down?"

Now he asks me? Should I tell him I've practically fallen over?

"Son, you have a brother named Ethan. He's about six years old, and a sharp kid for six. I got them a nice place out in the suburbs of Detroit, couple of dogs, big yard, a pool. I'm here on Tuesdays and Sundays when I can make it out. Like I told you, this is the best place to reach me. I don't need the Feds to think you're involved in my mess in any way."

And just like that I had another brother, and a Wendy, whatever she was to me. He didn't mention if his wife, Sue, was aware of this situation. Based on the way he was talking, I gathered she was in the dark about all of it. My focus shifted to the beachgoers periodically strolling by.

I was trying to piece together the bravado, the street lingo, the crime, the mistress, the other son. In the pauses between sentences my mind raced through dozens of scenarios. I pictured being questioned by the FBI, I imagined visiting Detroit and having to negotiate my father's double life, I saw my grandparents in a courtroom pleading for mercy from the judge, then visiting my father in prison behind thick Plexiglas in his prison blues, and on and on.

"Listen, son, there'll be a day when we'll all be together, be able to sit down with Granny and Poppa with big smiles on their faces. I just gotta get through this FBI thing and try to clear my name."

"Yeah, sure, that's right," I fumbled, still reeling from the completely unexpected direction I found myself propelled in.

"Don't worry, we're gonna get together soon."

Maybe my presence was now a burden. How could he possibly handle one more distraction, one more detour? "Dad, what about these letters from Sue? I hope I'm not getting in your way here."

"No, son, I knew she wrote you a letter, that's why I phoned your grandparents. Granny 'n Poppa been waiting for you for years now. Don't disappoint them; you stay in touch with them and we'll all get together soon."

"Well, sure, Dad. I, well, I just don't want to get in the way here."

"Listen son, you're not in anybody's way. We've been waiting for you. It's been a long time and we've got lots to catch up on."

Suddenly I asked, "Dad, why didn't you try to call me all these years?" I hadn't intended to ask it, the question just sort of escaped. There was a pause as he steadied himself before he answered.

"You know I did call once, son. I believe you answered the phone."

"Yeah, but you didn't identify yourself to me." My courage was rising to the surface.

"Now how would that have been, huh? If I had called and said I was your father? You were just a little kid back then. I knew your mother was married. I just called to find out how you all were doing. I think your mother was shocked but seemed to be doing all right."

"Why didn't you stay in touch after we left?"

"Look, your mother's family—her father—made it clear there was to be no contact. He hired a powerful attorney. My folks couldn't compete with that. They didn't have the resources, if you know what I mean. So I stepped aside but always had hopes that this day would come to pass. Your grandmother held on to your baby clothes, blanket, shoes, hoping that one day she'd be able to hand them back to you."

His vernacular smoothed out as the subject took a more serious turn. The weight of his admissions began to sink in. That little boy who lost his dad was so unaware of the complicated journey his life had taken. How much of the anguish and pain his parents experienced had that boy understood? At this moment, none, as far as I could tell. I felt great pain deep down, for both the boy I had been and for the family that lost a child.

"I'll call you again when things get a little more square on my end," he offered.

"Dad," I quickly interjected before I let him escape, "how is your health? Are you feeling better these days?"

"Well, let's just say I'm dealing with it, son. The doctors don't know what is happening, can't quite figure it out. But I'll get by. We'll talk again soon enough and in the meantime, don't be a stranger. Stay in touch with your grandparents, you understand? And trust me, we'll see each other soon."

"OK," I said simply, and with that, we hung up.

WENDY REVEALED

The end of the oppressive heat of that summer and my surprise-a-minute family ride couldn't come soon enough. I stayed in touch with my grandparents, talking with them every couple of weeks, telling them about the Hollywood world of faux finishing and the lives of the rich and not-so-famous. My grandmother was the primary recipient of my occasional updates, as my grandfather was a man of few words. We'd chat about the weather, my Detroit father, and our struggling business, then she'd fill me in on various points of family history. I told her how badly I wanted to come visit, and we swore it wouldn't be long before we had that opportunity. She wrote regularly, most times short notes scratched out in a sort of chicken scrawl, sometimes including photos, articles ripped from newspapers, and family scraps.

Hi Michael Sidney and Jo,

Trying to stick to my promise—there will be more as soon as the fall weather sets in. I am not a hot weather person. Do only what I have to do when it is hot and humid.

We have often wondered of your whereabouts, your well being— Truthfully I had expected you to have darkened our door some time years ago.

Talked to John Sid yesterday, things are somewhat turning his way and he is looking forward to a reunion with you and going on with his life.

Oct. 31st—Roy will be 79

Feb 23, 1993 I will be 80

We are fighting like _____—trying to hang in. We really have been blessed and living quite well—for the shape we are in— Smiles. Have frequent bouts with Arthur—Arthritis, smiles. John Sidney has kept us supplied with the best heating pads. There is one on my side of the bed and one on his side. One is in the back of Roy's recliner also. Smiles.

Do take care and if God is willing I do hope 1993 will be our year of rejoicing—Seeing each other. Good luck, love, joy and the best in all your endeavors.

Love, "Me"

Meanwhile, with the powder-room circuit floundering, we began to expand our repertoire. We took on projects we had little experience with but that challenged us to faux our way through. Our income had slowed to a trickle, and we accepted as a result almost any paying job. Patinas for outdoor railings, furniture painting, even the occasional scenic job—a faux finish artist's nightmare—were secured. I knew things had hit an all-time low when Jo dragged a braggadocio film director home. He wore a tan safari coat over an open white shirt, complete with a director's lens—a free-floating camera lens eyepiece used to help directors frame a shot—hanging from his neck. He took one look at our portfolio of painted finishes and commenced with the obligatory Hollywood gush of pretentious praise. He had this amazing script he was filming and the sets needed to be perfect, he told us. These colors and finishes were some of the most beautiful things he had ever seen, and so on. He begged us to do his movie and asked if he might bring his partner/producer back to see these absolutely magical pieces of art.

The next day, an identical, tanned, overweight, balding guy sporting a goatee dropped by the studio with the director. They cooed over our painted boards, asked what we might charge for such heavenly work, then perhaps sensing our financial predicament, pleaded with us to do their movie for half the price. Fortunately we had hiked our pricing, so half wasn't far off our going rate for such painted subtlety. The film could become one of the all-time greats, they claimed. It was at this point I thought to ask what kind of film was soon to become one of the most talked about pieces of celluloid in a town overstocked with such. Why, a piece of art, they proclaimed, an X-rated piece of art! Porno, in other words. We were being asked, then, to paint sets to make them look like something they weren't for a movie that would give the illusion of something it wasn't—while I was still reeling from discovering the life I had been living was based in no small part on a misconception.

That X-rated movie aside, we scrambled to piece together any kind of work just to keep the lights on and air conditioner humming. Summer turned into fall and the contact with my father grew increasingly sporadic. Updates were regularly forthcoming through my grandmother, but any fatherly conversation had now fallen off dramatically. Was this the "putting the relationship on hold" Sue had warned me about? Yet my grandparents said repeatedly he longed for conversation, he'd just grown more ill from his debilitating ailment. I was worried, but respectful of his instructions not to phone his home lest we wind up as audio fodder for some FBI mole. Then Wendy called.

––––––––––

"Hello, Real Illusions," I answered in my customary, upbeat business best one afternoon as I readied myself for yet another interview with a prospective decorator. The chipper female voice on the other end of the line identified herself as Wendy. So at last, here was the famous, or infamous, mystery woman in my father's life.

"Can you talk? Is this a good time for you?"

I set down my bags and sat at my desk. "This is fine. How are you? Or should I be asking who are you? I mean, I know who you are, or rather, I know of you." I was stumbling and stammering, attempting to weave my way through the awkwardness of our exchange.

"Yes, I know John told you who I am, and about your brother Ethan... You're probably wondering about, or perhaps confused by all this. I can't even imagine what this whole journey has been like for you. It must seem like an odyssey."

"Yeah, you can say that again!" I felt slightly lightened by her tone, her expression of understanding. "So, how did you become a part of this journey?"

"Your father and I have known each other a long time, from work. I was once an executive assistant for a client of his. He'd come into our office quite regularly, and we got to know one another over time. We saw each other for a while then kind of broke things off. I'd still see him through work, and when I decided I wanted to have a child on my own I asked John if he'd be willing to father it. No strings attached, just help me have a child and we could go from there."

"I see," I said with mounting skepticism. "So you had a child together?"

"Yes, well, I suppose it's a bit more than that. He's set us up in a house out in the suburbs. He's out here a couple days a week..."

"I know," I interjected, "he told me."

"Yes. He's going through a lot right now with the investigation, the loss of his job, you suddenly turning up. It's a great deal to manage."

"I'm sure it is," I answer curtly.

"He'd told me about you years and years ago. He is so happy you've found him. And his parents couldn't be more thrilled. They are ecstatic you've returned and are back in their lives."

"Well, I can tell you I'm pretty happy to be getting to know them as well."

"Listen, I won't take up more of your time. I just wanted to say hello and connect. We can talk more later. I'll send some photographs. Can you do the same? I'd love to see what you look like, where you live."

"I'll put together some things and send them your way. I gotta run," I tell her.

"Talk to you again, I hope."

And just like that, the mystery of Wendy had come full circle. It was awkward, even troubling, talking with my father's mistress about intimate details of his life. I still didn't know who knew, or what I was supposed to say or not to whom. Sue couldn't possibly have known, could she? And what about my grandparents? My father and I had yet to meet, nevertheless the family dramas kept piling up like a bad soap opera.

A few weeks later a large envelope arrived bearing a return address of Lathrup Village, Michigan. A suburb of Detroit, I surmise. I open the envelope and pore over the photographs inside. There are dozens of shots of a small, adorable boy playing, running with dogs, hugging his mom. There are photos of both the exterior and interior of a house as well, along with shots of a child's art projects and a drum set in an otherwise empty room. I glance through the contents and then come across a typed note:

Dear Michael,

A very quick note to send along with the enclosed photos:

I don't know what your plans/priorities are when thinking of John; under what circumstances do the two of you want to re-meet—privately or along with grandparents, aunts, uncles, etc.

Ethan and I do not exist as far as John's family goes. Their attitude is one of unacceptability and immorality and though they certainly have knowledge of Ethan, they have never bothered to say "hello" to him (and yes, you do hear anger).

Michael, I welcome you (and Jo and her son) to become involved in any part of our lives as you choose to. Ethan is your half brother and when John and I are gone, you will be the only meaningful family Ethan will have (this is not meant as a burden).

My future plans are to maintain a stable, healthy, enriching, loving home life for Ethan. John's future plans are uncertain and dependent upon other circumstances/people. If our futures share compatible goals, then perhaps we will be together. John has many loose ends to attend to and they require abilities that John may or may not possess.

Michael, please stay in touch. AND SEND PICTURES!!

She signed it "Fondly, Wendy!" and then typed their names, address, and phone number.

I laughed—it was the only thing I could do at the thought of having a secret relationship with my father's mistress. I still had not met my father, yet the story line kept unfolding. The photos now confirmed for me the existence of my half-black, half-Jewish half brother. What would my Jewish uncle have to say about this crazy racial concoction? And what kind of double-racial turmoil would Ethan face once he was old enough to understand the historical dynamics? How much of his mixed cultural heritage would he embrace? When will people start to reveal to him the kinds of damaging racial preconceptions full of misunderstanding and hatred they harbor? Does it begin when he says he is observing Rosh Shoshanna? Or how about when he says he prefers to eat soul food? Perhaps as he grows older he'll not embrace any of his diverse cultural heritages but instead become completely assimilated into American tech-pop culture. How then would this define who he is? What should we call him? Simply American? Simply a member of the human species? Can you deny your cultural heritage and still find a wholeness of self?

Ethan, circa 1972, age 7.

In hindsight, I see I got caught up in trying to place myself in Ethan's shoes, and in so doing I lost sight of how my own path of identity had changed. Or had it? Was I any different now than when I started this journey? Was I blacker? Did I understand more about myself? The only true difference I could detect was the influence of confusion and drama, which had turned what I thought would be an embracing of my roots into a melodrama of family crisis. In finding my biological father and subsequently discovering the missing side of my ethnic/racial background I had thought I would be able to feel more whole, more complete as an individual. With the continued unmasking of my family's—or better put, my father's—secrets, I found I spent more time trying to navigate the melodramas than understand what it meant to be half black.

And what of my father's indiscretions? I am certainly not a holier-than-thou type, but if what I'd gathered to that point were true, the revelation of a child out of wedlock couldn't have gone over terribly well with his religion-minded parents, my grandparents. An unaccepted grandson from an illicit liaison certainly put a decidedly twisted spin on the story. And it sounded as if Wendy had expectations of a future with my father even after she alluded on the telephone that they were just friends. How would I figure into that future? My Detroit father and I were most assuredly related by blood, but does that make us "family"?

Meanwhile, members of my Fosberg family had begun to express feelings themselves of having been left behind, as if somehow I'd abruptly shifted from being "white" to being "black," though it may have been that they were simply upset by my neglect. My siblings, my mother, my adoptive father couldn't understand why I was searching out these relationships. "Why are you *doing* this?" Translation: "You have a father, a family. We raised you, loved you. Why them, what did they do for you over the years?" I felt as if I were walking some kind of family/racial/emotional tightrope, constantly teetering above the abyss of perhaps losing them all.

Wendy from time to time gave me news about my father and began to share with me some of her bitterness toward my father and their situation. It was awkward, yet I occasionally enjoyed speaking with her about art and life. One day she called about him, quite perturbed.

"I can't get ahold of him, and he refuses to return my calls," she exclaimed.

Return her calls? *Where*, I thought, *would she be leaving messages?* Certainly not at his house! "I don't really know what to tell you," I said. "He told me not to call his house."

"I'm worried about him. It's not like him to not call or come over and see his son." However, I somehow felt it was more about her than her son. "I want to make sure he's OK. Will you please do me a favor?" I knew what was coming but couldn't figure out a way to dodge the oncoming bullet. "I need you to call him and tell him to get hold of me."

"Wendy, I'm not sure it's my place to do this."

"Well, aren't you worried about him as well?"

"Of course I am," I admitted.

"When did you last speak with him, did you say?"

"I didn't," I said simply, realizing that it'd been nearly three months. "I guess it's been a long time," I finally said.

"Don't you think that's odd? There could be something seriously wrong with him, and we'd never find out!" I thought back to the last time I had spoken with my grandparents. Surely they'd tell me if something was seriously wrong.

"I doubt there's anything too terribly bad happening," I offered with a less than ringing endorsement.

"Please, Michael, I think we should both know if he's in bad shape. Both you and your brother should know this at the very least. After all, you and Ethan are his heirs." A heaping handful of guilt. But already her manipulation was having an effect as I started to question why he hadn't called. Why didn't he just pick up the phone and say he was OK? What could possibly be happening?

"I guess I could try to call to see if he's OK," I answered unsteadily.

"Thank you, Michael. I'm sure you and Ethan will both be better knowing he's all right."

The next day I gathered the courage and dialed my father's house in Detroit, against my better judgment and against the wishes of my father's wife. The phone rang several times before Sue answered.

"Hi, Sue? This is Michael." I didn't even say my last name. I could feel hostility mount in the silence on the other end. "I was wondering if I might speak with my dad." I waited anxiously as she still had not answered. "Hello?"

"He's unable to come to the phone, I'm afraid."

"Is he OK?"

"Well," she paused, "he's doing better. He just can't come to the phone."

"Doing better?" I asked.

"Yes, however he can't speak just now. I'll let him know you called."

"OK," I said half-heartedly, and before I could offer anything else, she hung up. I wasn't really surprised at her chilly reception, but the finality of the click was painful. I felt foolish for having been used as a pawn in this mistress psychodrama in which Wendy had enlisted me. Sure, I wanted to get to know my father and see if we could lessen the gap the past thirty years had created. This particular exercise was just not how I envisioned achieving that connection. When I let Wendy know I'd tried to get her message to my father with little success, she railed against him. Her diatribe was mean, vicious. It made me realize I needed to step back and trust what my grandparents had told me— that there would come a time when all this would be settled and we'd have that reunion we'd all been waiting for.

IT'S KANSAS, DOROTHY!

Back on the superhighway after wandering some of Colorado's side roads, I was eastbound on Interstate 70 heading into Kansas. The spectacular scenery was now just a glimpse in my rearview mirror; in comparison, the plains of Kansas ahead were as flat as a board and as dry as sandpaper. My truck was now on autopilot as I tossed in the Steinbeck tape, *Travels with Charley,* and cursed the massive highways he derided for their commercialism, lack of character, and speed.

My destination was the farmland of friends near a town called Frankfort. It would be my last stop prior to meeting with members of my family who lived along the way east. It was here I would try to collect my thoughts and focus on the days ahead. What was I really trying to do? How would these family encounters play themselves out and what did I want to ask? What secrets would unfold, and was I prepared to hear them?

The heartache I'd set out with several weeks earlier was now buried deeply under the questions, fears, and doubts about my family, my self, and this journey. The landscape had changed not only physically, but for me mentally and emotionally as well. It felt as if I'd come from navigating the ups and downs of my failed relationship to what I expected was the heart of who I was. Still struggling to piece together the pages of my life, I was hoping for a week's quiet reprieve in this corner of the world usually silent but for the sound of wheat waving in the fields and the murmur of cows.

As I pulled off the main thoroughfare and drew near the farm, I listened to the last chapter of *Travels with Charley: In Search of America*, which is Steinbeck's attempt to explain the nature of journeys. Alas, just as he begins, his journey comes to an end, and he gets lost in rush-hour traffic near New York City. He pulls off the road and finds himself laughing uncontrollably: he is lost in his own town, unsure exactly how to get home.

My own journey began lost and had seemed to this point to be filled with disjointed crisscrossing of lanes, up and down mountains, through deep valleys and gorges, in and out of tunnels. Now on rolling farmland deep in the heart of the country, I felt myself to be on firmer ground.

A route number, a mile marker, a red barn, two miles after the sharp curve—these are the directions plied in the country. A long drive down a shaded dirt road leads to an opening, a small orchard, then a cluster of farmhouses. There is an old red barn, a converted silo house, two large classic white farmhouses, and off to the side a huge newly built stone cottage. There's an old tractor in a field off to my right, another parked squarely in front of a barn. Between the two white houses is a large vegetable garden with a few folks digging through the weeds. It is near the end of the day and the light is warm, vibrant, and golden. As I park my truck near the garage, through my open window I can smell the sweet aroma of tomatoes on the vine, freshly cut grass, and an assortment of other farm odors: cow manure, horse hides, and tractor grease. My legs are weary from the drive, my body rank from the long hours sitting and sweating, my mind overflowing with thoughts, ideas, and questions. I am warmly welcomed by a group of friends who met back in the sixties and decided to live as a group. It's a mishmash of personalities, intellects, and artisans who discovered long ago that "family" could be whatever you make it. Some have married, had kids, divorced, married others, but they all have always remained true to their core. They have lived a life of quiet bohemia, nurturing the land, raising families, and working hard. Because of their unique outlook on life and how it can be lived, I have always felt a certain connection. A kind of "all for one, one for all" feeling permeates everything they do. In an odd way this could be my family, I muse, my support, my connection. After all, what is family? Mine of Waukegan was certainly filled with warmth, love, and nurturing, but what of the missed connection to some core? There was an absence of a deep-rooted bond, a bond so mysterious and elusive it's difficult to explain its absence in my family growing up. Whenever I visited with these friends I never felt the absence of that bond, that deep connection, a familiarity in which words need not be used to empathize with one another's joy or pain. I was accepted for who I was even if I was still desperately searching for who that was. And whether we sat in silence or engaged in deep conversation about our lives, it was as if I was allowed to be comfortable being uncomfortable.

Watching other families in action as I grew up proved to be equally mysterious. No two families are alike. Whether it's different dynamics or different locales, I never found answers to my confusion in watching others. Maybe there are no answers, no mysteries to solve, no magic potions to make me feel whole with my clan. Maybe it had everything to do with me, and little or nothing to do with them, I wondered.

My first stop after the layover at the Kansas farm is the house of my great aunt, Marjorie Louise Robinson Anderson, youngest sister to my paternal grandmother, Lois Enoch Robinson Woods. This would be the first person on my father's side of the family I would see face-to-face. Marjorie was in her late seventies, living alone in Jefferson City, Missouri. Her husband, Charles E. Anderson, had been a professor of meteorology in North Carolina when he had passed away

The three Robinson sisters, Lois E. Woods (standing), Francis Johnson (seated left), and Marjorie Anderson (seated right).

Their husbands, Roy A. Woods (standing), Harry Leroy Johnson (seated left), and Charles E. Anderson (seated right).

a few years back. Marjorie decided then to relocate to the town in which she'd been raised.

I was also looking forward to meeting my great-uncle, Paul Kenneth Robinson, Marjorie's older brother. He was a bit of a cad, I'd been told. A fast living, hard drinking, chain smoking, Cadillac driving old coot who had called me out of the blue just prior to my journey.

"Michael?"

"Yes?"

"This is your Uncle Paul."

"Uncle Paul?"

"Yo grandmotha's brotha."

"Uncle Paul!" surprised by the adventurous nature of his call.

"I seen yer piture here and I'll be damned if you don' look like yo daddy," he told me.

"How'd you get my picture?"

"Yo daddy sent it ta me. Son, I spent many a days teachin' yo daddy how to enjoy life."

"I imagine you did."

"Used ta go visit 'im in Detroit just ta keep 'im in line."

"Really? I didn't know he'd get out of line."

"Aw you know I'm jus messin' with ya!... I hear ya may be comin' out dis a way, pay us a visit, me 'n yer Aunt Marjorie?"

"Well, yes sir, I am indeed."

"Well, I hope ya know ya can stay with me when ya git here."

"That's awfully kind of you, Uncle Paul, but I think I am staying at Aunt Marjorie's."

"Dat a fact?"

"I hope you're not offended."

"Can't say dat I am son... can't say I ain't."

"I certainly would like to spend some time with you, I hope you realize that. And maybe I'll see if Aunt Marj won't mind if I spend a night or two with you."

"Well, awright son, dat'd be fine." Aside from a photo my father had sent me of Uncle Paul standing next to the new Cadillac he'd just bought and driven to Detroit, that was my introduction to the notorious great uncle. My aunt was equally excited, I'd been told, so this was really going to be quite a remarkable reunion, I thought. Actually it would be more than a reunion, it would be a kind of initiation into a club I'd only heard about. This was more than family, deeper than discovering another lost childhood I could have had, far beyond just aunts and uncles. It would be a reconnection to my racial heritage. It was as if I'd been passing for all these years—which at some level I had, without my knowledge—and had now suddenly decided to come home to my newfound roots.

Passing—looking white, therefore able to be taken for being so—has a deep historical record within the black community. If circumstances were ripe, you could slip into white society and never have to feel the hardships of racism again. Passing would present a wealth of opportunities that were not normally bestowed on folks of darker skin. Many found themselves passing merely for survival, as told in the stories of hundreds upon thousands deserting their families of origin to pursue a better life. There was the writer and literary critic Anatole Broyard, for example, and a musician named Korla Pandit, who although born relatively dark realized he could pass for Indian and therefore be gainfully employed as an exotic musician from a faraway land.

The decision to renounce a part of their family for those who consciously could pass was often fraught with agony and confusion. The privilege of having white skin, of being identified as white, cannot be overlooked, and for some it was the difference between life and death. It is a permission granted to those who bear it for which there is no initial request. It wields a power and a preference taken for granted by all who are card-carrying members. It's as if there was an exclusive club the existence of which no one acknowledges. To pass yields access to this exclusivity. I had been a member since early childhood without having to bear the agony most of my brethren have had to endure.

Now I was climbing back across the fence to try to understand what this club was all about. I'd been passing for white without knowing it and yet had that one drop for which anyone was deemed black. I was, in a way, coming home. Click your heels three times and say it: "There's no place like home. There's no place like home. There's no place like home."

CONVICTION

The pain in my father's side turned out to be his appendix. It had been leeching poisons into his system for months, compounded by the stress of his pending trial. With a few quick snips he was relieved of the faulty organ and on the road to physical recovery, though with his trial set to commence. He went back to visiting Wendy and Ethan on Tuesdays and Sundays. She was apparently happy to see him, and life there returned to its abnormal normalcy.

As fall slid into winter of 1992 and what would be snow in the Midwest was now rain in California, I continued to stay in touch with my paternal grandparents, exchanging notes and letters every few weeks or so. Business was looking brighter, and for the first time Jo and I actually had money stashed away in a savings account. I bought a used car that turned out to be a lemon, we bought furnishings for our little walk-street home, and we felt fairly certain we would never again have to hand-paint sets for pornographic movies. We were closing out the year in the black for once, which now had dual meaning for me.

I was working ridiculous hours as the year came to an end, managing several small projects while trying to juggle bidding on some potentially amazing projects. Jo was pumping out sample after sample for commercial projects two years down the road. Work may have been getting more hectic but life was truly grand. I was sober and occasionally attending AA meetings and enjoying the bungalow, which we shared on occasion with Jo's son. Moving back and forth between his father's house and ours seemed to take a heavy toll on him, however. He grew increasingly lethargic and distant, and I recognized some aspects of my own past in his fractured childhood.

My father would call on occasion to fill me in on the progress of his criminal trial. It was a surreal relationship at this point—we'd yet to meet, and this courtroom drama could determine when that reunion might, or might not occur. Having experienced firsthand the psychodrama of Wendy and the racial drama of Sue, I was hesitant to press him hard for answers. Not to mention that when we'd talk, he would be at the home of his mistress! It was all I could do to just listen, hold back my questions, and tread with anticipatory caution, wanting so badly to meet the man I'd been named after.

"Looks like they're gonna change judges on us," my father announced one day.

"Well, what does that mean for your case?" I asked, unsure if I should and wondering if he even knew the answer.

"Not good," he said pessimistically. "The new judge is a real hard ass with something to prove, they tell me. My attorney's got a few tricks up his sleeve, but we'll see what shakes down." It felt so streetwise the way he described it. So bebop and cool.

"When do you think you'll know something, anything?" I asked anxiously, hoping to schedule a rendezvous.

"Don't know, son. I know it seems like it could go on forever. We just have to be patient."

It was well into the spring of the following year before he called again.

"Judge is a real asshole. We're havin' a hard time pleadin' our case. If I didn't know better I'd take the motherfucker out. Pop 'im in the ass with my gat."

I struggle again, trying to comprehend the streetwise vernacular coming from the mouth of my once-corporate, college-educated, well-read father.

"They're tellin' us two weeks. We'll know in two weeks. Keep your fingers crossed for me, son."

Then two weeks later came the call.

"Son, I think you and your gal should make plans to go visit your grandparents sometime this summer."

"Dad, what's up? Did they tell you something? What's the verdict?"

"Came back guilty. Gonna lock me up in the joint for a year. Shouldn't be too bad. Gonna put me up in one a those white-collar work-release places in downtown Detroit. I think they're gonna give me until the fall to get my 'affairs' together. So if we can plan some kind of gathering at your grandparents, I'll see what I can do to make it out there. Might be the only time we'll get to see each other before they lock me away."

And with that, my father, my biological dad, was now a convict. I'd waited thirty years to find him, and another couple of years just to see him, and once we get through that reunion, if we manage it before he goes to prison, I'll have to wait at least another year to see him again. What do I tell friends who ask me constantly about my ongoing

Ford official guilty

A purchasing agent for Ford Motor Co. pleaded guilty Monday to soliciting a bribe from a Detroit printing firm. According to federal authorities, purchasing agent John Woods told T.A.S. Graphic Communications Inc. in 1992 that Ford would no longer use its services unless it paid him a $50,000 bribe. In 1991, Ford purchased about $1.5 million in work from the company. U.S. District Judge Julian A. Cook Jr. set sentencing for Aug. 12.

family drama? As if the racial surprise wasn't enough for people to chew on! "Yeah, homey, I'm black and my daddy's goin' down to spend a year in the joint!"

When I told Jo, she encouraged me to set up a trip out east as soon as possible. I felt her love and support, and perhaps she even saw in a potential trip an opportunity to relive a part of her life she'd lost so many years ago upon the accidental death of her father. A trip to Virginia Beach during the summer. What a grand idea.

Who said "crime doesn't pay" anyway? The "Shadow"? My shadow, my dark side, my biracial past, or is that the present? I read somewhere that black men between the ages of 18 and 65 are seven times more likely than white men to have a prison record. That there are currently three times more black men in prison than in college. And with close to 70 percent of black children growing up fatherless in this country, it's a wonder how black men survive?! With my father's pending jail time we—he and I—had somehow become a part of those daunting statistics.

But I had to wonder, is this the proud male African-American legacy I've inherited? Has my haphazard and almost accidental flinging open of the father door divulged the muffled cries of other black men also searching for their own fatherly love? Was my father's near silence and distance over the past two years of attempts to reunite a by-product of the culture of American male blackness or just thirty years of a buried personal past? Or are these one and the same? Will we be able to pick up the shards of our lost common past and assemble them to form some kind of familial relationship?

I guess I would have to wait on this one to find out. I needed first to see the man, the part of me I'd known, yet not, and finally meet his parents in person as well.

LIKE FATHER, LIKE SON

So it came to pass that in early summer 1993, I found myself on a plane to Norfolk, Virginia, with Jo and her now eight-year-old son. Finally, I was going to meet my birth father, who was flying in from Detroit, and we would stay with the grandparents I had never met.

I was so nervous on the plane I could barely speak the whole flight. Jo was videotaping our journey with a borrowed camera from dear friends of mine, a black couple who upon hearing my race-changing news proclaimed, "We always knew you was one of the family..."

"Are you nervous?" Jo asked as she focused our borrowed camera on my head. I nodded my head in the affirmative and smiled sheepishly.

"All right, just checking," she joked as the camera shook in synch with the intermittent turbulence. The plane ride, which in actuality takes about five and a half hours, seemed to be taking ten and a half. Suddenly, a smooth southern dialect came over the loudspeaker; "Ladies and gentlemen, we are approaching the Norfolk/Virginia Beach area. At this time we ask those of you who are up to return to your race, fasten your seat belts, put your tray tables up, and return your seats to their white positions." I was now experiencing audio hallucinations.

My stomach turned. I shifted nervously. Would my father be there to greet me? What would it feel like? How would we react to one another? Would my grandparents be there?

When the plane landed and it was our turn to deplane, I hesitated, almost frozen in fear of the impending reunion.

"It's now or never, darling," said Jo.

I took a deep breath, grabbed our carry-on bags, and headed out through the plane. Walking through the dimly lit jetway, I slipped into my own little world. There was not another soul present. I was alone as I navigated my way quietly and in slow motion. Jo and her son were gone, as were the crowds of passengers who had forced their way to the front.

Once inside the terminal, I scanned the crowd and immediately spotted my grandmother across the concourse. Precisely as the photographs I'd seen, she was unmistakable, a large, beautiful, light-skinned black woman in a brightly colored dress with thinning gray hair and round glasses. When our eyes met, her face lit up brilliantly. She waved to me as I raced toward her and embraced all of her with my long arms. We locked in a clinch, oblivious to the airport clamor surrounding us. Her warmth and love were unyielding, penetrating, exactly, I thought, what I had been missing all these years.

My grandmother's smile is contagious. Something burst inside me and my tears flowed. She began to cry as she rubbed her eyes underneath her large-frame glasses. It is a tearless cry she later tells me, a result of her cataract operations. When we released our grip, we noticed Jo had circled with the camera and was now facing us. I laughed nervously and introduced her.

"Grandma, this is Jo," I said, pointing to my camera-holding girlfriend.

"It's my job. It's the only reason I'm here," Jo responded excitedly, shaking the camera and slapping an arm around Charlie. "This is my son Charlie," she blurted out nervously and gave him a little shove forward. My grandmother reached for his hand and greeted him warmly. Charlie smiled widely back and shook her warm hand. Granny then turned to me, pointing at the doorway from which we entered the terminal.

"I recognized ya the minute I saw ya step out," she said, wagging her finger.

My grandmother stood there, gazing up at me, shaking her head in disbelief as her eyes squinted under the weight of her dry tears. We walked down the corridor arm in arm toward the baggage claim, smiling and laughing through our tears, camera crew in tow. My grandmother was speaking, I realized, but I could not hear a word she said, just the sound of her soothing southern dialect.

At the baggage claim turnstile I was half watching for our luggage and half glued to my beaming grandmother. I reached for a bag that appeared to be ours.

"Here comes Poppa," she announced.

I turned around and found myself practically eye to eye with a tall, husky, handsome, older black man. It was the man who, in the pictures my grandmother had sent, stood next to his fishing boat named

Lois and Roy.

Michael Sid, Roy A. Woods, my grandfather. There was an awkward manly moment, then I dropped the bag, we shook hands, and I wrapped my free arm around his shoulder. He was visibly annoyed by Jo with the circling camera, but he smiled warmly and said little.

"Hey Lee," he says to me.

"What?" I ask.

"I say, hey Lee," he repeats.

"What are you talking about?"

"You 'n your father," he says most confidently.

"What do you mean?"

"Yo' father UG. You LEE. An' between ya, you the UG... LEE twins!" He was teasing me with a jest of "ugliness" with an obscure reference to the fact that my father and I apparently looked alike. He laughed heartily as he embraced my shoulders with his arm.

On the way to their house they explained that my father was expected to arrive the next morning. Their house was a two-story pine and brick in a middle-class housing development amidst some woods and set back from a frontage road. Inside, it was remarkably cozy and cool for such a hot, humid day. The shades were drawn to keep the midday sun from baking its contents.

Every nook and corner was filled with artifacts or antiques. The walls in the family room were covered in awards and plaques bearing my grandfather's name and likeness. There were pieces of African art lying about everywhere, masks, staffs, figures, carvings. The coffee table in front of their blue Naugahyde sofa was piled high with back

Discharge certificate for Talton Woods.

issues of *Jet* and *Ebony*. Stacks of papers and books and photographs lay haphazardly about. I walked around the house with Jo and her son Charlie, dazed by the collective weight of my family's historical portrait before me.

The walls of the living room were filled with antique clocks, paintings, nautical toys. There were pictures everywhere of my father, my grandparents, and what appeared to be their parents, and their parents'

parents. A framed document on the stairwell was dated August 29, 1863. It was a set of Civil War induction papers for a Talton Woods, making him a member of the black infantry unit, the 54th Regiment. This, I realized, was the very unit the movie *Glory* was based on. Talton Woods would be my great-great-grandfather. Next to that was a picture of a tall strapping black man in a baseball uniform in full pitching windup. It was her father, Charles "Lefty" Robinson, my

Charles "Lefty" Robinson, circa 1923.

Lefty's team in Jefferson City, the Mohawks. He is the last player on the right.

grandmother said. Framed on the wall next to the photo was a player's contract dated July 7, 1924, from the St. Louis Stars of the National Association of Colored Professional Base Ball Clubs.

The following morning, my grandmother was already busy in the kitchen when we got up.

"Poppa's gone to the airport to get your daddy. Y'all grab yo'self sumthin to eat 'n sit down fo he get back."

"Well, what are you doin' there, Granny?" I asked.

"Jus getting things together fo supper tonight. Y'all work around me."

While Jo, Charlie, and I put together our respective breakfasts, my grandmother recited birth and death statistics of various family members as she showed me the entries from her gilded Bible. The practice of listing important dates in the front or back of the family Bible is an age-old African-American family tradition she tells me. I leafed through the pages of names and dates, trying to grasp the significance of my newfound history through touch. Her Bible is old and well worn, interleaved with a letter here, a note there, a recipe—it's like a family scrapbook. Each page, each note, was a glimpse into a family—my family, my roots, my beginnings.

St. Louis Stars of the National Association of Colored Professional Baseball Clubs circa 1924. Charles "Lefty" Robinson, standing, sixth from left.

"Every player before signing a National Association of Colored Professional Base Ball Club contract should carefully scrutinize the same to ascertain whether all of the conditions agreed upon between the Player and the Club President, or its authorized Agent, have been incorporated therein, and if any have been omitted the player should insist upon having all the terms, conditions, promises and agreements inserted in the contract before he signs the same. If at any time, as the result of an official investigation, it is ascertained that an agreement of any kind between the National Association of Colored Professional Base Ball Club Presidents and a Player is not fully set forth in the player's regular contract or made a part thereof, then a penalty shall be inflicted against the Club and Manager violating this provision according to classification, the same to be paid into the Treasury of the National Association of Colored Professional Base Ball Clubs of which the contracting club is a member and the said contract shall be null and void and the player unconditionally released."

CONTRACT CLASS

APPROVED BY THE

National Association of Colored Professional Base Ball Clubs, Inc.

This Agreement, made this ..... 7th .... day of .... July .... A.D. 19..

between .... St Louis Stars Base Ball & Amusement Co .... party of the first part, and

Chas E Robinson

party of the second part, WITNESSETH:

FIRST. Said party of the second part agrees to devote his entire time and services, as a ball player, to said party of the first part, during the period of this contract.

SECOND. Said party of the second part agrees to conform to all the rules and regulations now adopted, or which may be hereafter adopted by the party of the first part, appertaining to his services aforesaid.

THIRD. The player further agrees that during the term of this contract he will not, except with the written consent of the President of the Club and the President of the Association, either during the playing season or at any time, engage in any exhibition game of Base Ball, except as herein provided, and further agrees not to use the Club uniform at any time or for any other purpose, and at the expiration of the playing season to return said uniform to said Club-owner.

FOURTH. It is further understood and agreed between both parties to this contract, that all the provisions and conditions of the National Agreement of the National Association of Colored Professional Base Ball Clubs be and they hereby are made a part of this contract.

In consideration of the foregoing premises, the party of the first part agrees: 1600

FIRST. To pay to the said party of the second part, the sum of $ 160000 .... per month, to be paid in equal semi-monthly installments, upon the first and fifteenth of every month during the championship season of the Association of which first party is a member, unless the ball team shall be away from home playing games, in which event the installments falling due shall be paid within the first week after the return home of said ball team.

SECOND. Said party of the first party agrees to pay the traveling expenses, board, and lodging of said party of the second part, whenever said party of the second part may be traveling in the services of said party of the first part and when not so traveling the party of the second part will pay all of his own expenses.

THIRD. It is further stipulated and agree between both parties to this contract that should the party of the second part sustain an injury on the playing field, while actually engaged in the playing of a game of Base Ball while in the service of the party of the first part, that immediately, continuously and wholly prevents him from service, the party of the second part shall be entitled to, as hereinafter set forth, and shall receive during the period of such continuous total disability the sum of his salary in full for the first two weeks,—further provided: that the party of the first part reserves the privilege, or option, of terminating this contract at the expiration of said two weeks without further liability.

FOURTH. The compensation of the party of the second part stipulated in this contract shall be apportioned as follows: 75% thereof for services rendered, and 25% thereof for and in consideration of the player's covenant to sanction and abide by his reservation by the party of the first part for the season 19........ unless released before its termination in accordance with the provision of this contract. The party of the second part shall be entitled to and shall be paid the full consideration named herein in regular semi-monthly installments, unless released prior to the termination of this contract, regardless of whether or not the contracting Club exercises the privileges of reserving the party of the second part for the season of 1925........

It is hereby mutually agreed by the parties hereto, in consideration of the premises hereinbefore set forth, that should the party of the said second part, at any time or times, or in any manner fail to comply with the covenants and agreements herein contained, or any of them, or with any of the rules and regulations of the party of the first part, which are now or may hereafter from time to time be made, or should the said party of the second part at any time or times be intemperate, immoral, careless, indifferent or conduct himself in such a manner, whether on or off the field, as to endanger or prejudice the interests of said party of the first part, or should the party of the second part become ill or otherwise unfit, from any cause whatever, excepting injury in actual service, or prove incompetent in the judgment of the party of the first part, then the said party of the first part hereunto shall have the right to discipline, suspend, fine or discharge the said party of the second part in such manner as to it, the said party of the first part, shall seem fit and proper, and the said party of the first part snall be the sole judge as to the sufficiency of the reason for such discipline, suspension, fine or discharge and in case of fine imposed, it is agreed by said party of the second part that he will pay the same or that the same may be withheld, as and for liquidated damages.

No non-reserve contract shall be entered unto by any Club member of the National Association until permission to do so has first been obtained from the National Board of the National Association.

Failure of the reserved player who has been tendered a contract on March 1st, to return said contract to the reserving Club on or before March 20th, may be reported for indefinite suspension, and same promulgated.

In order to enable the party of the second part to fit himself for the duties necessary under the terms of this contract, the said party of the first part may require the said party of the second part to report for practice and participate in such exhibition contests as may be arranged by said party of the first part for the period of 30 days of April , the party of the first part to pay the actual expenses of said party of the second part during said period.

It is further agreed that if the said party of the first part should desire the services of the said party of the second part, for any period of time after the date mentioned for the expiration of the term mentioned herein, or which may be mentioned in any renewal hereof, said first party shall have the right to the same, by paying compensation to said second party for each day, at the rate of one-thirtieth (1-30) of the amount herein specified, as the monthly salary of said second party.

In Witness Whereof, the said party of the first part has caused these presents to be signed by its officer thereunto duly organized, and the said second party has affixed his hand and seal on the day and year above written.

By R W Kent
President.

Chas E Robinson
(Player sign here) [SEAL]

_____
(Player's Home Address)

Lefty's Negro Leagues contract, July 7, 1924.

After breakfast we sat in the family room. Jo was chatting away with Granny about gardening, Charlie was possessed by the large-screen television, and I started to thumb through an issue of *Jet*. Suddenly my grandmother looked toward the entry and a smile moved across her round face.

Bible pages.

Me and Sid.

"They're home," she said in a singsongy voice.

Jo quickly grabbed the video camera as each of us stood there awkwardly, my grandmother, Jo, Charlie, and I in a kind of awkward anticipatory moment. My heart was racing. I heard the door open, and then shut. I looked over at my grandmother standing in front of her easy chair, hands on her hips, a huge smile affixed to her face. Finally, thirty-three years having passed, my father entered the room. He looked over at Jo running the video and laughed.

"Hey there, sweetheart," he said to her, "you got the camera going."

He turned and faced me and we stood eye to eye, both somewhat unsure of ourselves, both in amazement. I looked *exactly* like him: same smile, same hair, same way he moved his hands, same tilt of his head, the same resonance in his voice.

"Jesus Christ," he said, looking me over, "you're a good lookin' kid."

I laughed nervously, smiled broadly, and fought back the oncoming tears.

"And you're tall too, aren't ya," he added. I could see him fighting back the identical emotions, giving it his best shot at staying manly and in control.

We stood examining each other. I could sense the jubilation in the room although my attention was completely on the man, the mirror in front of me. He smiled at me, and I melted inside.

"Come here," he said, as he opened his arms wide and laughs, "and give your old man a hug."

We embraced. We gripped each other firmly, slapping our backs.

"How are you?" I asked him, my head buried in his shoulder.

"Real good," he answered.

We gazed at each other, then he winked at me, and thirty-three years disappeared in the blink of an eye. He turned and embraced his mother, whose enormous smile masked her tearless crying. Her sniffling was muted under their bear hug.

"You OK?" he asked her.

She sort of nodded, as he kissed her on the forehead. The reunion was complete. For most of the rest of the day I moved around half in a daze. I kept staring at my father, the uncanniness of our similarities. I watched him strut around the house, I listened to his stories about playing basketball, I looked at his hands with the half-bitten nails, I observed his vast collection of art.

That evening my grand-mother cooked up a sump-tuous, soulful, southern meal of fried catfish, col-lard greens, macaroni and cheese, sweet potatoes, and cornbread. It was the best food I'd ever tasted. After supper, she placed a cake on the table. Sticking out from

the cake were six tall, plastic holders, each with a photograph or handwritten note attached. The notes read "A Joyous Reunion," "In God We Trust," and "A Celebration." The photographs were old black-and-white four-by-

fours with ragged edges. There was the picture she sent me, of her and me and my father, all beaming. There was a photograph of my mother attempting to walk me down the street. And last there was a portrait of a beaming young man with short-cropped hair holding a child in his arms. If you didn't know any better, you'd think that the young man in the photograph was me.

COUNTRY ROADS

"I kept you when they went to get their marriage license. I went over to the apartment and babysat you. Then when yo' motha' went home to her grandfather's funeral, we kept you at our house. We were livin' in Bedford, Mass, at the time, had moved there from the big ol' house in Cambridge that yo' grandparents had owned. I put you in a crib right next to our bed cause you were so precious."

I'm in Jefferson City, Missouri, speaking with my great-aunt Marjorie Louise Robinson Anderson, the youngest of the five siblings in my grandmother's family. She is a small, frail woman, long hair, a bit hunched over, but with a soft scratchy voice that comes across with confidence. She was born November 4, 1921, in Hannibal, Missouri, the last child of Verna Francis Fraizer Robinson and Charles Eugene "Lefty" Robinson. My aunt Marjorie and her husband, Charles E. Anderson, lived in the Boston area when I was young and helped take care of me as an infant.

We are seated at a chrome-and-glass table in her basement family room filled with modern fixtures and furniture. There is a full mini bar in the corner with a mirror ball hanging over it as if she could throw a wild party at any moment. She shakes her head from time to time, smiling broadly as she stares me up and down.

"You couldn't deny yo' fatha on the darkest day."

I've spread old photos and letters over the table. I show her a photograph my grandmother had sent of me as a child in 1958 with my mother.

"I 'member yo' motha, she had beautiful long dark hair like movie stars. Very attractive. She was a good woman."

I open an envelope my mother had sent me, revealing a letter on a torn piece of yellow legal paper and a

Charles and Verna Robinson, 1955.

photograph, the only picture she had kept of my father. I begin to read the letter to Marjorie as she looks on.

> Dear Mike,
>   Please excuse the poor substitute for stationary but I'm still in kind of a state of flux and am not sure where everything is. I think my paper is still at the other house.
>   I know you were very anxious to get this

I know you were very anxious to get this photo so I went right over to the house and found it for you. Your dad was probably no more than 23 or 24 years old at the time and the picture was taken on the porch of the apartment we lived in at 23 Tavern Rd. in Boston. It was a quaint old neighborhood with some historic homes very close to Roxbury and "the projects," that is to say project housing, so it was cheap ($75 per month). It was also very close to the museum and you and I used to walk there (you in the stroller buggy of course) a couple of times a week. I loved that museum. We spent a lot of time there.

Sometimes we walked to the Fenway Park and there were other young mothers there with their children. You used to chase the pigeons to try and feed them. We had no car and the closest grocery store was about eight blocks away so once or twice a week we would walk there. I have many bittersweet memories of the time we spent in Boston and would be happy to share them with you if you are interested.

Your dad was a very good-looking, bright young man who had many good qualities. I'm sure you sensed that when you spoke with him. He was interested in art and literature and was quite well read. (Sense any similarities?) In the short time we were together he was never unkind or mean to either one of us and was delighted with you as a son.

"That's beautiful!" Marjorie says, as her face lights up with tears of both pain and joy and she is sent hurtling back in time. She stares at the faded crinkle-edged black-and-white photo of my father standing on our apartment's porch. He wears a big wide grin, head tilted, a cigarette in one hand. I show her another photo of my parents and me taken on the same porch. She smiles and turns to the inscription on the back: August 1958, Tavern Rd. She notes proudly and confidently that it is her sister's handwriting, my grandmother.

Next was a photograph of my mother attempting to lead me down the street with a dark-skinned man in tow. "That's Harry Lee! Harry Leroy Johnson, he'd be yor second cousin, son a my sista Francis. Well of all things. How 'bout that?" Her breath is short as the excitement from this history lesson catches in her throat. "I guess Harry had gotten out a the service and was livin' in Boston going ta school. Now isn't that remarkable that she had all those pictures while you were in the Boston area?"

John Sidney Woods.

My mother, second cousin Harry Leroy Johnson, and me.

"There's a whole lot more," I tell her.

"Oh really?"

"There's a whole photo album."

"An' Lois kept 'em?"

"My mother sent them to her. She sent the whole photo album."

"Why?"

"I think she felt guilty."

She shakes her head as she gazes at the photographs, the historical record. "Mm-mm-mm," she says. "That's 'cause she had deprived them of their grandchild."

"Do you remember me being around?"

"'Member?" she says, almost incredulous. "Course I 'member. We took care a you. My daughters played with you. We loved you and bathed you and powdered yo' bottom." She squints, forcing tears to cascade down the sides of her face as she pours over the documents and photos laying before her. "Then it seemed like you disappeared. I din't ask any questions 'cause I din't want it ta seem like I was meddlin'. I jus' gathered it was... my husband and I just had a feelin'... by yo' motha not takin' you home to the funeral. Then suddenly not too long after that, she disappears and we see you no longer..." Her voice fades. She raises her hand to her mouth and holds it closed as she continues to shake her head.

"Do you think it had something to do with race? The reason we left?" I ask her bluntly.

"It did run 'cross our minds, my husban' and I," she starts out carefully. "Why would she not take you ta the funeral, show you off wit all that sadness there—to see this precious child would bring joy, you know?" The searing pain of the past resurfaces. "Afta you left, then yo' fatha got polio and we had to leave fo' California. I 'member seein' him in the hospital wit tears in his eyes 'cause he was all alone. He had a double whammy." She stops to clear her eyes with a tissue she's held tightly in her hands. "It had ta have bin racial," she says with assured confidence. "Of course if they had ever met yo' fatha' and not seen us, they wouldn't a known if he was mixed or white, or anything. So I never asked yo' grandparents about it. I figured if they want a talk 'bout it they would. Evidently it broke their hearts so they jus' din't talk 'bout it; 'cause you kin see in these pitures how delighted she was." She stares down at the picture of my grandmother beaming as she holds me, my father next to her proud like a bird.

"Did you ever think you'd see me again?"

She smiles broadly, looking me over. "Yeah, I figured someday we'd find ya, see ya. We had driven from North Carolina where we was livin' at the time up to Lois and Roy's fo' Thanksgivin', and they were on air that you had bin there. They were delighted—it was jus' like God had arrived. And you know yo' grandfatha, he's very quiet, you know, and boy, all the nice things he said and what not. I remember while we was there the telephone rang and he jumped wondering if that was you callin', which is unusual fo' yo' granfatha. You know how he is. Since that incident he talks 'bout you all the time, and she does too." Her eyes lighten up as she looks back at the photos. "You know, you cain't go back. Now that they found you, jus' love you and keep on goin'."

She finds a photograph in the stack of her mother and father and holds it up. "My motha and fatha were jus' heartbroken 'cause they never got to see you. Johnny Pudd was like the heart of our family, 'cause he was the oldest, their first grandchild. He was king a the mountain, they worshipped him."

Johnny Pudd was the name she had called me as I stepped through the doorway to her brick and wood-trim home after having driven non-stop from my friends' Kansas farm. That was the name they all called my father as he was growing up. And now it was me, although my name was not Johnny. I arrived under a bright blue sky.

Judging by the way her house was appointed and by its great size and location near downtown Jefferson City, not to mention the brand new Caddy in the garage (although I'd been told she did not drive), I'd say my aunt's husband must have done quite well for his family. He had been one of the country's foremost experts in meteorological research. He had received an undergraduate degree in chemistry—along with being class president—from the historically black Lincoln University, a master's degree in meteorology from University of Chicago, and a PhD from MIT in 1960. He'd been a weather officer and captain in the U.S. Air Force for the famed Tuskegee Airmen and had experienced, my aunt said, "unbelievable, horrible, terrible" racial hardships. For a while he worked for Douglas Aircraft, then was recruited by the University of Wisconsin as a professor of meteorology, associate dean of the

The Robinson girls and their families. Back row, standing: Harry Leroy Johnson, Charles Anderson, and Roy A. Woods. On couch: Harry Leroy Johnson Jr., Kenneth Wayne Johnson, their mother Francis, Cheryl Elaine Anderson, her mother Marjorie and her brother Charles Edward Anderson Jr., Lois E. Woods, and John Sidney Woods, circa 1949.

graduate school, and organizer and chairman of the Afro-American Studies Department. He ended his teaching career in the Department of Marine, Earth, and Atmospheric Sciences at North Carolina State University. He had died just two years previously, at the age of seventy-five.

By mid-afternoon, Aunt Marjorie's brother, my Uncle Paul, was supposed to have dropped by to join us for dinner. By 7:30 p.m. we still had not heard from him, so my aunt, who says she never cooks, called for takeout. We had a lively conversation over some fried chicken until 9:30, when finally the doorbell rang. It was Uncle Paul bearing flowers for his sister. There was some standard sibling bickering: "Where the hell you been?!" "Yer not my watchkeeper." "Maybe it would help if you got a watch!" Then Uncle Paul settled down with the intention of getting to know his new great nephew. He is a gruff old codger, stout, with a full head of shocking Don King gray hair and a dollop of gray just under his lower lip. He wore an old rumpled, slightly soiled, cream-colored suit with a wide, plaid tie. He speaks in a slow, elongated southern drawl. He occasionally headed out to the garage for what I discovered was an opportunity to grab a smoke away from his disapproving sister.

"How'd ya like to come stay wit me tomorra and maybe we go fo' a short drive into Hannibal? I'll sho' ya' the family sights."

"Sure, Uncle Paul, if that's all right with Aunt Marj?" I look over to her for her approval, but she stands defensive and slightly incredulous I would even consider this proposal.

"You do what you like. I'll still be here when you come back."

That night I sleep soundly under the mirror ball in her basement party disco lounge on a pullout couch. The next morning over breakfast I ask if it's okay if I go to Uncle Paul's for the night.

"I'm fine with it. You might not be, however."

"What do you mean?" I ask.

"Bin trying to warn ya 'bout yo' uncle. He's a good man, jus' not terribly responsible is all. You seen how the man show'd up here yesterday? Practically ten hours late!"

Uncle Paul doesn't show up until almost 7:30 that evening. We dash off to dinner—I am starving—under the skeptical scowl of my aunt. We've decided to drive both vehicles back to his house, drop off his new car, then hop in my truck and grab dinner at the local Applebee's—a favorite choice among family members for some reason. After a leisurely but lively dinner, we're the last folks to leave as Paul has a smoke outside before we start off. He wants to drop by the home of some friends, he tells me, although it is now approaching 10:30 p.m. I find it odd but oblige him just the same. *I suppose he wants to show me off to his friends,* I tell myself.

We pull in to his friends' driveway about 11 p.m. Their garage door is wide open, lights all on, garage stuffed to the brim with bikes, lawn equipment, tools, and automotive parts. We knock on the door and are greeted by an older white couple. They are not surprised in the least to see Paul at this hour. He introduces me, then they proceed to gab for what seems like forever. They are a pleasant couple, but the time is edging after midnight and I am tired. We finally say our goodbyes and get back into my truck.

"I'd like you ta take me ta the Walmart," says Uncle Paul in his slow, deliberate drawl. "Need a few thangs fo' tomorra mornin'."

"Are you sure, Uncle Paul?" I beg, hoping he'll relent. "It's awfully late and we can get whatever you need in the morning."

"Naw, naw, now take me to the Walmart," he repeats in his slow-mannered way.

We pull up in the parking lot of the behemoth of discount stores. It is practically 1 a.m., but the place is jumping. Paul smokes another of his Benson and Hedges extra-long filtered, then searches for a motorized sit-down shopping cart outside the entrance. He stamps out his smoke, mounts the cart, throws it in drive, and slowly edges toward the overly lit aisles buzzing with activity. I follow dutifully, my aunt's warnings now reverberating in my head.

After a good hour in the store and five items later, we check out and head back to the truck. Uncle Paul lights up another long one as he climbs in on the passenger side.

"Uh, Uncle Paul," I stop him, "do you think you could finish that smoke outside my truck?"

"What?" he says, startled and agitated. "Oh fer cryin' out loud! What the hell's yer problem?"

"Well," I say, hoping to appease him, "I'd just rather you didn't smoke in my truck."

He grunts as he opens the door wildly and clearly agitated says, "I don' need this crap…"

I hadn't seen this coming. He had seemed to avoid smoking in my truck earlier, but now he was truly disturbed by my aversion.

He slammed the door as I looked down, shaking my head, almost laughing, at the ridiculousness of our disagreement. I sat there, my aunt's admonition running through my mind again. After a few minutes I look up. No uncle. I look out the side window toward the still bustling store and there is no sign of him. Finally, I see a figure far in the distance walking slowly toward the main road through the yellowed fluorescent light illuminating the night. *That can't possibly be him*, I think. But it is.

I start my truck and drive up alongside him, hoping he will stop and jump in. He does not. He won't even look at me. "Uncle Paul, what are you doing?"

"I'm goin' home," he says in a now disgusted growl.

"Walking?" I ask.

"You see what I'm doin', don'cha'?"

"Uncle Paul, please get in the truck." He says nothing as he walks slowly on. "Look, I'm sorry, I thought you knew I didn't want you to smoke in my truck." Still nothing. "Look, it's late, please just get in, and let's go back to your house together."

"You kin go on by yo'self," he pouts.

"Uncle Paul, I don't even know where I am! Please, look, I'm sorry." He stops walking, I brake the truck. He stands looking out straight ahead, takes a long drag off what is left of his cigarette, and tosses it. He climbs in, closes the door, and says, "Take a left out the parking lot."

We enter his split-level home in silence, exactly as we had sat the entire ride back. It's sparsely furnished and reeks of cigarettes. Overflowing ashtrays are everywhere, and everything is covered in dust. I put the bag of food on the sticky counter next to the fridge. I open the door and an otherworldly odor strangles me unexpectedly. The refrigerator is filled, bursting with spoiled food: meat in plastic packages that have ballooned from the distended gasses pushing to get out, fruit nearly black from age and furry, milk cartons seeping with congealed soured liquid. The walls are dark and could be covered in mold.

It is a chemistry experiment gone awry. I put the carton of milk we'd just bought next to the old one and quickly closed the door, hoping microbes from the souring experiment won't jump ship and spread to the new member.

Uncle Paul shows me the upstairs where I will be staying. The good news is that a window has been left open and the stench of cigarette smoke is barely present. The bad news is the room is unfinished—unpainted drywall, half-laid carpet, a bare lightbulb hanging from the ceiling, and a barren mattress in one corner with a pile of what might be clean sheets atop.

He shows me a bathroom off to one side, also unfinished: no shower fixtures, no mirror, no toilet paper. I mention the toilet paper and he tosses me up a roll from downstairs.

I try to sleep, frightened and curled up in a ball, scared there may be bugs or creatures of some kind living in the walls or floors of this nightmare house.

The next morning I wandered the house hoping to avoid food-borne creatures and dysentery and then ventured out for a walk. By three my uncle still had not risen. If we didn't get moving soon, our road trip to Hannibal would be in the dark. I finally knocked on his door.

"Uncle Paul? Uncle Paul? UNCLE PAUL?" I tested my volume, hoping not to piss him off like the night before.

"Yes?" came a raspy growl from beyond the closed doorway.

"Uncle Paul, we need to get going if we're gonna see any daylight in Hannibal."

"Yeah, yeah, I'll be up in a minute." I hear him stir.

An hour later, I am knocking again. "Uncle Paul? UNCLE PAUL?"

"Yeah?" comes the half-dozing voice once again.

"We gotta go, Uncle Paul, it's getting late."

"Yeah, yeah, I'm coming." Moments later I hear him actually rise and then the sound of water running.

Two and a half hours later, we are on our way along the country roads leading to Mexico, New London, and Hannibal, Missouri. A storm approaches as we hurry toward the family lands, hoping to catch a glimpse of the old farm, house, and graves of those that came long before me.

"I grew up on dat farm in New London. Spent summer's there workin'. We'd get outta school in the spring and work hard 'til Labor Day."

"Whose farm was it?" I ask.

"Why, that was my grandparents', Ma and Pa Braxton. It was their farm."

"The Braxton's?"

"Yes, Lucinda and Jack is what we called 'em. That were my mother's mother. I worked there wit my brotha' Rip, Charles Jr. We worked hard, 'n fought even harda. He was a big strong guy, but no guts. Pa's favorite. Every parent got a favorite grandson. After Pa died I became foreman fo' 'bout a year, but Ma din't pay much and was too set in her ways. I liked ta smoke and shoot craps and I needed money fo' that."

He tells me his father's mother was Mary Morrison Robinson. Her father, Arthur Morrison, had refused to raise Mary because she was fathered by a white landowner's son and a black woman—his wife, Jennetta Morrison.

"We used ta tease my grandmotha' all the time, we'd say, 'Gran Morris, when was ya born?' An' she'd say, '49. An'

Lucinda's first husband, Enoch Fraiser, circa 1890s.

Pa and Ma Braxton, New London, Missouri, circa 1920s.

we'd say, 'When?' an' she'd say, 'I tol' ya '49!' See she was born in 1849, 'fore the emancipation proclamation. She was born into slavery in Pike... or was it Rawls County, Missoura?"

The skies have opened up in a torrential downpour as I try to nav-

Margaret and Lewis Emerson outside their house in New London, Missouri, with Verna Robinson, early 1900s.

igate the now rain-slicked country roads in the area my family had its first roots.

"Uncle Paul, what was it like back then with separate bathrooms and drinking fountains and all that?"

"Hell!" he gruffs. "What difference does it all make? If you can take a shit where ever'body else does? You can go behind a guy that leaves a bad odor? Don't make no difference if he's black or white, it stinks! The fact that you kin go in the front door..." He laughs heartily. "That don't make... jus' as long as you kin git in the house, go in the back door..." His voice trails off as I see he notices something along the side of the road. "Now right down in here somewheres there's a tree—my father used to point it out to us, on the way to Columbia— where they hung the Negroes, very close to the road. An' the tree last time I saw it didn't have no foliage. They lynched a black man, hung 'im to this tree. That tree," he says emphatically, "right over there in that field. Seems a little far from the road but darn near looks like the one." Off in the distance I see a tall scraggly tree standing like a death mon-

Margaret Emerson, my grandmother's mother's father's mother, circa 1860s?

ument, the rain cascading off its branches, undoubtedly the very same branches men hung from at one time.

The rain lets up as we drive through New London toward Hannibal, the town made famous by Mark Twain. The skies lighten, the dark clouds pass, but there is little daylight left. Uncle Paul tells me about his life of odd jobs, hoboing, and military service overseas. It is a life full of disappointments and struggle.

"I'm not angry at people; I'm disappointed, depressed by everyone."

"Tell me about your relationship with my father." I encourage him to lighten his mood.

"I's always tight with John Sid. He's more like a brotha than a nephew. And when I first saw you I never been so elated about anythin'... to meet such a fine image! You look like a clone—well, as I understand clonin'. So mannerly and such a sweet young'un. Seem like a dream, didn't seem real. Took me back when John was just about the same size."

We drive in silence for a while, then he points out the house he was born in and other family landmarks of note. Just this journey alone has been an eye-opener. The weight of my family history, coupled with the implications of our nation's racial history, discovered along the winding rain-drenched country roads of Missouri, began to sink in.

It is difficult to fathom the prospect of lynchings, of separate drinking fountains and restrooms, of segregation. It all seems so long ago. And yet, as my uncle laughed off the ridiculousness of separate areas for blacks and whites as if this parting of the races would protect one from a dishonorable fate, I too cannot understand the absurdity of our racial history. How can the color of one's skin have played—and still play—such an important role in relationships between people? Why do we still so often regard this as a defining attribute?

ANGER MANAGEMENT

After Jo and I had visited with my father and grandparents for the first time that summer of 1993, we moved as if in an altered dream state. I stayed in touch with my grandparents, but my father had returned to Detroit and the off-limits zone his wife had established. The place for his yearlong incarceration he alternately described as a locked-down halfway house or, when he was polishing his street cred, as "the joint." Come November, when his sentence was to begin, I expected to have little contact with the Johnny Pudd of my mirror image. It was hard to imagine that I'd journeyed so far, experienced so much, and the relationship was suddenly to be locked down for a year. I'd still have my grandparents, though, and of course there was Wendy and my little half brother Ethan.

Somehow Wendy and my father had come to an understanding, which led her to put her house in the Detroit suburbs on the market and purchase (with my father's funds?) a log-cabin-style house in a rural area outside of Virginia Beach known as Pungo. We stayed in touch, and Wendy urged Jo and me to come out, meet my half brother, and visit with my grandparents.

Business was going well, and an opportunity to travel east to learn some new Italian plastering techniques presented itself, so we planned a trip for the fall—eerily around the time my father would be incarcerated. Little did I know how great was the animosity Wendy still harbored toward my father. It became abundantly clear that October, however, when Wendy sent a carbon of a letter she had written to my father.

October 9, 1993

Dear John,

It has really impacted me, how self-centered and childlike your behavior is. It makes me question just what twisted belief of love you must have. It appears that "love" to you is a feeling in one's heart and that it has nothing to do with behavior. I feel love, therefore I do love. You are wrong. Love goes well beyond feelings; perhaps that is where it begins. Then it must move on to action, behavior. It is not words. Love is interacting with, not speaking words to. The love of a child is a physical and emotional involvement.

John, you seem to have this naive, fantasized notion that love is only having to say the words, "I love you." You seem to be saying, "I love you and that should be enough for you." Well, it's not. Michael has a deep void in his life. His search for you and his discovery of you has been all his effort and though I cannot speak for Michael, I suspect that your lack of attention and interaction has been very disappointing.

And now, here is history repeating itself. Ethan will become 35, just as Michael is, and have that same deep hole inside that never got filled. John, your blindness is so deep, rather so dark. And what will your excuses be?

I stopped reading for a moment, trying to look away, yet fascinated by the horrifying presumptuousness of what she said. Why would she send me this letter? I have absolutely no business in their private affairs, yet she took the trouble not only to make the carbon, but to claim to know my thoughts and feelings even though "she cannot speak for" me. I turned the page.

As long as I live I will never forget you telling me the advice your parents gave you when you told them about me. "Just keep her as a mistress," they said. You have been a dutiful son. Your parents have been a strong influence in keeping you from the only meaning in your life—me and Ethan. Well done.

You can stay with Sue. We both know you never left her, and think how pleased your folks will be.

My household budget is attached. I expect you to provide the needed income until the house sells. In the future I expect you to send me child support payments and you will be expected to pay for whatever private school education Ethan will require.

There was no attachment to my copy, thank God, but the weight of her letter needed no additional backing. The anger and hurt she felt may have been genuine, perhaps even justified, but the fact she made a copy to send to me was so filthy and repugnant, it sickened me. And it was totally presumptuous on her part to draw a parallel between my life and Ethan's. She knew nothing about my relationship with Sid, nor my expectations, or desires of our reconciliation. I remained silent on the matter, but our upcoming trip was now loaded with so much more emotional baggage than I had anticipated. Not to complicate relations further, I decided not to share Wendy's letter with Jo.

———————

When Jo and I flew into Norfolk that November, we were again greeted by my grandparents, Lois in a bright dress again, large-rimmed glasses, and warm embrace and a smile. Roy, slightly hunched over yet still a commanding presence, was wearing his ever-so-sly grin.

"Lordy, you look so much like ya fatha, don't he, Roy?" Granny grinned as she embraced us.

"Uh huh," came the brief response from my man-of-few-words grandfather.

"Finally, my two boys home at last!" Granny proclaims as she pats me on the cheek.

I looked to Jo in slight surprise, as they apparently readily accepted the presence of their other grandson, Ethan. We'd been led to believe they had resisted open acknowledgment of his existence, but this happy welcome proved our suspicions wrong.

Entering their history museum of a house again brings a flood of memories from our first visit. Jo grabs my hand tightly, smiling as we sit sipping lemonade while Granny works feverishly in the kitchen preparing soul food delights. Wendy and Ethan will be joining us, she says, and this seems to delight her to no end. As the preparations continue, my grandfather has taken his customary place at his desk in the home office. He sits among shortwave radios and squawk boxes, a magnifying swivel lamp at his disposal, fiddling with knobs, and reading science magazines as he listens to the sound of the police scanners announcing the latest in criminal activity.

There is a knock at the door and my grandmother sets down her potholders, scurrying to the door.

"They're here! Roy, they're here. My boys are here!" She flings the door open and with an enormous grin welcomes Ethan and his mother. "Well, Lordy, look who's here!" She announces as if it's a surprise. "Hello shugga, how ya doin' today?"

The open door blocks our view as I hear a tiny little voice from behind it. "I'm good."

"Hi, Lois," a distinctly feminine voice adds.

Jo and I rise from our seats and step toward the entryway. My grandmother edges the door shut as Ethan, a small, frail, cute sprite of a kid of eight, looking vaguely like a cross between me and our father, steps out from behind his mother,

"Michael," Wendy, long dark hair and flowing outfit, greets me, leaning forward and smiling, "so good to finally meet you."

"Hello, Wendy." I hug her with a concealed caution. "Good to meet you as well." I look down to Ethan standing shyly with an uncontainable grin. "Hello, Ethan." I extend my hand in an initial handshake. "I'm your brother, Michael!" He takes my hand, and after a quick cursory shake, I pull him toward me enveloping him in an embrace as I squat down to greet him. "Nice to meet you."

"Hi," he says shyly.

We eye each other as my grandmother stands above us with the same grin I saw on her face the first time my father entered this very room on my last visit here. A phantom tear falls on her cheek as she sniffles and holds her hand to her face. My grandfather stands in the doorway between the kitchen and his office. He is a proud man, and this emotional stuff is not really his style. As he looks on I wonder what his real thoughts about this moment are. Does he hold some resentment for this awkward situation his son has thrown him into? Is he accepting of Ethan and his mother, or is this just a charade? Here stand their two boys, both white in appearance, one with Jewish roots, the other Armenian. Yet, at no time do I feel any kind of resistance to our presence or appearance, just the familial warmth of their complete embrace.

For dinner tonight it is pork roast, with green beans and sweet potatoes, followed by gooseberry pie, a delicacy my grandmother tells us she has baked for many years. Dinner is of course delicious, and talk ranges from a few words about my father—now doing his time in prison—to detailed family history. Granny does most of the talking. Her manner of storytelling includes the tiniest of details down to the shade of a dress or the step-by-step way in which laundry was completed. But her stories are not boring. Wendy seems slightly uncomfortable at times, especially when the talk turned to the subject of my father. She was much more reserved than I had expected. Several times she reminded Ethan of his manners, talking to him in a slightly condescending way.

"Ethan," her voice rising on the end of his name, "use your napkin, honey." He gazes downward and dutifully takes his napkin from his lap, wiping his mouth and hands.

"That's better, honey," Wendy responds as if she needs to.

I notice my granny peeking over at my grandfather, but he doesn't let on he notices; instead he eats silently, occasionally getting up from the table to bring us more food or help clear plates.

The evening is cordial and pleasant, filled with stories and warmth on my grandmother's part. After dinner, Roy executes his nightly routine in front of the sink, washing dishes as we gather in the family room across from his quiet clanging. I sit next to Ethan on the Naugahyde sofa, my grandmother across from us in her easy chair, while Jo and Wendy take seats around us.

"So, Wendy, how are you finding it here?" Jo asks, hoping to draw her out.

"We're still getting adjusted. We love our cabin though, don't we, Ethan?"

"You know, Mom," he starts, "we should get them to come see it." He looks up at me, smiling. "And I can show you my room, and you can meet my dogs, Precious and Freddy, and you can see the frogs next to the creek."

"Of course, honey," she responds. "We'd love to have you out," she says, turning her attention to us.

"Sure, we'd love to," I say. "Jo?"

"Absolutely," she chimes in.

The next morning, armed with detailed directions my grandfather has supplied, we head out to Pungo in his Honda. The narrow country roads are lined with the occasional farm as they wind through the swampland so typical of the southern Chesapeake Bay area. The sweet odor of corn, the humidity of the surrounding wetlands, and the random smell of wandering cows pierce the fresh air through our open windows.

We drive by rural country households with ramshackle garages and yards littered with vehicles of all kinds: pickups, mobile homes, trailers, four-wheelers, and motorcycles. An occasional flag is attached or flying next to a barn—invariably a Confederate flag. It is a startling reminder we are in the South and headed toward the home of my half-black, half-Jewish half brother. Is he aware of this sporadic southern separatist symbol? Would he even know what it represented? Does he even comprehend how it might affect the way he thinks about himself, and what others think of him? We pull in the drive of the large log-cabin-style house situated in a semi-wooded area with a gentle creek running along one edge of the front lawn. As we park, Ethan runs out to greet us with his two enthusiastic and friendly dogs.

"Hey there, Ethan! How are you?" I ask as I reach out and grab his hand.

"I'm great!" he says, taking it. "This is Freddie, and that is Precious." Wendy comes out the door in shorts and a T-shirt, smiling.

"Hi guys. Welcome to Pungo. Ethan," her voice rises, "you have to finish your room before anything else happens."

"But Mom..."

"No buts, get in there and do it," she snarls, then quickly changing her tone, "I'll take care of Michael and Jo."

We step inside, and I am immediately impressed by the array of antique toys, African figures, and American folk art pieces tastefully arranged about the large living area we've entered. There are brightly colored fabrics and quilts, richly accented kilims, and chestnut-colored furnishings filling the room.

"This is beautiful, Wendy!" Jo remarks, astonished by the rich array of art and crafts decorating the spacious area.

"Thank you."

"Not bad for being here just a few months."

"It's been a lot of hard work," she tells us. "But I've had nothing but time."

With plenty of time that means she hasn't had to work. And the decor is so stunning, I'm curious as to how this was financed.

"These are yours?" I ask, pointing to a set of ancient-looking folk art figures and toys lined up along a wooden shelf.

"John's really. He gave them to us." And suddenly the picture starts to become clearer. Gave them to her? So he is still their sole means of support? "Come this way." She beckons us to follow her into the dining room. In the center is a beautiful barn-wood table with antique chairs lining its sides. There are more figures and statues placed in corners of the room, a settee with an assortment of antique toys seated on top, all set on top of a big colorful oval woolen rug.

The kitchen is charming as well. Old varnished wooden cabinets with silver handles and linoleum countertops. Ethan steps out from a long hallway alongside the kitchen and is smiling upon his return. The dogs, who have returned with Ethan, paw at us again in their über-friendly manner.

Wendy opens a door leading outside.

"Come on now, out you go. Go run and play," she tells them. As she closes the door she notices a pair of shoes sitting on a mat next to the door. Her face and voice change in an instant as she shouts, "Ethan?" Her face goes flush and her body stiffens. "What have I told you about leaving your shoes here?" She points at the shoes and holds her look of death as Ethan cowers.

He looks both embarrassed and dumbfounded as he utters under his breath, "Mom?"

"Now, Ethan," she says talking down to him in a voice full of anger. He bows his head, reluctantly grabs his shoes and heads back to his room. "Ethan?" I call out, hoping to ease his frustration. "Why don't you show me your room?"

His look turns immediately to joy.

I leave Jo with Wendy and enter the now excitedly nervous eight-year-old's world. The room is crammed with all manner of toys, collections, and books, and yet extremely neat and well organized—almost methodical. He proceeds to show me his vast collections of toys, animal bones, feathers, coins, and all manner of games and books. He is excited and proud as he explains each item in great detail. Everything neatly placed in some sort of container or alphabetically on a shelf.

In a way, it's scary. Although I was raised by a strict hand of orderliness, his room is so neat, so impeccable, it's hard to imagine where the fun part of being a kid steps in.

When we emerge a half hour later, Wendy and Jo are setting the table, preparing us for lunch.

"Ethan, napkin please," Wendy orders when we all sit down.

I notice Ethan cringe and can feel the anger and frustration well up in him. It's as if his every move is judged and controlled. He drops his spoon in his bowl, reaches to the side of his plate, grabs his napkin, then splays it out on his lap. We sit and eat in silence for a few seconds before Wendy breaks in.

"Oh, I almost forgot, what would you guys like to drink?"

"A soda of some kind would be fine," I say.

"Yeah, what he said," Jo responds.

"I'll have one too, Mom."

"I don't think you will, Ethan," she admonishes him in her carefully controlled tone.

Ethan and me.

"But mom?"

"Don't start with me, I'm not in the mood," she snaps, with what looks to me a sickly smile on her face. The tension between them is so thick and troubling, Jo and I glance at one another, then down at our plates, embarrassed. Wendy lights off to the kitchen, retrieves sodas, and places a water in front of her resigned but disgusted son, as we sit picking slowly through our lunches.

On the drive back to my grandparents, I think about the

path this poor kid will have to travel. Living in a home bought and paid for by his now-imprisoned African-American father, deep in the middle of nowhere with reminders of racism just steps outside his back door, a Jewish mother who controls his every move with a condescending tone. How will he shape up? What identity issues will he grapple with as he tries to figure out where he fits in? Will it be the Torah—a rarely seen book in these parts—or soul food or dirt bikes flying confederate flags that shape his life? As the warm air washes by, I begin to feel an appreciation for what my mother endured, the fears she kept at bay, and the difficulties inherent in my subsequent upbringing. It was not easy, but not nearly as challenging as what lies ahead for this young boy.

THREE SISTERS

The road trip has brought me halfway across the country having had revealing conversations with my great aunt and uncle about the genesis of my African-American family. It was now time to delve into my Armenian roots as I return home to the Chicago area and interview members of the family that raised me.

What was known of my Armenian family history lay in fragments scattered among the memories and a few records and photographs of the last three remaining members of the Pilibosian family, my mother and her two sisters. The distance that separated them and the selective nature of each of their memories and stories would also frustrate my quest for a comprehensive historical picture. The most I could hope for, I thought, would be a good handful of stories perhaps linking me to my family's past, to my roots, to my Armenian heritage.

My grandparents, Garabed and Rachel, had passed away in the 1980s, years before I ventured off to search for my biological father. Their racial and ethnic views were not at all uncommon for immigrants who came to this country at the turn of the century (and perhaps yet for some who immigrate to America); they wanted their daughters to wed one of "their own." The fact that their two oldest daughters never came close to fulfilling their parents' desires for continuance of their ethnic line had been for them the source of great disappointment,

disappointment made more poignant because of the troubled times they'd lived through.

For many Americans, Armenia is an unknown (and probably unpronounceable) land somewhere out in the vast wilds of numerous other unknown, unpronounceable countries. In reality it is set between Iran, Turkey, and Azerbaijan, landlocked and isolated in what some consider a part of the Middle East, although growing up we never considered ourselves middle eastern. During the rein of the Turkish Ottoman Empire in the late 1800s and early 1900s, Armenia suffered at the hands of the Turks what has been widely acknowledged as the first modern genocide. It has been conservatively estimated that more than 1.5 million Armenians were massacred, and hundreds of thousands deported while reports circulated the globe and the world watched in horror. It was a religious conflict in part, pitting Ottoman Muslims against the Christian Armenians they ruled over. Armenia had come under strict rule during the period dating back to the sixteenth century. The Turks set out to systematically eliminate them under the watchful but silent eyes of Europe. It wasn't until sometime after 1919 when immense world pressure, the end of World War I, and a change in the political climate in Turkey, helped bring the killings to a close. However, to this day the official Turkish position has been to deny repeatedly that anything other than a common battle ever took place. They claim the Armenians were the aggressors and that the deaths are overstated to heighten the drama.

How my grandparents had survived this had been the stuff of family folklore. I wanted to find out more about the horrors they experienced, the sacrifices they had made, and how they had made it to America. Unfortunately the three Pilibosian sisters' memories, like our conversations, were fragmented and disjointed.

"My younger sister is the one you want to talk to." My mother sighed as a breeze rippled across the tiny lake on which her house was situated. "Diane's the one with the family history." She squinted as her eyes adjusted to the faint summer gust in the bright sunlight.

"Yes, but what do you know?" I asked. "He must have told you something. After all, he was your father," I said as we sat staring blankly across the lake.

Garabed Pilibosian had passed away before any of his three daughters had time to record his history. His death came well before I embarked upon the upending journey to find my biological dad and his family and to track down my roots in preceding generations. His account of the Armenian genocide was scattered and incomplete. Each daughter had

The Pilibosian family, Rachel, Garabed, Meline, Adrienne, and a cousin.

been holding on to fragments of his past while keeping an unspoken, alienated distance from one another.

Diane, forty-eight, was now the vice president of credit risk management and research for the Northern Trust Company. Her shock of gray hair, her road-weary face, and her nervous gesturing made her look more like her deceased mother than like either of her older sisters. Twelve years separated her from my mother, fourteen from her older sister Meline. As the years since my childhood passed, my early connection to her had weakened, and we found ourselves trying to navigate the same distance she and her sisters did.

She had spent years as a librarian and research specialist, and initially, in lieu of meeting with me, she had prepared a brief history with a stale dryness that bespoke her aversion to emotion. When I had asked if she would tell me about Garabed and Rachel's past, at first she refused categorically, then relented on her own terms—no meeting, no questions—and wrote a few sentences at her own pace. Were the memories too painful? The historical record too great? I could not discern what it was she feared.

She was at least able to tell me when Garabed was born and the significance of his name: "Garabed Pilibosian: first name means 'one who opens the gates' (referring to St. John the Baptist)." It continued, "Born February 15, 1904, in Village of Tadem (Kharpert Province) Armenia." Her older sisters weren't privy to this information. They hadn't a clue as to when he was actually born. Their amusing anecdote was that there had been no records kept, thus Garabed's age was fuzzy at best. This combined with the fact that he had entered this country illegally with another relative's paperwork, made them unsure of his exact age.

It was the eldest of the three sisters, Meline, who was able to fill in a few aspects of Garabed's early years. She was still living in Waukegan when I spoke with her. She had the same gray shock on her head as her other two siblings, but a smile more like her father's. She was a retired radiologist with a gardening obsession, the mother of four sons, and the wife of Allan, who sat next to her slurping freshly cut watermelon. His intimidating presence in my childhood memories was now tempered by my recognition that I now knew my "secret" identity, and he knew I knew, though we never discussed it.

"I can only remember pieces of it," Meline began. "This is why I'm so unhappy, I don't have a connected story. He used to talk a lot about... his uncle as a priest. One of the things he remembered very clearly, he used to tell me all the time, was that every morning his uncle said mass. My father had to be his acolyte and he would kneel for hours on those cold stone floors because the churches weren't heated, and then he had to go to school.

"His uncle lived with them, he was an educated man, and for that reason the educational standard, and also other standards in their house, were higher and stricter than in the village. That explains how my father knew so much, even though he had never gone very far in school because of the massacre. He was still considered to be an educated Armenian...

"Then he told us about when he... uh... he saw his mother and father shot by the Turks. He also told us that when the Turks would come, the Armenian people would flock to the churches, and the Turks would then burn the churches. I don't know if he saw this or was told this by other people who had escaped... Anyway, he escaped from the village. I think he was caught and taken as a slave to a Turkish family... He never said anything bad about them. They gave him enough to eat and they gave him clothes. Apparently a lot of other Armenian kids were mistreated. So my father really had good things to say about these people because they didn't treat him badly, but he still was a slave and he knew even at that young age that his life wasn't going to go anywhere as a slave. So... he escaped from there."

She rocked back in her chair and then continued:

"He told us a story about hiding in a church when the Turks came looking for him. He never forgot this... the nuns lied for him and they said he wasn't there. They saved him from being recaptured by the Turks and that made a very long lasting impression on him... He went to Syria, then the trail as far as I know stops. I know he got to Marseilles, there was a port there, and it was there he left for the United States."

———————

Back on the lake, my mother, the middle sister of the three, had an overlapping memory of her father. In the warm summer sunlight that afternoon she appeared as a blend of her mother's gray pain and her father's colorful cheeriness.

"He used to talk about when he escaped the Turks. He went to

Unidentified village boy with Garabed sometime after his escape from Turkey, probably taken in France, circa 1922.

Aleppo, Syria, because it was a refuge for the Armenians. There was an Armenian orphanage there. He was one of the older children in that orphanage. They helped him there, and he was able to get from there to France where he stayed with his sister near Lyon for three months. He then journeyed to Paris by himself to meet up with his aunt and cousin. This was a kid, maybe thirteen, fourteen years old who knew minimal French and no English; he spoke only Armenian and maybe a few words in Turkish. So he had enough money to stay in a hotel for a while, I guess, until they met up. When he went into the hotel, he had never seen a flushing toilet, because back home in war-torn Armenia, all they had were outdoor facilities, a hole in the ground basically. He saw people go into this room, and he saw them coming out, so he was very curious. He went in there and he saw the old pull chain hanging from the ceiling and he saw this bowl. He pulled the chain, immediately triggering this loud rush of water. He thought he was going to flood the place because he saw all this water coming up. He ran out of the hotel and ran around the block because he thought he was responsible for a flood."

She stopped and wiped the sweat beads from her browned forehead, a smile on her face. She lifted a glass of water to her lips and slowly drank.

"When he came to this country, he actually came under false papers. I think I remember it being his cousin's papers. He got off the boat in Boston, had no idea where he was, and didn't speak a lick of English. His cousins lived there somewhere. He was wandering the streets lost, when a policeman stopped him and recognized his speech to be Armenian. The officer knew of an area where Armenian families lived and he took my father there. As it turned out, his cousins lived next door."

Back in Waukegan Meline picks up where Adrienne leaves off. She shifts in her chair, combing the air for more details. Although disturbing gaps exist along with contradictions, what she does remember is vivid and startling.

"The story of his coming to the United States is a very peculiar one. His name was originally Misakian, Garabed Misakian. He had cousins in Boston and in Worcester, Massachusetts. His uncle in Worcester lied, saying that Garabed was his other son. This is how he got to the United States. After he got here he changed his name to Pilibosian... I'm not even really sure where Pilibosian came from. There must be something back there that made him want to

Garabed with an unidentified man, somewhere in France just after 1922.

choose that name, like other relatives or something... Why did he decide to change his name at all?... I do know that something terrible happened between him and his cousin in Worcester, not the father, but the cousin who was approximately his age, and they didn't talk to each other for what must have been fifty years. When the cousin was a really old man he tried to contact my father, but he still rejected his offers of friendship. So whatever it was had to have been really terrible because my father was not the kind of guy to hold a grudge like that. Maybe that's why he changed his name."

Diane has surprisingly finally agreed to see me in person at her condominium just north of Chicago in Evanston, and yet what she has to share is only in written form. She has composed a brief background on her mother, my grandma Rachel:

> Rachel was born on August 1, 1910, in the same Village of Tadem. She was one of three children born to Karekin and Sarah Der Bedrosian. ("Der" means "Lord" and refers to a family of Armenian Gregorian faith which has clergy in its background.) The "Der" was later dropped by Rachel's brother, John, who determined that shortening the name would be easier and less awkward. When John was a baby, his mother reported to Rachel that traditions were so rigid that young couples could not even kiss their infants in front of the parents/in-laws. (This may explain why many immigrant families from earlier generations did not display warmth and intimacy with their children.)

I looked up from what she had written out for me. She sat stiff and upright in a chair facing me. Her face unchanging, hands folded in front on her lap, her dark granny glasses slightly cockeyed. I was dying to ask questions, which she still strictly forbade. The annoying lack of personal connection to the history was like a shield protecting her, keeping distance between her and my probing curiosity. I read on:

> Rachel's grandfather, Hovannes ("John," after which her brother was named), became a citizen of this country sometime between 1890–95. That means he came to the U.S. during the "Great Wave," possibly as early as 1888(?). Unfortunately, after earning sufficient funds which he sent home to his family, he returned to Tadem and in 1895 was killed in the first of two major massacres.

I wanted to know more about the massacres, the genocide, the slaughter of the Armenian people. How did my grandparents speak about it? What were their feelings? How did it affect them? Why hadn't they spoken out more, told more stories?

"Can I get you a glass of water?" Diane asked. I wasn't sure if she was being hospitable or if she noticed I was choking inside in frustration.

The three pages she had written out were the best she had to offer. We went out for a quiet dinner which was followed by her reluctantly agreeing to send more information as her time permitted. I left yearning to learn more about my Armenian family's past. I somehow felt deprived of what should be mine, my family's history. I could only hope she'd keep sending me more descriptions.

Several months passed with no word. Finally, I phoned. She wasn't planning to send me any more information. "It was too painful," she said. "I can't help you." And with that, she hung up.

I sat with the dead receiver in my hand, confused and angry at the prospect of my Armenian roots being buried forever by my aunt. I wanted to help her somehow see that she was a part of me, I her. We were intertwined by our respective family histories. Perhaps she was afraid I would somehow sully her name, our family name. In what way was unclear, but the path through her recollections was now blocked. At least my mother was able to add a few details about her mother.

The picture my mother showed me is a portrait of Armenians from the turn of the century. It is a faded black-and-white shot of a group of Armenians, mostly men, bunched in rows, seated, kneeling, and standing. It was taken at the orphanage in Allepo, Syria, to which my

Orphanage in Aleppo, Syria, 1922. Garabed is on the left, second row from top.

Armenian friends at the park, Garabed on the right, and Rachel, bottom row second from right.

grandfather had escaped shortly after fleeing enslavement by a Turkish family. My mother sat back and recalled how her mother eventually emigrated to America.

"It wasn't easy," she says holding her hand up to shield her eyes from the bright sun. "She came on a boat with her mother and mother's brother, but was so distressed by the journey that she cried constantly. When they docked in America her eyes were bright red from all her tears and the immigration officials feared she had some sort of eye disease. Back in those days they would send anyone back who might have a chance of spreading disease. Her mother pleaded with the officials, explaining her daughter did not have conjunctivitis and that her condition was solely related to her sorrowful tears. The officials finally relented and let them pass through."

Rachel's engagement photo.

Garabed and Rachel, 1934.

"How did your parents meet?" I ask her.

"They met years later. My father had been living out east with his cousins—well, not actually even a real cousin I guess, more like his best friend. Something had happened between them, a rift he never spoke of, and he came to the Midwest to find work in the steel mills. I think he met my mother through friends, in the Armenian community here, and the rest is history."

The details of our pasts, why don't we ask? I too could have inquired of my grandfather and grandmother, yet mistakenly, and perhaps some would call foolishly, I was too narrowly focused on my need to fit in, my need to be loved, my need to feel connected. What I failed to realize until it was too late was that connection I sought, the love I so badly desired, my need was right there in front of me in the form of my parents, my grandparents, and

Garabed (on left) at the lake with friends, 1931.

the stories of their struggle and survival. I couldn't see how their struggles, their journey could have anything to do with me, when in fact they had everything to do with me. I was so obsessed with my need to find where I fit, I didn't bother to look in my own backyard where roots of my heritage already abounded.

SIBLING RIVALRY

I t's July in Chicago and the humidity ranges as usual between just bearable and nonstop drip. Despite the heat and humidity, the city is alive with all manner of outdoor festivals and celebrations. Maybe it's because it's so cold for so many months here, when the warmth finally arrives, people go crazy with outdoor activities. With the relatives I've talked to and the questions I've managed to ask so far, a picture of my life, my family's life, has come increasingly into focus, even if many mysteries remain. I'm beginning to feel a sense of historical depth made possible by what I have been learning. Having set out on this quest nervous, slightly overwhelmed, and justifiably unclear on the actual process of how I'd go about conducting these conversations, I'd now settled into a kind of rhythm and flow. It hasn't been easy posing some of the more personal, even delicate questions, yet I've forged ahead hoping to gain a greater understanding of my family's trajectory—and mine.

I've stopped in the Chicago area on my eastward travels to learn mainly from my siblings what I can about their perspective on the family. I anticipated that these conversations would somehow be easier than those with my parents, aunts, and uncles. What could they possibly reveal about my past that I didn't already know? We'd grown up together—though I was quite a bit older than my siblings. We loved each other as siblings would, stayed in touch from time to time, and gathered as a family for major holidays. However we did not hang out together much, or share a great deal about our lives, or have friends in common. Whether it was age, differences in interest, or simply growing apart, it was clear to me I did not share the close bond Lora and Chris had forged with each other over the years. Being only a year apart and growing up side by side gave them a closeness and familiarity I could never capture. What component of this was biological, what part learned? Did I have less of a connection because I was born with a different father? Or could the distance be explained mainly by the age discrepancy and the differences of experience in and out of the family that went with it?

This distance between us had never really been acknowledged by anyone but me. Lora and Chris seemed to exist in a bubble of sibling euphoria separate and distinct from my world. And it was as if there was something wrong with me that I felt this gulf. The bond I so desired with the father I'd grown up with, with my siblings, had gone unfulfilled, unrecognized by others, and a source of enduring pain. Could I ever recapture what I sought? Would the reconnection with my biological father

Lora, Christopher, and me.

bring forth the dream of that father/son bond I felt I'd lacked? And would my current quest help unite me with the family that raised me, or push us further apart?

When I realized the importance of these questions to me and my long-simmering internal debate about them, I recognized how much more difficult these conversations would be. The love shared between us as siblings could not mask the distance we might not be able to bridge. It's an odd, sometimes uncomfortable feeling to have such a strong love for family and yet feel somehow so disconnected. As I thought about the conversations I hoped to have with my brother and sister I decided it would be best if I just listened to what they had to say as much as possible. Call it a premonition, but I think I realized there would be things difficult for me to hear. Rather than seeming preemptively defensive, I decided to just let them speak their minds.

"Christopher was the kind of kid who laid around and watched TV all the time," my sister said, describing our brother.

"And do you remember what kind of kid I was?" I ask, hoping to get her childhood impression of my youth.

"Don't know what you did."

As we sit opposite each other in her spacious art-filled loft in Chicago's up-and-coming hip area known as Bucktown, I realized I had been around for such a small portion of their lives. By the time

they were eight and nine, I was gone except for the occasional visit. I went to college and never returned home to live after my freshman year.

The sun pours in from the industrial skylights positioned high above our heads. Her usual doll-like voice is tempered now. As she navigates a more serious terrain, her voice takes on a slightly deeper and more earnest tone. It has been a pattern of hers for as long as I can remember, one I am just now aware my mother shares. In a serious mode—not often experienced in our household—my mother would speak more directly and with a solemn tone. Yet when either one wishes to attract fawning attention or get someone to do something for them they resort to the gently manipulative cuteness a childlike voice can solicit. I suspect they are both subconsciously aware of it, but practice it almost unconsciously.

Lora is seated on the old leather couch our parents once had in their home on Pacific Street. She looks much like our mother with a good dose of her father thrown in: slender with short brown hair, a great big smile, white white teeth, fleshy cheeks, willowy neck, and slim fingers.

"You weren't around much," she continued. "Nor was dad around much. Didn't play with us really. I wouldn't say that he was a really involved parent. He was involved in discipline. Of course when I hit adolescence, neither was around much. They both worked and nobody was home when I got back from school each day."

"Were you always close with Christopher?"

"Not in the beginning. We fought, beat each other up all the time. When we were little, I was bigger and stronger and could beat him in things. That wasn't supposed to happen—he was a boy, I was a girl! But he wasn't into athletics. I was a real tomboy. I wanted to get dirty, I wasn't afraid. I was also pretty spoiled 'cause I was the only girl so I got a lot of positive attention. It wasn't until junior high, and then high school, when we started having the same friends, that we became really good friends. We looked out for each other and we were really close."

"Do you remember family dinners with our cousins and grandparents?" I ask, wanting to understand if she could recall the dynamics of our upbringing when I had still been around.

She looked at me directly and in her most stern and somber tone said, "I'll just say this about family dinners: we were raised to be accepting and loving of other people whether you knew them or you didn't, no matter what color skin they had or whatever." There was a finality to her words and I suspected I should push no further. She'd said it all anyway, so I moved on.

"Do you remember our grandparents and what they were like?"

Hoping to shift the tone, I decided to ask about our favorite Armenians.

"I know you told me that grandma and grandpa were partly responsible for the breakup of your parents but I never ever thought they were racist."

The unexpected bluntness of her response was far from what I had anticipated. I hadn't asked a question about their racial beliefs. Where did this reply come from? I felt a sudden need to defend the question, perhaps steer the conversation, then remembered my commitment to sit back and listen.

"Did you ever ask Mom about her father?" I ask instead, thinking I may find a clue to the previous response.

"Mom said that he was really, really, really strict. That her older sister could do no wrong and she could do no right."

An oscillating fan blows warm air our way from a corner of the large room. After Lora talks more about the family, I decide it's time to ask how she reacted to my news of actually finding my biological father, a different father from the one who raised us. I am uncomfortable but forge ahead.

"I remember you telling me and feeling kind of shocked. I was very surprised to see how much you looked like your father." I'm sitting across from a sister who looks so much like her father, whose brother, our brother, looks so much like their father. I began to wonder again just how much biology plays a part in who we are. I look so much like my father, as does she and Christopher theirs, but how much of what we are given biologically becomes who we are?

"Did you ask Mom about what had happened?"

"I remember her telling me she thought it would be really hard on you as a child to go through life knowing that information and that you'd feel isolated and left out. I think she felt her decision not to tell you was a good one because you never felt isolated and left out because you were black. She didn't have a responsibility to tell you. When you finally asked her, she had a hard time with that, but she eventually did tell you. I think she has a lot of guilt about her history. But it's her stuff; she did it, she lived it, she suffered in hell for it. I don't know this, but my feeling is she probably doesn't really want to get into it because she's probably like, 'Let bygones be bygones, my God! I was just a kid!' and at the same time she wants to be able to give you what you want to know even though she doesn't want to talk about it at all. She already paid her dues for it. And I hope you won't force her to tell you things she doesn't want to."

I bit my tongue. My sister's anger and fear radiated across the years of distance that sat between us, as did the strength of her urge to protect our mother and her family against anything that might disrupt it. In her world I should just shut up and toe the line. This was the past, we had a family, don't rock the boat. Biological, emotional, or historical needs be damned.

I stuck to the vow I had made to myself, pressing on with questions. Knowing how close she was to her brother, how the two had shared a lifelong bond I had never been a part of, nor would ever conquer, I wondered what the two had shared.

"Did you discuss the situation with Chris?"

"Yeah," she laughs, "we both had some good laughs about it." Her tone lightens and the tension dissipates slightly.

"What do you mean, laughs?" I ask.

"Well, we were like, 'Can you believe that shit?! His dad is black?' We were both like, 'My God, he's had the craziest life!' It was so crazy and so wild, we couldn't even believe it!"

Trying to temper my once again rising urge to defend myself, I ask, "I'm just curious when you say that I've had the craziest life, what did that mean to you?"

"Well, until you ran the painting business with Jo, I've never known you to have a job. Then you leave a business that is thriving. You've moved a lot. You were a drug addict for awhile, got sober—you had a crazy life. I mean, nothing in your life in my opinion has ever been necessarily ordinary. Not that that's bad, it's just not real predictable, or steady, or secure. You never know where the next paycheck is coming from. It doesn't seem to bother you, you seem very comfortable living that way. Chris and I are very different from that. Neither of us is very comfortable with that at all. I may be an artist, but I still work thirty hours a week."

I sat stewing in what seemed like her judgment. My chest was tight with anxiety. I heard cars and heavy trucks on the pavement out front of her apartment loft, their weight now mine. The nearby El went by, punctuating the silence between sentences. If this is what Lora and Chris thought of me, what must they tell other people?

"Do you talk about it with other people?" I almost didn't want to know for fear I might explode.

"I tell other people, and I think the most amazing thing to me is how this happened in the late 1950s, a time of extreme civil unrest in our country. Martin Luther King was marching, black people were being hosed down with fire hoses, beaten in the streets. And my mother who lives in Beantown marries a black man. It's so unbelievable that she did that, and she couldn't handle it and pulled out. And you were left with no history, no traces of that brutal time in her life."

The weight of this statement fills the room as we sit silently before she goes on.

"Since you've found your father, in some ways I think your life has really changed and you've been able to settle into who you are. I mean, I don't have any negative feelings finding out my brother is half black. I'm totally not—race doesn't mean anything to me. I never look at the color of people's skin. You know what I'm trying to say? It's never been an issue for me. I think you are going to have a really hard time because of it. Because I think that you're really positive about it and very happy that you made this discovery. But I don't think that you'll ever know what it means to be black. You'll never be able to feel the racism that is out there. You are only going to have the good parts of being black not the bad parts... 'cause you're just not black enough."

———————

After the left hook my sister delivered, should I expect something similar from my brother? Still smarting from the derision, I summoned my best brotherly smile as a kind of balm to my already blackened eye. I felt embarrassed at the way I'd been perceived by my sibling. Nothing I could do or say would change my past's blemished record in her eyes. My "crazy life" was now fodder for conversation between her and her brother. The discovery of my African-American roots was perceived as an albatross. The journey to find a lost family, from her perspective, was more of a self-serving mission that would undermine our already fractured family dynamic. With my once wagging tail between my legs, I arranged to meet up with the sibling eight years my junior.

Christopher seemed slightly reluctant to talk and even more confused by my purpose in asking him to do so. He'd moved to London in a transcontinental job shift to trade commodities on the interna-

tional exchange. He was back visiting his hometown to participate in some of the summer pastimes he'd missed while living overseas. I grew more nervous as the time to talk approached but once again vowed to let him speak, to avoid interrupting or getting defensive. Christopher was still rail thin, much as he had been when we were kids. Nightly childhood dinners were seldom without his habitual food protest, then hours spent seated at the table long after we'd all been dismissed, forced to finish what had been set before him. We dubbed him the most finicky eater on the planet. His shaggy brown hair was also unchanged, flopping over a narrow face with his familiar grin sporting slightly buck front teeth. His green eyes pop out from his customary bronze summer skin. This was the kid I remembered from so many years ago. His voice, however, had changed, and oddly, it now sounded very similar to mine.

"What do you remember about our growing up together?"

"Not a whole lot. You left when I was nine never to be seen again. I kind of remember a station wagon full of stuff and you leavin'. And I kind of remember mom cryin'. I think I have stronger memories of you when you moved back to Chicago, and even still we didn't see each other loads. I was never aware of you having any drug problems — didn't see any of it. I just remember you were doin' all right, you had your theater going. It always seemed like you were into the Chicago theater scene."

"When did you become aware that I had a different father?"

"I can't say that I knew when you had a different father. I just always thought that Dad was Dad and that was it. I think that probably has a little something to do with why now it's kind of weird that you've found a different father. That's kind of weird to me."

"Why is that weird?"

"I think that, well, all right, to be perfectly honest, I think it all came too easy in the fact that you have found this guy and... I don't know, for some reason I don't think — and I'm not trying to knock you or anything—but I just think there's something in the back of my mind that tells me that you should not have unconditional acceptance for this man like you should for John Fosberg. I think it probably hurts his feelings that, well, first of all, you and Dad are really different. You've never been super close. I think I'm probably closer to Dad than any of us 'cause I can relate to him the most. I think the correct approach to the whole thing—and I'm not saying you're doing it wrong—but because of what you're doing and because you are searching out a new family, Dad needs to be reassured. So that it doesn't feel like, 'Thanks for bringing me up but I got the blood over here and blood is thicker than whatever.' Know what I mean?

"I think that a father is a kind of sacred thing. You know what I mean? It's something that everybody needs, and obviously you can get away without having one, but if you've got it, you're a really, really lucky person. It can only help you in life and it's something you should hold really dear to you. And I think that I can't relate to having two."

But what if you have a dad, or two for that matter, and can never really find that connection, that bond, that sacred thing he is talking about that makes that father/son thing so very special? What then? I did indeed now have two fathers and was struggling to understand what that meant and how to navigate a path I'd never learned to traverse. He grew up with a dad he looked, sounded, and acted like. My foray into bio-daddom had yet to produce the desired results.

"For you and Lora, it was Mom," he continued, "for me it was Dad. He had a workshop and that was his game, and I thought that was cool. That didn't interest you. He was always there for me, whether it was in his shop showing me how to take things apart or put them back together, or fishing out on a lake. I get the impression you think he wasn't there for you, and you carry some kind of resentment about that."

His stinging assessment was close, but the deeper resentment I felt lay in the fact that I desired the connection he so naturally found in his dad. The sacred connection born between them. How could I resent a great guy for not being what I wanted? My anger lay not in who he was, but in the absence of what we never found.

Christopher's cautious protectiveness was wholly understandable, yet painful for me to bear. I resisted the urge to defend my position and tried to move beyond the catch in my throat.

"Do you remember how you felt when I told you I found my dad?"

"I was hurt. You see, the thing is, you've always been part of the family, but not part of the immediate family. You haven't been around much. And I just kind of felt this was another step in that direction. I just didn't think it was a good idea, that was my first impression. But as I thought about it more, it was probably really a good idea. It's good to know more about yourself. But in the back of my mind I thought, I hope he keeps his focus on who his family really is. And that's the way I feel about it. The Fosbergs are who your family really is."

I was certainly learning more about myself now. Where I stood, how I was perceived, what I was made of. I sat across from Chris wondering if he understood the weight of his words. The distance established since our early days would not shrink in this setting. I felt small and insignificant, as if I'd been wiped off the family registrar. It was all or nothing, like much of what we seem to be fed, you're either with us or against us. You can't have it both ways, you can't have two. You can't be white and black.

"Have you talked to Mom about this?"

"I told her I don't want her to be forced to tell you things to make her feel guilty. And I almost think it's selfish on your part, the fact that you want to open up all these old wounds for her. Easy for me to say, but it's hard for me to relate what you're going through with all this. I sit back and say, 'He's got a dad, what's this all about?'"

"Did you discuss this with Lora?" I ask, knowing full well he had.

"Yeah, me and Lora talk about everything. And you are often the subject of conversation, I won't be afraid to tell you. I think some of these feelings developed because Dad might be feeling neglected and hurt.

That pissed me off. And, because I was angry, that made me think negative things about what you were up to. There was something about the fact that you were so excited to meet this guy. And the fact that you were so excited he was black.

I talked to Lora about that too. I mean, it didn't matter to me; it doesn't matter either way what this guy is. But I think, to be honest with you, it might affect you. I think if the guy was white it might be different. I kind of feel that certain things need to be left alone and not stirred up, and this is kind of one of them."

How does one react to being told basically to sit down and shut up? Take what you are given and like it? I'd asked for his honesty and his sister's, and I seem to have received it in full unedited blunt form. Would it have been better if I'd cautioned them to go easy? Could I have asked for perhaps a little compassion and understanding? How was what had happened, the choice my mother had made so many years ago turned into such an awful, terrible affair? How did the negative spin get spun around what I now saw as a way to heal an old wound?

Sure, there was pain, the pain of loss, the pain of mistakes, the pain of revisiting what might be seen as stupid youthful transgressions, the pain of introducing another family into the mix. Why did my siblings seem so distraught by what had happened? I couldn't really fathom it at the time.

As we sat facing each other, me on the verge of internal implosion, he with perhaps the relief of finally having said his piece, he added one last note, this of positive reinforcement. "I think it's pretty cool to sit down with you and do this interview. I think it's pretty cool that you're doin' this with other people. I think it's totally healthy and cleansing. I think it's a great idea."

Is it such a great idea? In listening to their thoughts, their feelings, and now writing down their words, would it be a healthy cleansing experience, or just more of the self-indulgence my brother and sister pronounced me guilty of? Could we inch closer to understanding one another, or will these thoughts, words, and feelings cause us to move even further apart? Will I always remain an outsider in my own family? Who decides if I'm inside? Me, or them?

A CHANGE IN SCENERY

The year my father spent incarcerated seemed like two. Having no way to communicate with him left me with just bits of news relayed through my grandparents. My connection to them continued to grow stronger as we wrote and spoke on the phone quite often.

Little did I suspect that my personal life would soon take on what would look like a disaster shortly after my felonious father was locked up in the slammer. Jo and I had finally carved out an income sizable enough to allow us to purchase a fixer-upper Victorian near the canals of Venice, California. It was on the cusp of this long-hoped-for success that our relationship began to unravel. What had once been a mom-and-pop operation had been catapulted into a full-fledged faux-finishing factory. At times we had as many as twelve artist/painters working for us, slapping paint and Italian plaster on the walls of the likes of the Ahmanson Theatre in downtown Los Angeles, the corporate headquarters of Nissan Motors, and—having graduated from powder rooms— entire homes of wealthy Bel Air/Hollywood wannabes.

I was now manning our studio office, peddling our painted wares to the largest and most prestigious architectural firms, overseeing job-site work, ordering materials, and doing our corporate paperwork. Jo would concoct the various painted samples for each project in our spacious rented loft studio and occasionally visit a job site to make sure the crew was applying the finish to her specifications. The workload was daunting and our respective responsibilities unbalanced. Tension grew as I got further behind in my workload and as we began tearing apart our Victorian in an attempt to restore its grandeur. We had gone from living in a cramped, nearly unfurnished, one-story rented beach bungalow to shelling out the big LA real estate bucks to possess our very own two-story charmer complete with two fireplaces, outdoor Jacuzzi, and Japanese garden. We bought new vehicles, took separate trips to interesting destinations, and began quarreling with one another over everything, business and personal.

Couples therapy only pushed us further apart. Jo's complaints were numerous and unrelenting. "You don't know a lick about business," she'd complain, as money poured in and jobs stacked up. "Why aren't we making more money on each job?" she'd lash out.

When I'd tell her we had a better than 50 percent profit margin on most of our contracted work while the industry standard for most painting contractors was closer to 20, she'd hit back with, "Oh what the bloody hell do you know? You're just a washed up actor who barely worked." Her once supportive and loving tone grew more distant as the relationship with my father stalled in the face of his incarceration.

We got lost and hardly knew it, as the engine of our ever-growing workload kept churning and demanding more focus. As if there weren't enough on our contentious plates, Jo was repeatedly struck with some mysterious ailment that no doctor could ever diagnose, let alone cure. The latest troubling pains she described as heart attacks, about which the fourth in a long line of specialists suggested she see a psychiatrist.

Ironically, the precipitating episode in our breakup occurred in the midst of one of our most interesting assignments. We had agreed to take on a job for a group of friends who had created a sprawling Spanish estate along an abandoned coastal area near the southern tip of Baja California, Mexico. We'd worked for their contracting company on a project in Bel Air, a ten-million-dollar home owned by a television soap opera producer. Jo created beautifully subtle paint washes for every wall in the house, earning us a sizable profit and putting our company on the map.

The Baja getaway this group owned had to be seen to be believed. A dozen or so classic Mexican structures dotted the hillside overlooking the vast turquoise ocean, each a richly colored and textured stucco structure topped with a palapa thatched roof and hand-carved doors opening onto balconies overlooking the coast. We'd been asked to create an Old World plaster finish for the walls of a great sitting room with arched glass windows facing out onto a balcony that overlooked the sparkling Sea of Cortez. It was a magical place. We were housed in a cute casita with a beautiful Mexican tiled floor, ornate fireplace, oversized wood-carved bed, and classic iron furnishings.

Our hosts were a group of aging hippies who had checked out of the traditional American family life years ago and attempted to create their own all-for-one, one-for-all kind of utopia. This friendly, intellectual, artistic bunch had forged their own way despite the many negative reactions to their collective lifestyle they had encountered. I immediately felt at home with this group of bright, loving people, which made me begin to wonder what truly constituted family. If I could feel so at home with a group of near strangers, why didn't I have the same sense of connection with those I'd been raised with and known almost my entire life?

Jo, on the other hand, did not mesh so seamlessly with our hosts, and the tension became more and more palpable as the days unfolded. Her manner could be cold, abrupt, or negative, and she possessed that typically dry British sense of humor. During meals when we'd all gather in the dining house, members of the group maintained a respectful pleasantness toward Jo, yet it seemed to mask something I couldn't explain.

Then all hell broke loose during a dinner one evening near the end of our stay. The usual intelligent dinner conversation led to a contentious debate between Jo and the matriarch of the family. Words were exchanged, a disagreement ensued, followed by an awkwardly long silence. I could feel others in the room holding their collective breath as Jo and the matriarch searched for a way to navigate the impasse. Engaging conversation was suddenly replaced with silverware clinking on plates and the sound of glasses plunking against the table. The matriarch looked down at her plate then slowly up at Jo.

"Can I ask you, did you suffer a great loss as a child?" she pushed forward gently but with a firm voice.

"What?" Jo asked, confused.

"As a child, did you suffer some kind of great loss, or hardship? Perhaps some kind of traumatic event that gave shape to a painful upbringing? A hurt that you have carried your entire life?"

"I don't know what the hell you are getting at!" Jo hurled back with such force it exposed a pain she'd carried all these years. Plates were still now, and those drinking held their glasses, as if the small act of placing them on the table could somehow jeopardize the flow of the encounter.

"Look, Jo, I have the sense you experienced something when you were very young that has left you with a deep grieving, a sense of loss. This loss has been translated over time into a barrier, a protective shield if you will, that has manifested itself into a cold and negative exterior."

Jo lashed back with a ferocity I had seldom seen except during the worst of our most recent disagreements. "Who the hell are you, and what right do you have to judge me like this? You don't know me! You have no idea of who I am, or what I've been through!" She turned toward me for support, a desperate lost look deep in her eyes. Gazing back, I saw in her eyes what I had not seen, had not been willing to look at, for the past three years. The very woman who had helped give me the courage to go off on my own journey to find my father and confront my pain and fears of the past was sitting here sinking under the weight of her own painful past. I glanced downward quickly, not knowing what to say or how to return what she had given me. I knew the matriarch was right. Jo had suffered the terrible loss of her father and the subsequent harshness of her mother's wrath, a mother who never really knew how to love her and had more than likely blamed three-year-old Jo for the death of her husband.

I too had lost a parent at a young age, and in Jo I had found a person with the same pain, the same hurt, but magnified. Yet my discomfort of loss at such a formative age had become transformed, at least I liked to think so, into a compassionate caring for people, rather than a cold negativity. I had opened up to avail myself to others, rather than closed down, as she had done to protect herself from more pain. My mother hadn't blamed me for the loss and acted inappropriately. Instead she carried me along as a young boy, she loved me, and tried as best she could to prop me up on her frightened shoulders.

"You have no idea of what you are talking about! Bloody hell! This is fucked up!" And with that, Jo glared at me with her red, tear-soaked eyes, terribly disappointed in my silence, threw her napkin on the table, and bolted for the door.

I looked around at a table full of people deeply disturbed by the turn of events. Awkwardly making eye contact with the few who sat across me, I knew, they knew that I knew what I had come to realize about Jo's painful past.

Two women hurried after Jo, perhaps to comfort her and help edge her closer to the realization we'd all felt. *How did they know?* I thought as I looked around this room of people I'd just met. How could they have understood when they know nothing at all about us, our pasts? Yet each face stared back at me with an understanding compassion. They knew. They'd been through it. I could see by their pained yet sympathetic gazes they'd been down this path before. Was it fair of them to confront Jo, a person they barely knew, with an understanding of her painful childhood neglect? Could they then see not only into the childhood pain she carried forward, but into my similarly afflictive abandonment? And why didn't I respond with some kind of defense, a compromising position, perhaps a conciliatory voice?

This family abandonment revelation was one I'd felt deeply for the past several months and had begun to experience in ways unrecognized by me. The discovery of my father and family, the uncovering of my identity, the opening of the door on my memories of loss had been playing itself out in my life, and yet I had little understanding of its significance until now. Over the course of the past year, the mounting difficulties and tensions between Jo and I had been compounded by her pain—now uncovered—and my inability to recognize the source of her growing discomfort. I'd been too focused on my journey to notice the pain emanating from her lack of one.

Later that evening, after long conversations with members of the group, Jo and I sat silently in our four-poster bed, a fire across from us. Jo's face was stained and sagging from the weight of her tears and anger. I was numb yet enlightened by the enormity of the evening's revelations. Breaking the silence in a sudden a fit of anger, Jo sparked another round of sparring.

"Why the bloody hell didn't you say anything? Not a goddamned word out of you. What the hell where you thinking?"

"Jo," I tried to say peacefully, "I didn't know what to say…"

"Didn't know what to say?" she shot back incredulously. "How 'bout coming to my defense? Huh? What the bloody hell did you think was goin' on in there? I was being attacked, and it was as if you couldn't lift a finger. Jesus, Michael! God, I feel sick!"

"What did you want me to say?" I said stupidly, avoiding sharing my true feelings and discovery about her.

"You've gawt to be jokin', right? How 'bout explaining to them that they have no right to attack me like that? How 'bout letting them know they don't know what the hell they are talkin' about? What the hell is wrong with you? You sat there with that pathetic smirk on your face as if you believed what they were saying, as if you knew they were right or something. You make me sick. I am sick. Sick of your pathetic response. How can you be such an arsehole?" Her voice was shrill now. She sat lashing into me. I probably deserved it. I had sat silent while she suffered a public humiliation at the hands of strangers. I certainly could have at the very least defended her right to privacy, yet spoke not a word to uphold that right. Watching it unfold for her, I too found my own feelings of abandonment, estrangement, and dissatisfaction rise to the surface, and yet I was too afraid to utter the truth.

And yet, as supportive as she'd been on my familial quest, I began to feel so angry and resentful that I'd spent these years with a woman who was so often harsh, cold, and uncompassionate, who treated me as if I was some kind of idiot, who saw me as some sort of failed non-artist. I lashed back, having now seen the other side of her so clearly.

Grabbing her, I shouted, "Look at you! Every time you get confronted with some kind of truth, some kind of personal revelation, you break down in pain. What the hell do you think has been happening the past six months? Why do you think the doctors have yet to diagnose your myriad of ailments?"

Light from the fireplace flickered in her pained face as tears rolled down her cheeks. We sat still, looking straight ahead across the room. The anger had subsided for the moment. It was late, and neither the blackness outside nor waves crashing along the shore seemed to penetrate our darkness within. We sat next to each other with nary a body part touching as Jo wept quietly. She cleared her throat, trying to speak.

"When I was a girl," she began, "I would always get sick, or have 'accidents' to get attention. My mother was so mean to me that I thought I could gain her sympathy if I was somehow injured or needed care." She took a deep breath and continued. "After my mother remarried, I lived in the top floor of our 'ouse an' her husband would come in my room and fondle me. It was so ugly and dirty, and I couldn't do a bloody thing 'bout it. When I tol' my mother she'd just laugh it off as if I'd made it up. So I'd keep getting sick or have some kind of accident to get her attention—walk through a plate glass window or whatever. And by the time I had a real accident, like the time I fell off the cherry picker on the kibbutz in Israel, her level of compassion was completely lost."

She sat silent for a moment, almost out of breath, trying to regain her composure. Her immense revelation lay between us like the ocean outside our door. It swallowed us whole and now there was no place to hide.

It wasn't long after our return from paradise that I moved out of our still-under-construction Victorian rehab. We'd gotten lost and knew we couldn't find our way back. Revelations aside, we still harbored the anger, pain, and distance that night in Baja had exposed. The breakup, although inevitable, was devastating, and I beckoned for help from the group that had helped expose the festering wound between us. They loaned me a room in one of their homes in LA as Jo and I tried to navigate the rocky split in our personal and business lives. We eventually sold the dream house after sinking wads of money into it just to make it saleable. We argued and fought over our now-burgeoning business. She claimed she didn't want it; I knew I didn't, but I refused to let it go for nothing. We settled, I sold, she resisted paying, then balked further as she discovered I'd met someone else and moved on.

Was I a misogynist racing around destroying the lives of the women I'd loved and lived with? I found myself desperately clinging to beauty, hoping to capture the longing I'd lost in the absence of acceptance from father and family. I needed to be loved by someone because I couldn't find the love for myself in myself.

The next someone was a natural along the dysfunctional lines of my racial self-discovery, Victoria, a tall slender black woman of mixed heritage holding a past filled with loss and rejection just like mine. A black mother who'd spent time in a mental institution, a white Irish father who physically abused her as a child, and an upbringing in the projects of the Bronx were just a few of the hors d'oeuvres on her biracial plate. There couldn't have been a more apt course for me to traverse if a psychologist had ordered it. I was black-identified, needing to date black. I wanted to feel proud of my black heritage, show my newly found African-American family I was down with the race, and to somehow give proof to myself of my blackness.

Victoria was beautiful, an unemployed struggling actress/writer connected with many of the up-and-coming young black stars then making their mark in Hollywood. I found myself attending black Hollywood functions, attempting to fit into a world where I had a) no job, no prospects, and no money, and b) no color—but I had growing cachet as people slowly learned about my story. It felt as though once people learned I too had black ancestors, an unspoken acceptance was conveyed, and I was made to feel that I'd become one of the club. Smiles would appear on people's faces, black handshakes would be greeted with laughs and sudden changes in tone. A certain formality would melt as idioms of black culture would surface in dialogue. The livelier and funkier exchanges led to obstacles I'd not foreseen: my difficulty in deciphering vernacular, a self-consciousness at the prospect of sounding too "white," and conversations to which I was now privy that turned on resentment of whites.

Navigating these was just a sideshow to the relationship with my biracial black beauty which was moving so fast I lost control. Immersion in a world I wanted so desperately to understand, combined with her stunning good looks and my unquenchable need to be loved by someone, made our engagement a fait accompli. And with the sale of the home Jo and I had previously owned, I was now flush with cash to lavish on this relationship.

Soon I'd bought her a car to replace the clunker she'd been continually repairing. We rented a quaint but fashionable house along a canyon in Bel Air, complete with outdoor Jacuzzi and sauna. She charged elegant and elaborate furnishings to my credit card as we set up house and began what we would call our future together. Friends saw us as the budding love couple as we flitted about from party to event, Victoria wearing the large rocks I'd purchased for her finger. And with Christmas approaching, I had a newfound sense of pride, ready to introduce Victoria to my birth father and his parents, the black prodigal son returning home with a black woman.

A CHRISTMAS STORY

It is Christmas Eve, 1995, the first Christmas together with my father and grandparents. My father, having done his time and fresh out of "the joint," was back living at his parent's home in Virginia Beach. I, along with my love symbol of newfound identity, was returning "home" to my biological family, filled with a sense of pride and happy to be reunited with the family I'd had little connection with most my life.

As I weighed the significance of this holiday gathering, I observe my grandparents glow with a radiance I hadn't seen. There are large smiles, hearty laughs, incredible soul food meals, and yet more detailed stories of family. They immediately take to Victoria and make us feel warm and embraced. Granny digs through mounds of fabric remnants hoping to pawn them off on an elated Victoria while Poppa reclines in front of his large screen television fixated on the day's news.

"Here, son." My father hands me a large envelope.

"What is it?" I ask him.

"Just a bunch of odds and ends I saved and put together for you." I opened the envelope and cautiously peeked inside. "You may want to sit down and take your time with this later," he says.

"Thanks," I tell him, unsure if I should be sarcastic or grateful.

Later that evening, while lying in the guest bed with my fiancée, the mixed-race partner of the fate I'd chosen, I open the envelope and out spills its contents. There is a full page bio of my grandfather, Roy A. Woods, listing his many accomplishments over the span of his eighty years: his five degrees in mathematics and physics from universities across the country, membership in five honor societies, extensive teaching and scientist credentials from Pearl Harbor to Norfolk State University, and numerous community service awards, appointments to boards of directors, and civic contributions.

Included in the envelope is a family tree from the Woods side of the family dating back to the mid-1800s to what would be my great-great-great-grandfather's time. A program from a funeral service for a great-great-aunt on my grandfather's side. An old blurry picture of my father as a strapping young teen boarding a train with the tall dapper man he was named after, my great-grandfather's brother, Uncle John. A copy of a sale notice dated March 7, 1936, for the family farm in New London, Missouri, which had belonged to my grandmother's grandmother. There is a necrology—an obituary notice—from a science magazine for my great-uncle the meteorologist Charles E. Anderson, husband of my granny's youngest sister, a man who cared for me as a small child when I lived briefly in Boston.

Sid and his Uncle John, for whom he was named.

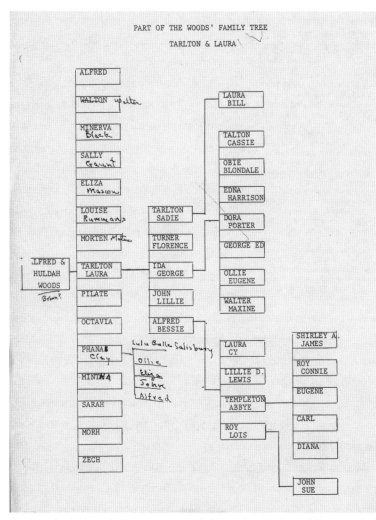

PART OF THE WOODS' FAMILY TREE

TARLTON & LAURA

Also in the envelope are a copy of the notice in the public record of the suit for divorce between my mother and father, dated April 13, 1961, and a copy of the adoption petition my father signed, essentially handing me over to the Fosberg family, August 23, 1963.

I looked over each item carefully, gently touching the pages as if I might feel the history within. My mind was swirling with what I knew of my history, my heart was bursting under the rush of feelings. My fiancée leaned over and kissed me on the cheek, caressed my head, and

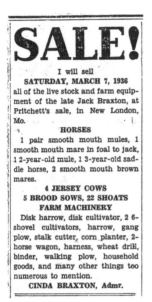

SALE!

I will sell
SATURDAY, MARCH 7, 1936
all of the live stock and farm equipment of the late Jack Braxton, at Pritchett's sale, in New London, Mo.

HORSES
1 pair smooth mouth mules, 1 smooth mouth mare in foal to jack, 1 2-year-old mule, 1 3-year-old saddle horse, 2 smooth mouth brown mares.

**4 JERSEY COWS
5 BROOD SOWS, 22 SHOATS
FARM MACHINERY**
Disk harrow, disk cultivator, 2 6-shovel cultivators, harrow, gang plow, stalk cutter, corn planter, 2-horse wagon, harness, wheat drill, binder, walking plow, household goods, and many other things too numerous to mention.

CINDA BRAXTON, Admr.

wrapped her arms around me, holding me in an embrace that felt both safe and comforting.

As I sifted through the papers, I noticed a stack of handwritten letters photocopied and neatly stapled, including copies of the fronts of the envelopes. They are addressed to my father at 23 Tavern Road, Boston 16, Massachusetts. The handwriting looked familiar — it was my mother's. The distinct looping of her l's, the roundness of her n's, m's, and o's. The third letter of the group confirms my suspicions of where she was at the time: the return address reads, "A. Pilibosian, Los Angeles, California" — our pregnant runaway destination — and it is postmarked November 24, 1957, exactly sixteen days after I was born. The return address on the fourth and final letter reads "A. Woods, Waukegan, Illinois" and it is postmarked August 5, 1959, putting this approximately two weeks after we'd left my father in Boston and went to live with my mother's parents.

I sat very still, staring at the pages before me. The beautiful looping handwriting, the set of three-cent Liberty stamps attached to each envelope with the words "Air Mail" carefully handwritten and under-

lined in the bottom left-hand corner, the postmarks complete with location, date, and time — spelling out in historical terms my birth, my early life. The first lines of the letter postmarked November 12, 1957, read:

November 10, 1957, St. Mary's Hospital

Dearest Sid,

Honey, you should see the baby. He's just beautiful!!

I couldn't go any further. My throat was choked with emotion, my eyes were red and running. I sat rereading those words over and over.

I wish you could see him now — you would be so proud of him. He just does the cutest things. I haven't been able to pick him up cause I have the flu but I saw him through the glass and he just wiggles around and yawns — he hasn't cried once, and he makes the cutest faces.

As I read each sentence, each word, I felt transported back to the context of a childhood I'd thought lost.

You can't tell what color his eyes will be yet, they are just kind of bluish now like all new babies but I imagine they will be like yours… I knew the minute I saw him that I could never give him away even if you didn't want us.

"Give him away"? What did she mean, "give him away"? Was her plan to give me up for adoption? Had I been that close to growing up with neither of my true parents?

I doubt if we will be able to leave for at least three weeks, but I will try to make it in time for Thanksgiving — depending on what the doctor says. I'm going to write my folks in the morning and ask them for sort of a long term loan, but I can't tell them why yet cause I just couldn't tell them in a letter; so if this is okay by you, after we get back to Boston somehow or other I will have to go home for a weekend or so and explain things and get my clothes, and I'm hoping they will understand enough to want to offer to do something financially.

I lay there in silence unable to move, my fiancée next to me, completely riveted by the pages I held gently in my hands. We held each other tightly with the letters scattered about us on the sheets. She rocked me

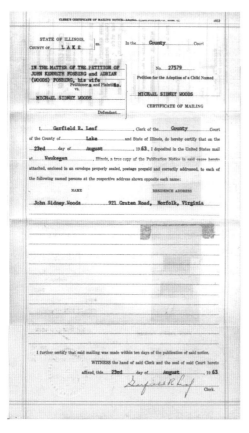

gently and we stayed that way the entire night.

The next morning I said nothing to my father about the contents of the envelope, whether out of fear, uneasiness, or just plain shock, now having read the letters and seen the difficult choices both he and my mother had faced. Perhaps like my mother—and maybe even my father?—I feared too much exposure of feelings, so therefore was content with the evidence so far shared. Besides, I was elated at the opportunity to finally spend a Christmas with my missing family and felt such a sense of black pride to have returned home with a woman not only so beautiful, but visibly and culturally part of my newfound heritage.

That trip to Virginia, a subsequent journey to New York City to visit my fiancée's family, and everything in between was funded in full from my dwindling bank account. My fiancée grew sullen and distant as we finally began to see how wrong we were for one another. She needed a financial caregiver, which I couldn't be. I wanted a woman to love me, but she lived in a different emotional world.

Her moods swung wildly, and I tried to hold on for dear life. She began staying with friends, and instead of giving us the space to discover what we were really in this for, I held on tighter. She'd disappear for weeks at a time, and I grew despondent and helpless. One day I returned home from an outing with friends to find all her belongings had disappeared. There was a note on the dining room table. She could no longer be a part of this relationship, she wrote. Not knowing who she was, or what she wanted, I was suffocating us both and she needed out. She left the rings, she said, as it didn't feel comfortable to hang on to something so sacred. She pleaded for the car and asked me to grant her time to settle in before she would repay her debt, return the car, and make things right.

I went ballistic. I'd spent thousands and wanted it back. I forced the issue, got her to return the car, and decided it was time to pack up the house and hit the road. What I wasn't willing to examine was why I had let all this happen. What made me think it was a good idea to get engaged to a woman I really knew little about? Why would I open my wallet so carelessly and allow her to spend all my savings so freely? More important, what was I trying to prove to myself through this biracial relationship? Did I think it somehow made me blacker to date a black woman? What made me think I could affirm my own racial identity by connecting myself with a black woman? I had worn her like a trophy and didn't even realize it.

I needed to get out of Los Angeles, I realized, to get a fresh perspective on my life.

RETURN TO SENDER

It is Saturday, July 4, Grayslake, Illinois. I am now ready to face my mother, nervous, yet determined, carrying my mother's letters which Sid had given me. It is a breezy, hot, sunny day, and we are sitting in Adirondack chairs out on her deck overlooking a tiny lake. A few small rowboats navigate around as children dive from a platform set out in the middle. She seems to have moved on since her recent divorce and there is a peacefulness about her at last.

I begin to ask questions, nervously at first. After awhile we both begin to loosen up, and her stories start to flow more easily. I realize I must tell her at some point about the letters I have, but for now she is telling me about her childhood, growing up in a strict Armenian home, her sisters, her rebelliousness. Her face twists, her brow furrows, her eyes dart off to one side as if she can picture a specific moment. She is in pain one moment as she talks about her father slapping her across the room, and then she laughs as she recalls what may have prompted him to strike her in the first place—her continuing to date a black boy in high school when her parents had strictly forbidden it.

I begin thinking about how to approach the first years of my existence, in Boston, 1957 to 1959. What a time that had been in our nation's history. In the beginning years of the civil rights movement and marches for equality, with segregation still rampant in society, and the beginnings of some of the most important work by Martin Luther King and Malcolm X, my mother had taken up residence in one of our nation's most segregated urban cities and had a child with a black man. Yet I was not born there as my mother fled to Los Angeles hoping to find a solution to her "problem"... me.

"So, you went to California to visit your friend there?" I am asking.

"Yes. My girlfriend was out there, she introduced me to this lady from Catholic Charities, Mrs. Layden. I went to live with her, and she placed me in a couple of different jobs."

"Did you tell her about your predicament, about Sid?"

"Yes, I went out there thinking I was going to give up my baby. But I knew I could never give up the baby."

She looked away, squirming in her chair under the hot sun. I was shocked by her admission, having yet to grasp how radically different my life might have been if she had chosen differently some forty years ago.

"You never told me this," I said. "You went out there thinking you were going to have the baby and give it up?" Speaking as though it weren't I, perhaps to shield the pain, distance myself.

"That's the pretense under which I thought I was going to go out there. I could never have done that, I knew I couldn't do it. I knew every day that I was there, I couldn't do it. But I guess I didn't know what I was thinking."

"You thought you would go out there and give up your baby and then go back to Boston?"

She continued to backpedal but the pain and discomfort were too much for her to hide.

"I guess. I guess that's what I thought. But even on the plane out there, I knew that I couldn't do it. I remember that thought going through my mind. I remember thinking, 'What are you doing? You're not going to be able to do this.' And then I thought, 'What choices do I have?' So when I talked to Mrs. Layden, I led her to believe that I was going to give up my child, and I knew I wasn't."

She sat quietly, pensively, squinting in the bright sun. I noticed her hands shaking ever so slightly. Mine were as well. I already knew the pretext of her decision, but her honest confession was jarring. "I... I... need to... to tell you..." I broke the silence awkwardly, looking away across over the lake hoping to find strength in the calm of the reflecting waters.

"What?" she said, looking up. I could feel her stare. "Say it."

I struggled to find the words as I took a deep breath and plunged ahead.

"I have some of your letters that Sid kept." The sentence escaped from my mouth. I slowly turned and looked into her face as her eyes searched for a response. I fidgeted with the papers I had lying in front of me.

"What did they say?" She asked, looking down at the papers in my hands.

"You can read them if you like."

"Yeah, I'd like to. What do they say?"

Her tone had changed. It was soft, sober. It felt safer to proceed.

"There are four letters. Three of them you wrote between the time I was born and Thanksgiving when we went to Boston to live with him. The final letter was written after we had left and were back living at your parents' house."

"Yeah, I'd like to read them."

I pulled the letters from the pile of papers and handed them to her. She sat up, a bit startled, not quite ready, and took the stack from my outstretched hand. She looked uncomfortable, but it was hard to tell the true nature of her discomfort: shame, fear, or disappointment. Small drops of sweat fell from her forehead onto her bare legs. The bright sun combined with the lack of her reading glasses made her squint at the page. Her sun-browned hands trembled gently as she recognized the handwriting as her own. She began to read, her face solemn, eyes watering, head nodding, body slightly convulsing, the outline of her past becoming transparent.

She looked back and was sent hurtling forward. Bits and pieces, fragments of her memories, forty years past rushed toward her. I watched as an enormous weight of history descended upon her the moment her eyes met the page. A look of confusion crossed her face. She shook her head. She read the letter dated August 6, 1959, the last letter.

Dearest Sid,

I'm sorry to be so long in getting this letter to you...

I'm going to try and explain how I feel—I hope you will understand all of this—first of all I do love you very much. I thought that was one thing you were certainly sure of and was very surprised that you should question it. I realize we had a bad start in marriage and that I was and still am immature in many ways. We didn't have time to adjust to each other before Mike came which caused a lot of problems plus the money problem, it wasn't easy. But I'm sure all of those things could have been worked out—they were only little things.

I think you know what the big thing is—I don't like to say it because I know it hurts you but I guess I will have to try and explain this... I don't consider you and even the word Negro as related while to you this is a part of you which makes it synonymous with your very being—that is the problem I have never thought of you as belonging to a "particular" race. I just knew I loved you and assumed that our life together would be happy and what for a lack of a better word, I will call "normal"... However, after we were married I found that this was not the case and it wasn't a situation of my not wanting to accept it but of not being able to. Maybe it was because I was so in love and had missed you so much that I just wasn't thinking of anything but our being together at first. After we got married I had a lot of time to think and look into the future—probably too much time. Also I was afraid—I'm not even sure of what—maybe for Mike, maybe for myself, or for all of us—I don't know but I was afraid. I just could not bring my son up that way. It seems too unfair and cruel and I guess I'm just not a brave enough person. I realize that it isn't fair either that Mike doesn't see or know his daddy anymore and I tried to be reasonable in thinking of that...

This probably seems strange to you to think that I can say I love you and yet leave and take Mikie too. Well I'm not happy here at home and I miss you terribly. I don't like being alone without a husband and I feel quite lost except for Mike—but I still feel I am doing the right thing and that keeps me going— At least I'm not afraid anymore and I can't tell you how good it is not to be afraid. I do get depressed and lonely but not like before. I can try to make friends now anyways because I'm not afraid of being rejected.

As far as Mikie is concerned, he has almost everything he could ask for—love and affection as well as material things. And he has a chance to grow up to be or do whatever he wants. He doesn't have his daddy and I don't have my husband—I wish we did—we need you and want you very badly... I don't think I can adjust my life to be without you always but I also don't think I could adjust my son's and my life to live as Negroes.

I hope all this makes sense to you—I've explained it the best I could on paper—please write soon. I will be waiting to hear from you.

I love you, Adi

Her eyes were swollen and red, shaking teardrops down the page. Her voice, once creaky and sad, had disappeared. Unable to speak, she looked up from the page, her face pleading. There were no apologies to be made. She sat up, trying to gather her thoughts, her composure. She wiped her face with her bare hand. After a long pause she spoke, "You can't blame your life on anyone else, there are choices that we all make in life and these were just... you know..." Her voice

broke. She waited for the stillness to surround her, then tried again.

"I remember making the decision and then not acting on it. And then finally acting on it. I don't know what to say, I guess that's the way I felt. I don't even remember writing that letter. Isn't that interesting? I look at that and I think, holy cow, how many years has it been since I saw the word 'Negro'? Isn't that incredible. I think white people judge color by how much education they have, and the more education they have, the more compassionate and understanding you are.

You're willing to open up your mind. Where we were, it was just... I could have lived in a biracial world, that would have worked. If we were at a different social status, if we were at some kind of intellectual milieu, or if people were somewhat more tolerant, that would have worked. I could have brought you up as a black child. I couldn't have done it where we were. I just couldn't do it.

"I don't know that I ever felt like I was married to a black man. I mean, I know I was, but I don't think I ever thought of black or white. Then suddenly it was like it wasn't just he and I anymore, there was a baby, and that made all the difference in the world. What did I want for this child? God, how hurtful that must have been for him, how horrible... Jesus."

Her head shook back and forth, eyes almost shut, trembling hands, her breath slow and measured. I sat quietly and felt how horrible her pain must be as if it were my own. The afternoon shadows were beginning to lengthen as her lakeside neighbors prepared for their Fourth of July celebrations. In the midst of all the preparations, the setting sun, the glowing smooth lake, and the occasional bursting firecracker, it seemed somehow appropriate we—my mother and I—shared this personal discovery. There was a sense of relief between us as we walked back toward her house to prepare for our own independence day celebration.

AN UNCOMFORTABLE
CONVERSATION

From the beginning the conversation I had dreaded most on my journey was the conversation with the *father* who had raised me about my recently found *father*. I was meeting John Kenneth Fosberg at his spacious new home in a suburb of Waukegan. He insists it actually lies within the boundaries of the township in which we grew up, but the area for me bears no resemblance to the world I remember from my childhood. He built this expansive prairie-style home with his new wife, whom he married during the frigid winter of 1994.

I'd had a phone conversation with my adoptive dad back when I first discovered my biological dad, but now came the face-to-face moment when we would try to forge some path forward. I wanted to expose our pasts and find a way to discuss the elephant in the room, my race, and our future. I felt nervous and uncomfortable as I turned into the circular drive in front of his house, with lingering thoughts of the two-hour dialogue I'd had with my mother just the day before. Each conversation I had had so far with members of my family on this trip had seemed to blow open doors I never even knew existed, and this one was likely to hold revelations of its own.

We sat in the open two-story living room in huge overstuffed furniture. The ice clinked in our water glasses as we tried to get comfortable. I felt I first needed to clear the air by saying something about my feelings about him and how awkward I felt talking to him about Sid.

"Dad, I just want to say that this is an uncomfortable situation for me to discuss at times because, well, I have a lot of fear. I don't want to hurt you. I love you. You're my father. I just happen to be very lucky in that I have two fathers. You raised me and I learned a *lot* from you— a lot from you! And it's a little uncomfortable talking to my dad about my dad, you know what I mean?" I looked up at him, his straight no-nonsense face staring back at me. I looked away, uncomfortable about meeting his gaze. "It's awkward and I don't know if I'll ever get totally comfortable with it—and I don't know if you will either, I don't know." I looked back at him as I struggled to find words.

"Probably not," he answered plainly, "because I probably have some of the same fears you have. I don't want to say something that's going to hurt you or be negative or something. So yeah, there's some of that for both of us. I hope I didn't make it hard for you to tell me you found your biological father?"

"You didn't make it hard for me, I made it hard for myself," I tell him as we enter the world of a father-son discussion unlike any we've ever had.

"You know," my father began, "I don't know where all the pieces have fallen through all this—you were never told about your heritage or anything, you had to discover it. I wasn't either. You're the one who told me… You wonder what happened. And who tells who what. You had no control."

"I have no control over that or anything anybody thinks about me now," I replied.

"Well, just so we have no misunderstandings, I love you like a son."

"I know that, I'm not worried about that."

"And whatever you told me about your heritage or anything, I think I can honestly say there's nothing there that affected how I felt about you in the tiniest amount. I still felt the same, it didn't matter."

We are barely into our conversation and already I see that both of us are flinging expressions of feelings back and forth as if we did this all our lives, yet holding back the related emotional outbursts. It is a careful path we tread, one we needed to take years ago. "I thought about it a lot relative to your mother and I have no animosity toward her not telling me about your heritage. Your Grandmother Fosberg said to me, 'Don't you think Adrienne should have told you about this?' I said yes, I think it would have been nice if she had told me sometime, but I'm not angry with her because the question was, when would she do this? When? When would it ever be the right time? The day I met her is she supposed to say, 'I wanna tell you about my son's heritage'? Day two? Day three? When do you do this? It was never a good time."

He takes a long drink of water as I try to keep my emotions in check and push forward. I am wondering if he felt cheated by her omission.

"You mentioned my heritage made you think about other things?"

"Well, I thought about your mother, and her parents, and characters that I've never met. I mean, did I ever tell you I talked with your father one time?"

"No," I say, startled by this revelation.

"He called our house—'Is Adrienne Fosberg there, please?'—I said sure, just a minute. I handed the phone to your mother and walked out of the room. When she was done talking, I said, 'That was Michael's father, wasn't it?' She said, 'Yes.'"

I sit trying to piece together whether the story my mother had told me about my answering the phone when he called was in fact this call instead. I ask, "Do you remember when that was?"

"I know we lived on Pacific Avenue so it was after 1966 or something like that. I would probably guess around 1970, '72?"

"How'd you know it was my father?"

"You know how things get you in the heart, the gut, or someplace?"

He looks at me with a gaze that can only be described as fatherly. It is a knowing glance that says we are father and son. I feel I know exactly what he is talking about, as I experienced the same kind of connection

Johnny and me.

when I was told the news of my race. He chuckles to himself as if a private moment is about to be made public.

"Do you remember when we were in the judge's chambers where you were adopted?"

I shake my head and smile awkwardly. "No, I don't. What was that all about?"

"You have to appear in a courtroom as part of an adoption and stand before a judge with your attorney. The judge asked if you were cognizant of what was happening and you replied in the affirmative. And he asked you some things like was it OK, and you were a very young boy, about five, I guess, five and a half."

"When was this?" I ask him, trying desperately to find memory traces of this intimidating childhood moment.

"Summer of '63. The judge asked you some things, then he asked me a bunch of things about the adoption. I was surprised cause I thought this was kind of a rubberstamp deal. I was a little taken aback by the length he took and the number of questions he asked of you and me." He sat trying to recall the moment, apparently to no avail. He hesitated before he started in again. "For a long time in my life I was not very good about asking questions. My life style prior to your mother and with your mother was not communicating about things— especially if they may not be what you want to hear."

He leaned back, deep in thought. I felt as if I'd been having a conversation with someone other than my father, a different person, someone who was unafraid to open up. Was this the father-son relationship

I'd always wanted? Feeling slightly more comfortable in my discomfort, I glanced over at his silver-gray head of hair with a sense of deep compassion. He caught my gaze with a troubled look of resignation.

"I remember a friend of mine who married a gal with two sons and it was the damnedest thing. I look at that and, well, the father of those boys won't..." His voice trailed off as he tried to navigate his fears. "Well, he's a factor. The boys see him and they use their father against this friend of mine when he disciplines them or something. And he's just trying to do a good job raising these two boys! And there get to be things about money—their father is very successful but won't contribute beyond what the law decreed. There's animosity and other things like that.

"I didn't get any money to raise you, but I'll tell you one thing, that's the best money I never got in my life. Because when I listen to a thing like that, even while I was poor, wouldn't be worth it, who needs it."

"Tell me about the first time you met me and my mother," I ask, hoping to brighten the mood.

"My first real remembrance of you is..." he looks off in the distance as if searching for the memory somewhere above. "We were on Glen Flora Avenue, and I saw your mother driving in her green Ford Falcon. We stopped to talk and you were in the backseat of the car. You had some kind of hat on—you were a hat kid—and you had on glasses, looking at me from the backseat. I just remember you looking around at me—that's probably the first time I saw you—it's one of the most vivid memories of you."

"I actually remember that, now that you are describing it."

"You do?"

"Well, I remember meeting you in the car, the Ford Falcon," I tell him, suddenly registering my car memories. "I had it confused with another time, but I remember that I met you when I was in the car."

"I'm surprised you remember that and you don't remember being in front of that judge almost a year later."

"I don't remember the judge, but I thought I remembered meeting you when we got in an accident in the car."

"Your mother and I were already married." Recognizing the accident I am referring to, he puts it in historical context.

"That's what she told me as well." We sit quietly for a moment. I can faintly hear birds chirping outside in his wooded yard. A clock ticks steadily from the kitchen under the sound of his wife making some household clatter. "Do you remember doing stuff with us as kids?" I ask, having a vague recollection of limited quality time.

"Well, my recollection is, I didn't do a whole heck of a lot with you kids. I mean, we went to relatives' houses and did holiday things together, but I didn't do a whole lot outside of that. I remember going to your plays as far back as grade school."

"Yeah, I played William Shakespeare in my first play."

"Well, I kinda remember that."

"Do you remember taking me fishing?"

"Oh yeah," he answers abruptly. "You didn't like it. It was not a good experience."

"Why do you say that?" I wonder what my behavior might have

been like back when he tried to drag me out on the boat.

Johnny with a big catch.

"It was raining out and I said we were going fishing anyway—that was a fisherman's way of doing things. You didn't wanna to go. I think then finally one time I asked you if you wanted to go and you said no. And I tried to talk to you about it and it finally dawned on me—this kid really doesn't wanna go fishing. Is that correct?"

"I guess so. I didn't like fishing."

"Yeah, but I mean I'm thinking when I was a little kid my dad took me fishing. Everybody liked to go fishing. I liked to go fishing. I was gonna take my son fishing. It was also the connotation of what a father oughta do with his son, and I sure wanted to do with my son what everybody else did with their sons."

"I was into basketball and tennis," I mention, but he hardly hears me as he is fixed on admitting his belated discovery.

"It took me a long time to figure out that this kid doesn't wanna go fishin'. Now Christopher loved fishing with me up in Canada, except he wouldn't eat anything."

"Yeah, but Dad, he never ate while we were growing up. Don't you remember, he was a skinny kid and people picked on him."

He laughs as he remembers. "Michael, do you remember he used to get bussed to a special program at West School and he hated to go on that bus 'cause there was always this one kid picking on him. I remember you saying, 'I'll take care of this.' And one day you went on that bus with your brother and told that 'Johnny-rotten-kid,' 'If you touch my brother again I'll beat the shit outta you every day!' or something like that. Christopher never had another problem on that bus."

"Seriously?" I ask incredulous.

"Seriously," he states emphatically.

"I did that?"

"Yep, you did that. Christopher was coming home all upset, and we didn't know what to do and you said, 'I'll take care of that.'"

"That's funny because I was just about to ask you if you recall me being full of fear when I was a kid."

"Yeah, but that was earlier. I remember that day I met you when you were in the backseat of your mother's car looking out at me like you were scared of the world. You were peeking out, so scared. And I don't think that changed for a long time."

"Do you remember when it changed?"

"Well, obviously it started to change when you started getting up on the stage. I don't remember specifically, but there was quite a period in your life when you were hesitant to do anything."

"Yeah, I remember going to camp and you had to come to get me 'cause I couldn't handle it."

"I don't remember that, but I remember I didn't want to leave you there. You were crying your eyes out. I mean, why is it so important you go to camp? You didn't like it there, and it wasn't a nice camp."

"I just remember a lot of swimming and I didn't like to swim, never liked it, never been a swimmer. I mean, I can swim, but, well, there's two things going on here; one was Laurie—you remember her, my high school sweetheart who drowned trying to save a couple of kids while working as a life guard—and two, when we were in high school—you probably had to do this as well—the boys didn't have bathing suits during gym swim class. And I thought that was—"

He interrupts me before I can even finish telling him of my

traumatic high school experience. "I didn't like it either 'cause I was a skinny little kid. Didn't start to mature until sometime in my senior year and so many of these young guys were all practically men already. It was very embarrassing for a guy like me. And these coaches were just the biggest bunch of dipshit jockstrap guys that just...

"The only kids that were good at that were the mature kids who were big and strong and could do all the things they were supposed to. If you were a skinny little kid like me and couldn't swim, they'd just as soon see you in the bottom of the pool."

"Yeah, I wasn't as skinny as you but I didn't like the idea that we had to swim naked. It just really bothered me no end."

"I couldn't swim well either and I didn't like gym."

"You weren't really into sports?"

"Not at all. I went and hid in the grocery store for four years. I didn't go out for any sports or do any extracurricular stuff in high school or anything. My uncle offered me a job at his grocery and I worked there after school four, sometimes five days a week and all day Saturday."

"Did you feel like you perhaps missed out on something with your kids?"

"I didn't feel any of that until later. In hindsight I was always busy doing other things and not doing things with my kids. But, you can't change the past."

He sits reflecting apparently on his absence during our childhoods, an absence for the first time revealed in his searingly honest admission. As the light from a second-story window shines across his face, his normally contained emotional front seems somehow delicate and fragile. I reach for my water apprehensively, like a person who laughs nervously when confronted with an uncomfortable truth. I am amazed at how alike we are, and yet different. I wished we had had conversations like this as I was growing up. I couldn't help think how these shared experiences might have taken the edge off our troubled relationship. I felt like I was just beginning to get to know him.

"Tell me about your impression of our relationship when I was in high school and college."

"My impression was that you and I, we were on two different wavelengths. And your mother was in your corner all the time, and in hindsight it was a darn good thing because I'd have run your life in a different way if she hadn't been there.

"You were a senior in high school and we were trying to figure out where you were going to go to college. I finally figured out you were gonna go to college for dramatics, or theater, or something and I gave in to that. Wasn't what I thought a person should do because I thought that wasn't a substantial enough way to make a living, but OK, that's gonna happen.

"So I read about the different universities with your mother, and I determined that Southern Illinois University had quite a theater program and it was a state school, and I said that's where you oughta go. You and your mother decided you oughta go to University of Minnesota. So we were discussing this and you stood up—and I'll never forget it—and you started screaming at me that I didn't know anything and that the only thing I cared about was my damn money. Then you left, walked out, and you went to Minnesota. And that tells you kinda how it was, the atmosphere between you and me."

"I remember I got accepted at both schools."

"I didn't even know you applied at SIU."

"Yeah, I got accepted there and Minnesota, and—" I suddenly remembered how my mother had stretched the truth about my birth father's heritage, "I think I got accepted at either Dartmouth or Cornell 'cause I checked American Indian on my application!" He joins me in my amusement of this memory.

"That's something, you should say that! The only indication your mother ever gave me about your heritage is one time she said she thought you might have a little Indian in you, and I just kinda shrugged my shoulders like, 'so what?' I know you got into that minority thing at some point in your life, about having Indian in you."

"I kinda rode that for a little while 'cause that's what she told me."

"I know."

"It never fit really, but..."

"Well, did your father have any Indian in his family?"

"Not that I'm aware of."

"I said to your mother just recently one day, what does he look like, Sid. And she said—and I assume she hasn't seen him in thirty years or so—and she said, 'Just like Michael!' Is that accurate?"

"You can see for yourself," I tell him as I reach across the table and open an envelope, retrieving a stack of photos. What may have at one time seemed like a fearful event—the act of showing my father photographs of my father!—was now a fearless endeavor. I rifle through a few shots before pulling out a photograph of Sid, Roy, and me from that memorable first trip to Virginia Beach during the summer of 1993. I hand him the photo and he looks over it slowly, slightly confused.

"Who's he?" he says, pointing to my grandfather in the middle of the photo.

"That's my grandfather," I tell him.

Aunt Marjorie, her youngest daughter Linda, Uncle Paul, and Cheryl, Marjorie's oldest daughter.

"Which one's your father?" he asks still gazing at the photo confused. "Oh, wait, that's you!" he says, pointing to me on one side then, "Jesus!" He goes suddenly silent as I see a look of shocked recognition pass over his face. "Truth is, I didn't recognize you there. That's amazing," he says as he shakes his head at the uncanny resemblance.

I quickly pull out more photos and show him shots of my Aunt Marjorie, her daughters Linda and Cheryl, my Uncle Paul, and Uncle Charles. "He's eighty-two," I tell him as I show him pictures of me standing in Charles's apartment with my cousin Harry Leroy. He points to a picture of a young light-skinned man with an afro clearly shown on the back wall of Charles's apartment and asks, "Who's this?"

"That's Charles's son."

"Because you didn't look a whole lot different than that when you had your big hair in high school."

We sit back as he shuffles through the photographs, taking in my new family. He seems fascinated by each image; I sit transfixed, amazed, and exulted by his fascination. As he comes to the end of the picture show, he looks up, his face full, and hands me the photos. He takes a long slow drink of his water and sits back in thought. Looking straight at me he says, "You know, I often thought about all the people, including myself, all of our family members, and tried to remember how we addressed race, how we talked about blacks. And I've thought about your mother in that position because of you. I mean, we grew up in a very bigoted society,

Uncle Charles, aka "Rip," second cousin Harry Leroy Johnson, and his wife Nancy.

in a bigoted family, that's the way it was. And your mother taught me all kinds of compassion and understanding without ever letting me know why. She gave me a terrific education in becoming more liberal, more considerate, becoming more appreciative of the situation. From every aspect she gave me a great education without ever telling me why."

His honesty is sincere and piercing. He looks off into the distance, bringing us closer together than even he knows.

"You know when you got engaged to Victoria, your black girlfriend, and there was this potential wedding with families, I told your mother that she needed to talk to my mother and tell her about what was going on, about your heritage, about this wedding that was gonna take place. So then your mother went and talked to Grandma, and I talked to my sister. I thought your mother never got through to her, but she did, it just took Grandma a while to start talking about it. And the life she comes out of, Michael, is very bigoted. We've had some conversations, nothing to do with you, because before you and the revelation of your heritage,

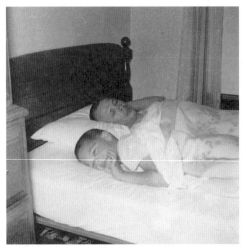

Me and Johnny.

she was unbelievably out of the Old World. Great lady, good honest woman but wants to come up with arguments for discrimination, I don't know how else to say it. Doesn't even know what she's arguing about, that she's arguing for discrimination; she'll tell you she's not."

We sit in silence. There is nothing to be said. I feel the depths of his sadness in the weight of these admissions. I also feel that the bond, the never-had-it-don't-really-know-what-it-is-or-means father-and-son bond has at last found us.

BACK TO THE BEGINNING

I arrive in Boston and am shuttled off to the Forthill home of the same group of people who watched over me in Baja and also made me feel so welcome on their farm in Kansas. This, their East Coast location, includes several old Victorian homes dressed up to match their age; detailed polished molding and trim in high-ceilinged rooms furnished with well-kept antiques. Again I feel embraced and comforted by a group of friends like family, yet not by blood. I find much solace in the ease with which we communicate. Etta, a large mothering black woman with a big smile, calm voice, and steady demeanor, takes me under her wing, offering to show me the neighborhood where I spent my first two years of life, Roxbury. I've come full circle, it seems, and my past has finally caught up to my present. I am excited yet unsure of what to expect, how I will feel, whether the experience will bring long lost memories to the surface. I was barely two when we'd left, what could I possibly remember?

After a cup of tea, we set out for Roxbury. It is literally just blocks down the hill from their home, and we wind and weave the crooked streets descending the hill. Before I know it, Tavern Road is upon us. It is a small one-block street set against the burgeoning Northeastern University campus. The block currently has no homes—as Joni Mitchell lamented, "They paved paradise and put up a parking lot."

It is university parking with no sign of its former self, my lost neighborhood, or my old tenement home/apartment.

"Are you sure this is it?" I ask, hoping she's made some kind of geographical error.

"This is it. Twenty-three Tavern Road would have been right there." She points out across the lined blacktop.

I struggle to hide my disappointment as I sit quietly, trying to imagine the street as it might have been, the feeling of what it may have been like.

After a time, Etta turns to me and touches my arm gently. "Are you ready to go?" she asks softly with a warmth radiating from her eyes.

"Yes," I say, still looking out over the landscape. "Let's roll."

On the way back to the house, she drives me through the wider neighborhood, giving me a glimpse of the areas I may have walked as a child. The university has now sprawled across many blocks and the freshness of its growth overshadows anything that resembles my historical context. She tells me something of the neighborhood's history as we glide through the angling streets of what is still a pretty tough neighborhood. As if I am in some sort of dream state, people and places pass before me in a slow-motion blur, surreal, snapshotlike. I gaze out on the streets, searching for something, a clue, a face, a memory. Watching people cross the streets, children playing, cars passing, I grasp a sense of community, a place people now call home. In some abstract way, my life seems to intersect with this place, these people, this environment. As we move slowly back up the crooked streets toward the hill upon which my friends live, I feel suddenly consumed with a sense of melancholy. The journey "home" is finished yet not complete.

The next day, Sunday, Etta takes me to a church in Watertown where my second cousin, Harry Leroy Johnson, a layman, is giving a sermon for the vacationing pastor of his congregation. Harry is the son of my grandmother's sister, Francis, and lived in Boston when I was just a child here myself. He encouraged me to attend when we spoke on the phone the day I'd arrived in town. We enter the church just after the service has begun, and Harry turns to acknowledge my presence with a huge smile as we scurry up the center aisle searching for an empty pew. He is dark, short, and stout with a neatly trimmed mustache hanging above his engaging smile. I smile and wave back as the parishioners take brief notice of our exchange.

St. John's United Methodist Church is a large cavernous stone edifice with a soaring bell tower, built sometime in the 1930s, I'm guessing. Etta and I find a seat, slide in, and take a breath as we listen to a variety of passages being read from the Bible. A song, a prayer, then more readings. The parishioners seem a mix of middle-class people, black and white, connected through their faith. Finally Harry takes the pulpit and with a flair for the dramatic he begins the morning sermon. His delivery is folksy, exuding self-assured confidence, at once engaging and personal.

"You know," he is saying, "as I come here each Sunday to share in the joys as well as heartache with you, the members of my extended family, I am reminded of the miracle of brotherly connection afforded by our faith." His voice is soft yet reassuring as he looks over the congregation. He looks my way, smiles.

"It is sometimes with family that we can reflect on the past, where we've been, where we are, and where we may be going. It is that sacred bond of blood that is a true gift of God's miracle. Today I personally have that opportunity to reflect on my past with grace by the visit of a long-lost and dear member of my blood family." As he smiles, I begin to feel a new lightness about my Boston past as if it was coming into focus. I can't remember any of it, but I do. I can't picture it, but it is there for me. "I can feel God's presence shining down on me, on us, and guiding our paths—once so apart—together again and allowing us to reflect on our past in the grace of his love."

I gaze at him, feeling a warmth and love lost years ago in that apartment on a street now covered in blacktop. Etta sits still beside me, her presence reassuring. I sense the support and love of the strangers sitting around me; it is as if they are lifting us and holding us up in a communal embrace.

Harry launches into what appears to be his prepared sermon, "In Praise of the Village." It is a beautiful recollection of walking through his Brookline neighborhood on a perfect summer evening and becoming aware of the rich tapestry of human existence surrounding him. Friends and neighbors of all colors and creeds, businesses established by folks brought there from all parts of the planet, and a maze of churches from all denominations. Rich, varied, and all within walking distance of his home. The village of mankind, the village that enriches and complements who we are as human beings. He ends his sermon with this:

> Are we not, you and I, part of a village, limited neither by race nor gender, by geography nor time, bound to one another by the irrevocable love of God? As you move through the day and the week ahead, pause, I pray you, to call to mind those members of the village who, in this generation and all generations, have shone a light onto your path. Remember and give thanks.

After the service, Etta leaves me with my cousin, and he and I make our way to his house in Brookline. It overlooks a green in the midst of a homey neighborhood with churches, boutiques, and coffeehouses—the very ones he described in his sermon. We settle in the cluttered living room with tea. I mention the universality of the story I am discovering in my journey—how two families in a way were brought together for a brief moment in time, then went in their respective directions only to be reconnected through me thirty-two years later. He nods his head frequently in agreement.

"One of the things I discovered in retirement," he tells me, "is there is a whole world called daytime television that I was totally unaware of and that is made up of two essential ingredients. There are of course the ongoing dramas, the so-called soaps that are in some cases thirty years old—five episodes a week, fifty weeks a year, for the last thirty years. I've been told by people you can miss a whole month at a time and plug back in and you haven't missed anything.

"The other is the so-called talk show. Our daily newspaper lists all the shows and who the guests are. What has been fascinating to me in reading those over the past years is how many of them deal with finding lost family members and making reconnections.

Harry Leroy Johnson.

There is a strange fascinating appeal to it, an emotional investment that is hard not to get caught up in. The incredible power of reconnection."

Knowing my background in theater, he suggests a stage play—and having been a subscriber to the Huntington Theatre and having seen all of August Wilson's plays, he suggests there is enough room on their stage for two full rooms. One family on one side, the other family on the other side, with me as the courier going back and forth between families.

We sip tea, the phone rings, and his wife Nancy, a petite white woman with a curly blonde perm, answers as we continue our conversation. She interrupts from time to time, relaying phone messages and occasionally sits in on our conversation.

Harry Leroy tells me more about his grandfather, my great-grandfather, Charles "Lefty" Robinson. "He had but an eighth grade education and yet he was known as the 'Black Mayor' of Jeff City. Whenever there was some kind of problem or disagreement in the black community, they would always call on him. He held down several different jobs, always trying to piece together a living. He was a black Republican who worked as a doorkeeper at the capitol building. And, he was the only black undertaker—working on the side for the largest white funeral home whenever they had a black body needing to be prepared for burial."

As we talk about Jefferson City and the racism that pervaded Missouri (and elsewhere) in the 1940s, I mention going downtown with Aunt Marjorie and stopping off at the local dress shop.

"Oh yeah, Milsap's, been there for maybe seventy years now. She probably remembers when she couldn't try anything on in that store. You can buy it, but you can't try it."

"Aunt Marjorie came charging out of that store with a big smile of satisfaction as an older woman carried her bags to the car," I tell him. "As she stepped into the car and we pulled away, she said, 'This woman wouldn't give me the time of day when I lived here as a youth, and now she's carrying my clothes to the car!'"

"That's it. You got a taste of it. It was a strange culture with strange rules most of which were understood, and all of which were honored by black folks."

He circled back to the subject of Lefty. "He was the founder of

the local chapter of the NAACP and the president of the community center. He persuaded the city council to build the first pool for blacks."

"When I was in Jeff City, Aunt Marjorie proudly took me by the city's maintenance building, which is named after him."

"He never did a day's worth of blue-collar work in his life, that I know," Harry LeRoy continues. "Although it doesn't surprise me that that's what they would name after a black man instead of something else. It seems to fit. It's a logical part of the tradition."

"He never worked for the city's maintenance crew?"

"Not a day in his life."

"So why name the building after him?"

"Well, it was an honor and lent some credibility to him, and the white power structure had to acknowledge him in some way. Remember, he was the black 'mayor' and he really did keep a lid on a lot of stuff. To his credit he also marched with the young folks in the civil rights demonstrations when he was in his seventies."

This seems like a great opportunity to ask about his wife, who is white. I wonder how this relationship stood strong, while my parents couldn't make it last. "You're a product of that civil rights movement. Is that how you wound up marrying your wife, Nancy?"

"Your father and I each in his own way ignored the rules in white society. I did it with a great deal of self-consciousness. Nancy and I got married and the baby was born two years later. Here, thirty-five years later we're still together. But we also function in what is essentially a white world. For better or worse, that's the truth. I function very comfortably in the black culture. But the black culture in places like Boston is less hospitable to Nancy than the white culture is to me."

"Has that been a difficult path to walk at times?"

"I think generally accepting integration happens easier at the lower level than it does in the middle class. I don't meet many interracial couples at the same economic and intellectual level as I am. Where I meet them is at the blue-collar level. Ninety percent of the interracial couples

Proclamation:
Office of the Governor
State of Missouri

WHEREAS, Charles E. "Lefty" Robinson of Jefferson City is a friend to many Missourians and to many worthwhile projects and causes; and

WHEREAS, Mr. Robinson has long served Missouri as a dedicated advocate of human rights; and

WHEREAS, he is the only remaining founding member of the Jefferson City Chapter of the National Association for the Advancement of Colored People (NAACP); and

WHEREAS, on the fiftieth anniversary of the founding of the Jefferson City Branch of the NAACP, it is fitting and proper to honor Mr. Robinson and pay tribute to him, his hard work and his ideals that have helped make a better community for all of us here today; and

WHEREAS, Jefferson City and Missouri owe a debt of gratitude to Mr. Robinson for his work, not only in the NAACP, but as past president of the Community Center Association and the many other community and civic endeavors in which he has participated; and

WHEREAS, we are happy to honor Mr. Robinson and his work on the occasion of the semi-centennial of the Jefferson City NAACP:

NOW, THEREFORE, I, CHRISTOPHER S. BOND, GOVERNOR OF THE STATE OF MISSOURI, do hereby proclaim Sunday, November 4, 1973, as

CHARLES E. "LEFTY" ROBINSON DAY

in Missouri in recognition of Mr. Robinson's contributions to Jefferson City and his work to improve the quality of life for all Missourians during his 82 years as a resident of this great state.

IN TESTIMONY WHEREOF, I have hereunto set my hand and caused to be affixed the Great Seal of the State of Missouri, in the City of Jefferson, this 2nd day of November, 1973.

GOVERNOR

ATTEST:

SECRETARY OF STATE

I see are black males with white females, not the other way around. Now your father traveled in this fairly narrow jazz subculture. He was into jazz, had a lot of records, wore a beret, I think I recall him having a goatee. He had the walk, always a drink or smoke in his hands. I was scared of it, not something I was totally comfortable with. But it was one of the subcultures that was integrated—but very few black women, a lot of white women."

"Do you think this is how my parents met?"

"Well, I don't really know, but Adrienne always seemed much too sweet, too innocent, and much too naive to fit in with that crowd. She was the last woman on earth I would have expected to end up with your father. She was not like anyone else I'd seen your father with. Just incredibly sweet and such a nice, nice, nice person."

"Did you spend much time with my father?"

"John Sid and I did not travel in the same circles. Your father traveled in what would have been considered a fast crowd. I was studying philosophy and religion."

"Do you remember what he was studying?"

"No, I don't. I was not a confidant of your father's so I didn't even know your mother was pregnant until she was far along."

"Do you remember what their relationship was like?"

"I stopped over at the apartment just a few times. I remember sensing the strain. And I don't know that I was sophisticated enough at that time to have any awareness of what the nature of the strain was, other than what I had always suspected and that is, they were just from two different worlds having nothing to do with color at all."

"Did you get any sense of what they were like with me?"

"My sense was, and this sounds judgmental, your mother was by definition your caretaker, and John Sid was still functioning like a single person involved in the scene. And my recollection was that he was still going out to the jazz clubs and she was tied down at home with you. So, when the breakup happened I was not surprised."

I pull out some photographs, the ones I have of him, my mother, and me. I hand him the one of him and me sitting next to the toy chest. He grabs his bifocals, wraps them around his head, and stares down at the old black-and-white photograph. A look of puzzlement, almost painful, comes over his face.

"Do you remember that?" I ask.

"Yes I do!" A broad smile moves slowly across his face. His eyes tear. "I made that chest." He shakes his head as I gaze at him feeling the weight of our history together. "And, what fascinates me," —his voice catches in his throat—"is you wouldn't believe how much this looks like my son at the same age. You absolutely would not believe it. It is remarkably like Mark's pictures. Holy shit, is that amazing! That is amazing." He is glowing with pride, history, and affection as he wipes his eyes with the side of his hand staring down at a boy, me, just a few years older than his own son. "And seeing this—there clearly was a lot more than I recall."

"Did they seem in love?"

"They certainly seemed to care a lot for each other, but if you told me to place a hundred dollars one place or another, I would have said at that time it seemed like she was more in love with him than the other way around."

"It seemed maybe he wasn't prepared for this."

"Absolutely. There was not a lot of money. Didn't have a car. Tavern

Me and Harry Leroy.

Road was not prime real estate, next to the projects. I remember your father clerking in a music store or something. Money was tight."

He returns to the photographs in front of him and gently finishes thumbing through the stack. He smiles as he reaches the last picture, a shot of him, my mother, and me walking, or attempting to walk, down Tavern road, our backs to the camera. In the photograph he is distinctly dark, my mother light with dark hair wearing a long white coat and saddle shoes. They look back toward the small, chubby child waddling behind them pulling what looks like a toy.

"I remember thinking that because there was no history of success in our family in a relationship between black men and white women, I might have a difficult time after your parents had split up, and I met Nancy just six months later."

He hands me the photographs as the afternoon sun peeks in through the lace curtains. Nancy has come in and taken a seat in a corner of the room facing him.

"You OK?" she asks, as he smiles broadly with his gleaming white teeth.

"Yes," he says. "We've had quite a conversation."

He turns to me and says, "I remember one of the last times I spoke to my brother; it was in '68 after our daughter was born. I was standing outside his car and speaking with him and his wife. Nancy was on the passenger side of the car talking with his wife. You remember this?" he asks his wife.

"Oh yes," she confirms.

"I was talking with him on the driver's side and the last thing I remember him saying was, 'Harry, don't trust the honky motherfuckers, they'll screw you every chance they get.' I remember it because of the irony of it. He's saying that to me, and I'm married to someone who he identifies as a member of the enemy camp."

Nancy sits still, shaking her head slightly, almost hiding a look of resignation.

"And I think there's always been that tension in our family, and I don't mean just my mother and father, I mean in the larger family. I think—and others in the family would probably deny it and would resent my saying it out loud like this—I think there were certainly elements of that kind of tension around your father and Adrienne. I don't know if family so much disapproved of it as thought it unwise."

Harry Leroy and Nancy glance at one another. She leans forward, reaches out, and grabs his hand as they smile and look back at me, content and loving. The complications of life, of race, of family—my family—sit smiling right in front of me.

I ventured to Cambridge the following afternoon to pay a visit to my great uncle who is 74, my grandmother's brother, Charles Robinson Jr., named after their father, the great pitcher, humanitarian, and founder of the NAACP chapter in Jefferson City. Uncle Charles— Rip—lives in a tall public housing building off a busy intersection. It is a basics-only type place, built with cinderblock and cheap labor. I take the clean, barely functioning elevator up to the eighth floor, and he greets me at his door. Rip is very fair-skinned, tall, lean and still well built, though he's on crutches as he welcomes me inside. He suffers from a recent hip replacement, bad knees, and some kind of nerve damage. A World War II veteran of America's segregated army, he complains that he gets only 10 percent of what white soldiers with the same ailment get. His apartment is small, cluttered, and hot. A fan churns on high, and the noise forces us to speak slightly louder than necessary. There are photographs on the wall of him in the army, him with a woman—presumably his former wife—and a photograph of a young dark-skinned boy sporting a huge afro—his son, he tells me, still lives in the area, but he rarely sees him. He speaks with a high, raspy voice and his face strains and contorts as he pushed out the sound.

We have a seat in his living room. He tells me he resided in a different part of the city when I was a child living there with my parents. I was the first grandchild among his siblings and there seemed to be a great deal of pride and joy throughout the family at my birth. He remembers playing with me at my Aunt Marj's, his sister's, and even vaguely remembers the apartment we lived in.

When I ask about race as a factor in the split between my parents, he shakes his head and his voice grows louder.

Charles "Rip" Robinson.

"Always has bin a prob'em, always will be." He tosses back his head, then leans forward, bracing himself on a crutch as his eyes probe my face.

"I 'member when I was jus' a boy an' it was Lady dat saved my life."

"Lady? What lady?" I ask, confused by his response.

"We had two horse back den on the farm."

"Ma Braxton's farm in Missouri?" I ask.

"Yep. Dere was Lady the work horse and Matt was the buggy horse. Well I was on Lady, went into town by myse'f to the show. Cost twenty-five cents. Ten cents fo' de theater—had ta go up in the loft—ten cents fo' popcorn, a nickle fo' soda. Afta the show, pitch my saddle horse ta come home and I was attacked by fo' or five white kids in a model-T Ford. They shot at me an' WHOA," he shrieks in such a high pitch it causes me to jump slightly in my seat, "I took off on the horse as they come down the hill. They had ta chase me 'cross a bridge an' I ducked the horse down under the bridge. Dey crossed and din't see me. I know that dey were out to attack me."

"Why?"

"Whites afta a black boy by himself, dey can do anything."

"How old were you?"

"I was prob'bly about twelve, it was," he looks toward the ceiling trying to do the math, "reckon it was 'bout 1926."

He looks agitated as he sits leaning against his crutch in a worn, overstuffed chair. The fan pumps hot air across our bodies as sweat trickles down his forehead. Pulling out a clean handkerchief, he wipes his head and begins to relate another racial tale. He tells me about enlisting in the army in 1942 and being sent to Toledo, Ohio. He was mistaken for white back then and spent three weeks in the white barracks before they found his birth certificate and shipped him to Ft. Lee in Virginia and put him in the black barracks. At this point he pulls out his military disability papers to prove his earlier contention about being shortchanged on account of his race.

I hold the papers in my hands while he continues to tell other stories drawn from his life and our family heritage. He confirms what others had alluded to—his mother's grandmother, Granny Emerson as she was known, was a slave who did laundry work for the family she was indentured to. Sitting cramped in his living miniature museum, soggy from perspiration, and swimming in sordid stories about our country's, and my family's, racial past, the hot flow of air blasting from the fan fills me with both deep sadness of the history and hardship, but also a sense of satisfaction in the acceptance I've felt and the sense of belonging I have.

As I leave my uncle's, I reflect on the conversation I had with my second cousin, Harry Leroy, when I asked him if he had any advice for me. "Who you are is significantly more important than what you are. Who you are is significantly more important than what you do. Therefore, knowing who you are is incredibly important. I'll give you some advice on this odyssey you are on. Follow it wherever it leads you for as long as the need to do so burns within you. Because it seems to me that to be robbed of a parent and thus that parent's family and history, as you were at an early age, is in fact to be every bit as crippled as a person who is missing an arm, or a leg, or an eye. If truth is the ultimate search of the human spirit, then truth about oneself ought to be very much a part of that. You can never know who you truly are until you have some sense of where you and your kind have been.

"I think you are among the privileged of the earth even as I think my children are, in that your kind is more complex than most people's kind. If indeed bridges are to be built on which we as a civilization can walk and connect, the bridges are going to have to be built by people whose kind live in both camps. So though the breakup of your parents' marriage may be measured by one yardstick—a terrible misfortune in the evolving of your life—the fact that you are searching to find out about that whole half of your history that you did not know growing up may be the most important work you do in your entire life. And, if having found that truth you find a way to document it and share it, whether in a play or a book, or just in conversation, it makes it all that much more vital. That's God's work, and even if you stop right now, you have done very important work."

What a remarkable idea, I thought, one that could transform a lifetime of hurt into a privilege offering a way forward.

THE INKWELL

I'm on Martha's Vineyard and it is a spectacular day, bright blue sky with scattered creamy clouds. It has been just three days since my conversation with Harry Leroy and my Great-uncle Charles, and I've come to visit Cheryl, a second cousin who played a significant role when she was a teenager during my Roxbury years. Along with her mother—my Great-aunt Marjorie—and her sister Linda, she took care of me when my young mother needed help.

She's on the island visiting with a friend, and we've arranged to meet for a late lunch. She is dark and well built, wearing a summery flowered dress that is a bit loud but not half as overpowering as the stingingly sweet scent of her perfume.

"Oh my goodness! Johnny Pudd! Johnny Pudd, Johnny Pudd! Lemme look at cha. You look sooo much like ya father! Johnny Pudd, that's what we called him, Johnny Pudd! Baby, I can't get over it, you the spittin' image of yo Daddy."

Our food is decidedly secondary as Cheryl stares at me throughout a course of the traditional Vineyard fish and chips meal. Afterward she takes me for a ride around part of the island I had yet to see. As we cruise the shoreline, she shares stories about changing my diapers while I blush. She says she wants to go to the beach, and when we arrive at the particular one she'd been in search of, we circle the lot searching for an empty space.

"It's awfully crowded here. Are you sure you don't want to try another beach?"

"Honey, there is no other beach on this island!" she states emphatically. "You don't come to the Vineyard and not visit the Inkwell, baby!" The Inkwell... the infamous Inkwell has been the number-one vacation spot for African-American families for decades, and it's the beach immortalized in the 1994 Hollywood movie with the same name.

As we step from the car after scoring a choice spot up front, the beach unfolds in front of me. It is packed with every shade of black person you can imagine. It looks like *Soul Train* meets MTV... people dancing, laughing, joking, struttin' their stuff.

Cheryl starts calling out to folks and before I know what is happening, dozens of people are stepping up to say hello.

"Donitra, this my cousin Michael from Chicago."

"Chicago, huh? I gots family from up near 'round there. Where you stay?"

"Well, I don't actually live there at the moment. I'm out in LA," I tell her.

"California! I know you lovin' dat!" She waddles off laughing as we continue to press the flesh of those we pass. My years of "hangin' wit da brothers" in high school comes in handy as I grip each hand in a clench of black appreciation and pride. A distinguished-looking gentleman approaches us.

"Hey, Skip, I want you to meet my cousin Michael. Michael Fosberg, Henry Louis Gates, Jr."

I choke momentarily as I recognize the name as that of one of the country's foremost black intellectuals and a writer from Harvard University. I grab his hand awkwardly. "Mr. Gates..."

"Skip. Nice to meet you, Michael."

"It's a pleasure to meet you, sir."

This goes on for what seems like hours. There is waving and laughter, jokes and stories, a few handshakes, slaps, and hugs. People coming and going all in the span of ten or fifteen minutes at most.

"Hey, Shirelle, this is my cousin Michael."

A tall, sexy, sultry, long-haired, dark woman eyes me up and down as she saunters toward us. "Hey, Michael, how ya doin' baby?"

Does Cheryl know everyone? I wonder. "I'm doin' great, thanks."

"Baby, we havin' a party tamarra night. Whatchu doin'?"

"Ah jeez, I'm going back home tomorrow morning."

"Oh no, baby, you can change dat. You gots ta party with us!"

"Well, I'll see what I can do." I'm hoping I can change the date of my departure and participate in the black culture I was unceremoniously deprived of so many lost years ago.

"We gon bring the house down, baby. You gonna wanna piece a dat!"

In that instant I suddenly have a vision of what my life might have been like, summers on the Vineyard, the parties at the Inkwell, hanging with the sistas. As I reveled silently in the pleasure of those images, in that same breath I realized the other side of that picture—confusion, racism, hardship, ridicule, unsure of where I stood. How would I have fit in? What race am I? Am I white? Am I black? Does it matter?

For thirty years my source of family history, of self, was the rich Armenian heritage with which my mother's parents surrounded me: a sense of Old World traditions, a thick and complicated language, pungent spicy foods, exotic yet danceable music, and a closely knit community, a family history dating back to slavery in a Turkish state. My overall family picture was formidable, celebratory, and yet one-sided. My non-birth-related heritage, the Fosberg's Swedish roots, were for the most part buried, uncelebrated, and unrealistic for me to grasp, given my dark complexion and wild curly hair.

I asked my mother about the time when her mother came out secretly to visit us in Roxbury while my father was away at work. Upon seeing our impoverished situation, she begged us to return home to Waukegan.

"What if I'd had darker skin, Mom?" I asked. "What would my grandmother have said then?"

"We would probably never have returned home to live with my parents," she replied. "Your life — our lives — would have been entirely different."

In the end, I was not raised black. I didn't live through the black experience, was not a target of racism, was not singled out because of the color of my skin, and was not spurned or called names. Does that make me any less a black man? Do you have to have that experience to be black? All my life I wore a disguise, a mask of identity. Incognito is defined in the dictionary as an adverb meaning *"with the real identity concealed... with one's identity hidden or unknown."*

So what am I now? Who am I? Which box have I been checking off on applications, or in the 2010 Census?

- ☐ White
- ☐ Black, African American or Negro
- ☐ American Indian or Alaska Native
- ☐ Asian Indian
- ☐ Japanese
- ☐ Native Hawaiian
- ☐ Chinese
- ☐ Korean
- ☐ Guamanian or Chamorro
- ☐ Filipino
- ☐ Vietnamese
- ☐ Samoan
- ☐ Other Asian
- ☐ Other Pacific Islander

Or what about...

- ☐ Mulatto?
- ☐ Octoroon?
- ☐ High Yella?

How about AAA, African-American-Armenian! Is there a box for that? More important, do I need a box to fit in? Frankly, there isn't a box big enough for me to fit in. I've got too much history, too much family, too much culture, to stick my roots in some box.

I slide between worlds, between cultures, experiencing everything from both sides. I live in between. I walk both sides. A box doesn't tell you who I am. I'm more than a label. I'm more than a race. I'm a kid with two dads with two heritages.

I am Michael Sidney Pilibosian Woods Fosberg.

ROOTS

I am a teacher in a small southern college. My desire to teach survived and grew in spite of some determined attempts on my part to crush it.

I have wanted to be a radio engineer since high school days. I made my first radio as a ninth grade pupil and have been making them ever since.

As valedictorian of my high school class, my first year in the local college was assured, but the college had no engineering school. I majored in mathematics.

After my first year in college it was evident that teaching would be my life's work. But, of course, I was determined to be an engineer.

I am a teacher in a small southern college. My desire to teach survived and grew in spite of some determined attempts on my part to crush it.

I have wanted to be a radio engineer since high school days. I made my first radio as a ninth grade pupil and have been making them every since.

As valedictorian of my high school class my first year in the local college was assured, but the college had no engineering school. I majored in mathematics.

During my freshman year I was fortunate to have had a teacher who had a profound conviction of the worth of a teacher's work, a man with a sense of the greatness of his profession—of its significance for society, or its power to benefit mankind. Here was the inspiration, and during the next three years I was instilled with the conviction that skillful teaching is essential to the strengthening and enlightenment of every citizen. Various specialists participated in imparting to me the process of teacher education.

I learned to believe in freedom and the worth of each growing personality; that respect for others and self-respect are essential to the creation of freedom. Friendly respect for others is, of course, basic to the establishment of sound community relations.

As a teacher, I believe that my chief function is to try to help produce intelligent, rational, enlightened individuals, who, regardless of what else they may be, will first of all be worthy and responsible citizens of a world society. To be a better teacher I must have a program for self improvement. It is essential that I should be able to give expert help to students in satisfying their interests and inquiries. Moreover, the world situation at this time, and the serious scientist shortage in the United States at present, make it imperative that we do not allow Russia to overtake the technological lead upon which the preservation of our society may depend. We need to train new scientists, technologists, and engineers. We must increase our supply if we are to cope with other nations in this dynamic world.

In a stack of papers my father has given me, I find the missive above. It was obviously typed using a manual typewriter, the pages now brittle and yellow. It is neither signed nor dated, but I expect my grandfather composed it sometime in the 1950s, owing to its reference to "teacher in a small southern college," which presumably would be Norfolk State. Whatever the date, it captures something of my grandfather's sense of mission in life and his integrity.

Roy Alexander Woods was born October 13, 1913, in Columbia, Missouri, the son of a hard-working truck driver, Alfred Woods, and an equally hard-working mother, Bessie. He was bright from the get-go,

Roy A. Woods, circa 1932.

becoming the valedictorian of his high school class at the all-black Douglas School. He was awarded a BA in mathematics from Lincoln University, the historically black college in Jefferson City, where he graduated magna cum laude. He earned an MA in mathematics, an MA in physics, a PhD in physics, and a doctorate of education in science from Boston University. He held certificates in radio and electronics from the University of Missouri and the Illinois Institute of

Technology. He was a radar instructor and technician at Pearl Harbor and a member of the scientific research team for the Upper Atmosphere Research Laboratory at White Sands, New Mexico—known for its work on the atomic bomb. He founded the departments of science and engineering at Norfolk State University, and he also served as the school's director of instruction, director of summer school, dean of academic affairs, and vice

Roy (right) with his sister Laura Ann Woods, circa 1916-17, Columbia, Missouri.

president for academic affairs before he retired in 1978.

His accomplishments were legion. He was the first African American appointed to the Virginia Beach City School Board, a position he held from 1966 to 1982, and the first African American to serve as vice chairman and chairman of that panel. He served on the board of directors for the Planning Council, the Committee on Childcare and Childcare Assurance Plan, and the United Way Family Center of Virginia Beach.

Most important to him, however, was his role as teacher and resource leader of the Roy A. Woods Bible Class for fifty years and his work as a member and chairman of the Board of Christian Education at the Bank Street Memorial Church of Norfolk, Virginia.

We sit in my grandfather's office at the back of their house on Wesleyan Drive, on the Norfolk-Virginia Beach border. He is surrounded by ham radios, CB radios, police scanners, AM/FM tuners, an array of parts, tubes, and electronics. On the walls are shelves of electronics books and plaques from various committees he's served on, and above the doorway to the garage hang several antique rifles. A man of few words, he chooses his moments carefully and interjects with wisdom befitting his years of experience; his speech is slow and slurred, yet steady.

He tells me about growing up in Columbia, Missouri. They lived with his grandparents, of whom his father's mother, Laura Woods, was head of the household.

"We had all kinda animals where I grew up. We had pigs, an' horses, an' cows."

"Did you live on a farm?"

"Not really. It was not too big a town back then, wasn't much

Roy at his desk in his home "office," circa 1940s.

developed. Columbia was still a kuntry town. My uncle John, my fatha's brotha, lived 'cross the street. He was a hard workin' man, a good lookin' man. His wife died early an' so he took all his meals with us. My grandmotha prepared the food ever' day. An' she had chickens over on his lot. She'd start out 'cross the road an' the chickens would come on down ta meet her an' turn 'round an' go back with her 'cause they knew she was gonna feed 'em."

He regales me with stories from his country life, filling in details and anecdotes as if he were spinning a yarn. I ask how he'd become so interested in school, growing up as he had out in the country.

"Just was. I loved school. I was the valedictorian of my high school class an' a fella that taught history wanted me ta go ta Wilberforce. He claimed I had a scholarship an' so he set it up that I could go. I did for a year but then he never paid the people that I stayed with. So, I

Uncle John with the neighborhood kids.

didn't go back the second year, I went to Lincoln. My wife tells me I went to Lincoln 'cause I met her that summer an' I couldn't stay away from her!" He laughs, recalling Lois's influence.

"Met her at a dance, they had a little dance floor, someplace 'round there in Columbia. I had a cousin lived with us an' I don't know how they met, but she knew Lois an' introduced us at this dance. Anyway, that was the beginnin' of sixty-three years!"

"Did you know any of her siblings?"

"Well, not really. I don't 'member anythin' Paul did except that he

Bessie Woods, Roy's mother, hand-colored photo, circa 1902.

was a ladies man. They all were crazy 'bout him. He knew I loved ta hunt so I went down to New London an' he was there at the time with his grandmother. I 'member a little girl walked three miles from town out ta see him. Oh, I thought that was sumthin'! An' she was a nice lookin' girl too!"

We laugh thinking about Uncle Paul, my wacky great-uncle still carousing the streets of his hometown. Poppa—as I now felt familiar enough to call him—leads me through a brief history of his education and travels across the country, a marriage, a son, a war, homes bought, money tight, more education sought. His memory is a bit fuzzy, but when he wanders he then finds the path as we weave our way through time. We've finally arrived in Boston and the meeting of my parents and my subsequent birth.

"John Sidney went ta Boston University fo' one year."

"Just one year? What did he study?"

"I don't know. I don't think he studied anythin' but Adi." He laughs, referring to my mother. "I tol' Adi that if they were gonna live t'gether they had ta get married—they were living t'gether on Tavern Road. I 'member you as a baby in the arms of yo' fatha standin' in front on the house there."

"Do you remember when my mother and I left?"

"I knew he was real upset... I like ta tease him... he was runnin' 'round takin' pictures, camera over here, and camera there, an' tripod here... takin' pictures of anythin'. Had ta do sumthin' to keep busy, I guess. He was just tryin' ta get over the fact that you all were gone."

We sit still, my grand-mother busy in the kitchen nearby. The cat, Miss Priss, purrs under my grandfather's feet, which somehow breaks this sorrowful spell. He tells

Huldah Woods, Roy's great-great-grand-mother, circa 1870s.

me more about his teaching life until retirement. Although justifiably proud of his achievements, he speaks with complete humility and grace. I ask if he has any advice or hopes he'd care to share with me.

Turner Woods, Roy's father's brother, a Pullman porter, circa 1920s.

"I think we all need ta really be a little more concerned with our neighbors than we are. An' I cert'nly hope that this thing between blacks and whites..." His voice trails off as if he almost would like to retract what he'd started to say. "But it will never straighten itself out. But I cert'nly hope that sumday it might be a little betta."

"Do you feel it's gotten better?" I ask, having not heard him express any racial animosity up to this point.

"Not much. You know the state of Va'ginia is talkin' 'bout how Norfolk State doesn't graduate as many students as it should. But no one has ever stopped to really

Roy at Lincoln University, Jefferson City, Missouri, circa 1932-34.

study to find out why that is, why we don' have more four-year graduates, or five-, or even six-year graduates. An' I definitely think they can find out what the reason is if they really tried to."

"What do you think it is?"

"The reason is socioeconomic. I'm pretty sure 'bout that. These kids start in school... they just don' have the money ta go ta school in the furst place, an' they cert'nly don' have the money ta come back the next year. You got ta sit there an' worry about are you gonna get in school or are you gonna eat. It's no easy job."

"Now what is it you wanna know?" My grandmother's rich southern drawl lingers smoothly across the ticking of the antique clock in their living room. She wears her customary summer flowered dress and large-framed glasses, and today her "beauty" as she calls it, her soft black-and-grey hairpiece that covers her dwindling scalp.

She pulls out a Bible, then another, and another, now a fourth. She mutters as she fumbles through them, searching for information she wants to share with me.

Lois E. Robinson (Woods), circa 1932.

"Ever'body I know in 'r family kept dates—births, marriages, deaths. Din't always keep up with 'em, but kept dates." She finally comes across what she's been searching for, a list of births in her family beginning with her father and mother:

Chas. E. Robinson Sr.
Mar 2—1891 at New London, MO

Verna Francis Fraiser Robinson
Mar 3—1887 at New London, MO

Then her and her siblings:

Lois Enoch Robinson
Feb 23—1913 at New London, MO

Chas. E. Robinson Jr.
Oct 24—1914 at New London, MO

Paul Kenneth Robinson
Aug 23—1916 at New London, MO

Francis Elizabeth Robinson
June 4—1919 at Hannibal, MO

Marjorie Louise Robinson
Nov 4—1921 at Hannibal, MO

Then a listing of family deaths in her family:

Mrs. Margaret Emerson closed her eyes in death Feb 6th 1924 at 2 o'clock. May her soul find rest.

Mr. A. W. Braxton passed away Feb 27th 1935 at 12:30 o'clock, buried Mar 2nd (?). Peace to his soul.

Mrs. Jennetta Morison was buried on Mar 2nd 1933. Buried at Hannibal, MO.

Mr. Lewis Emerson closed his eyes in death Oct 27, 1936.

William "Son" Robinson—Died at Gary, Indiana, Oct 29th 1939.

Mrs. Mary Robinson passed Nov 28th 1948, Hannibal, MO. Buried in New London, MO, Dec 1st 1948.

Maw Baxton died Sept 8, 1955 Buried in New London Sept 12, '55

And a list of Roy's family with ages:

Woods Family

Laura–grandmother	01-15-1852–09-16-1931	79
Tarlton–grandfather	12-10-1844–05-16-1916	72
Bessie–mother	10-09-1881–09-14-1926	44
Alfred	08-18-1879–05-26-1942	63
Pilate–grandfather's brother	1847–1950	103
Laura B.–sister	03-21-1904–03-21-1950	46
Lillie Dale–sister	10-09-1905–07-06-1951	45
Templeton–brother	08-10-1910–08-23-1974	64
John C.–uncle	05-29-1876–12-30-1974	78
Roy A.	10-31-1913	

It is a great if fractured historical record of my grandparent's families. It is my window back in time, in several cases back as far as the slave days. I'd seen these names and numbers briefly on a previous trip, but now knowing something of the family stories, they were taking more three-dimensional shape. My history felt close, immediate, real. How close might I have been to have met some of these very people called my family? Some dark, some light, just like me.

"Mary Robinson was Charlie's—my fatha's—motha. A slave owner was her fatha. She was very fair skinned, very kinky hair."

"You know, Granny," I interrupt, "all your brothers and sisters say you look most like your mother."

"Ever'body seem ta have thought that, an' there was jus' a difference in complexshuns. She was very fair..."

"She was very fair also?"

"She was 'bout the color you are right now!"

She spins yarns about growing up, her parents, her siblings, meeting Roy, their life together moving from town to town, and on and on. Her slow melodic voice and recall of minute details is hypnotic. At times I must pull her back to the topic at hand after she has departed

Charlie Robinson.

*Verna Francis Fraiser Robinson,
New London, Missouri, circa 1910.*

on a tangent of minutia, a verbal tour through someone's home, an in-depth description of how clothes were washed, recipes for a complete meal recited from memory. I am anxious to hear about her version of the events surrounding my birth.

"I was eager ta get ta Boston ta see my grandchil'. An' you were a li'l fat piggy peach. I visited a few times an' Marjorie was there. I thought you were a precious doll."

"Do you remember my mother?" I ask her.

"I could tell she was unhappy, Adi, she jus' din't show signs a happiness. I din't know the circumstances completely, an' the feelin's until… You could tell the family had bin there."

"Do you remember when my mother and I left? What was it, 1959?"

"He called, very depressed. Afta sum time he got terribly ill, a cold, fully congested. Marj called, said you betta get ready ta come, they gonna put John Sid in the hospital. I took a flight up there. They didn't know what was wrong with him. Finally, maybe week later, they tell us he's got polio."

"Afta he moved ta Detroit, Sid kept wond'rin where you were. I think if he had bin able ta have fought that on his own," she says referring to the divorce between my parents, "without askin' us fo' help, he would have fought it, but he couldn't—din't have the money. Then when he found out 'bout the adoption, he was furious. There again he

Lois (second from left) at Lincoln High School, Jefferson City, Missouri, circa 1928-30.

din't feel he should come back ta us 'cause he knew we had taken on too much already and were hurtin'."

"Did you..." I start, trying to force my way through the pain of the moment, "was there ever a time after we left that you or Sid thought about trying to make a connection with me?"

"Seems ta me that his feelin's were hurt. Felt kinda stomped on 'cause he was colored, or Negro, African American. I think he made two calls after he got back ta Detroit. I thought a him when he was feelin' rejected an' I tol' him, be a man—M.A.N."

I felt such a sense of deep loss for her, and for myself. Remembering her joy during the first call to me just a few years earlier, I ask her, "Do you remember when he called to tell you he had spoken with me?"

"Oh Lord! He called an' he said, you cain't guess what. Now what, I says. He says I have talked ta Michael... Fos...? what's yer name agin?"

"Fosberg," I laugh as she winces, smiling.

"Michael Sidney Fosberg. I said, you mean ta tell me Michael called?

He said, I jus finished talkin' ta him. I said, where is Sue? He said, she's not here. I said, you gone tell her? He said, Hell naw, not right away! Then the next call I think he was sick or sumthin' and he was really hurtin' cause Sue had taken these thangs and put 'em in the fireplace and burned 'em."

"What things?"

"Pictures an' thangs."

"What pictures?"

"That you had sent 'im. He said, but she don' know I'm gone jump ahead a her. I said, how's that? Those were the prints I had made, I have the originals! An' I made sure he sent me copies of those, don' cha know."

"Do you remember calling me?" I think back again on that morning when she woke me from a deep sleep with her smooth southern drawl.

"I believe I do. He gave me yo' numba." She smiles and grabs my hand squeezing it tightly. "There seems ta be so much closeness now." The journey has come full-circle and the prodigal grandson has returned. There is a closeness now, a joy, a historical connection, a lost life found.

"An' that is it," she says, as if placing a period on the conversation.

"Thank you," I say, thoroughly grateful for her remembrances.

"I'm glad ta have lived ta know ya," she adds.

"It's not over yet," I tell her.

IN THE MIRROR

I t is late morning as we sit across from one another in the office my father now occupies at the Lois E. Woods Museum on the campus of Norfolk State University. He's now curator of the collection. His office sits just outside a large room filled with beautiful and rare African artifacts his parents and he have collected over many years. Each notable piece is encased in a Plexiglas case protecting it from visitors who have yet to arrive. The museum space is still undergoing renovation in order to bring it up to the standard my father considers acceptable.

The collection is massive and mind-boggling, ranging from masks

The now defunct Lois E. Woods Museum of African Art, formerly on the campus of Norfolk State University.

to staffs to figures to ivory carvings. I am dumbfounded by its significance and breadth.

We're sitting surrounded by items ancient and striking which have spilled out from the galleries and fill his office area, classical music playing in the background. As I face this reflected image of myself, I wonder if I will age like him. It is an uncanny resemblance from hairline down to vocal resonance. I imagine how difficult it might have been for my mother as the years passed not to have the courage to tell me about my father and heritage, yet seeing more of his features in me each day. I wonder, too, about growing up seeing the image of oneself in another. Do sons often recognize this phenomenon, and how does it affect their image of self?

Sid lights a filtered cigarette as I pause, wondering if I should ask him if he could refrain. I decide to put up with the smoke so he'll be more comfortable talking about his background. I'm nervous, but he starts right in, telling me about his grandfather, Lefty, and the Hamburg hat he was known for donning, then darts off to say something about his father's mother, then quickly reminds me of family lore that Al Woods was a first cousin of the famous abolitionist John Brown, a story unconfirmed but worth telling.

Occasionally I try to interrupt to ask a question I have in mind, but he adeptly dodges my feeble attempts to reign him in. Perhaps it doesn't matter, I tell myself as I sit back and listen to him roll on.

"... then Wendy did her thing... I loved her, I really did. We broke up, got back together... I signed a deal with the devil," he says as he pauses a moment taking a slow drag from his now long-ashed cigarette. He picks up in the middle of nowhere.

"I was the first black that any automotive company allowed to spend their money—purchasing. It was a bitch. When you're dealing with purchasing people in large corporations, suppliers would kill their mothers for their buyer, 'cause your signature is their life. You become a god." He was now gaining speed by the second as he careened from family toughness to business cool.

"I liked to mind fuck with people. I used to say, 'Woods is the name, mind fuckin' is the game!'"

As he went on, his dialect got cooler and more street tough; it was as though I were listening to a gangster or some kind of street hood. His cigarette burned slowly, smoke billowing toward the ceiling as he flicked his ash in the iron ashtray atop a desk strewn with small African artifacts and figures.

"We were spending close to $800 million in my little department. I was the only one in five years that never got a merit increase. I don't ask for any merit, I don't believe in that shit. I wouldn't go ask, try to coddle the boss, or kiss his ass. Screw you, man. I'm doing a job and if you can't see to give me a merit increase, I'll look and get another job. Or, I could do some of the things I did, or I'll find another way to make up for it.

"There was a lot of cash around. I was a VIP. I had about 385 suppliers, and I was spending close to $150 to $200 mil a year. I never twisted their arms. I didn't ask; they gave, and I always got more than ten times what was coming." Was he talking about kickbacks?

Piecing together his tale, I began to understand how he amassed the money he did, and perhaps even portions of this massive impressive collection surrounding us. He took money from suppliers to take on their business. He awarded contracts based on rewards. It was a scheme I knew was not uncommon in the world of big business, but highly illegal. I was fascinated by how he made it sound so cool, how he related the story as if he'd been wronged, thus somehow seeming to absolve himself of responsibility.

"Did your wife know?"

"I told her if you don't know, then they can't ask. Asshole motherfuckers." He shakes his head spewing out a rant to preface a further twist to his story. "Three black guys out of Chicago had a printing company in the suburbs, and I put them together with an Italian guy with a huge printing business in Detroit that was looking to sell. He did about seven mil with Ford. So they tell me, if this thing goes you gotta finder's fee comin', it's fifty grand. I tol' 'em fine, that's against Ford policy, but I'll think about it. I went to a bunch of meetings with all a them and finally they got a bank in Detroit to cough up seven mil to buy the joint.

"I got into a situation where I needed money. I was trying to get to a situation where I could pay off the house for Wendy and Ethan, and I was gonna send you ten grand."

I stiffen as I hear my name mentioned in conjunction with his criminal activities. Would he really have done that? I bristled at the thought of being offered dirty money.

"So I talked to the Italian about the finder's fee. Had a meeting with the brothers at the Ritz and we discussed a finder's fee. I mentioned it frequently. As I talked to this guy, he was wired. Interstate commercial bribery. I was looking at eighteen months. Got twelve months in a halfway.

"I would have only had to worry about the maintenance on the house so if something happened to me, Wendy wouldn't be strapped with payments. Bought her the house, added rooms, redid the pool, alarm system, a ton a furniture inside. She had a car; she never had to work, I always took care of them. I sent Ethan to the best private school for first grade—$10,000 a year. Sent them to museums, art, twice when Pavarotti was in Detroit, Ethan and Wendy were front and center. He had a lot of exposure. Michigan–Michigan State game, fifty-yard line halfway up; hockey, the Pistons, usually got a box in the center. I'd call a guy, say I want the box, and I don't want anybody else there but me. And I want Jack Daniels and shrimp, you know what I want. And I'd get it there, it'd all be there."

I tried to keep as cool a demeanor as the mirror image across from me. The basic story sounded simple enough and sleazy, yet there was something about the details that reeked of hyperbole. Lavishly furnished houses? A four-year-old and Pavarotti? Football, hockey, the Pistons with Jack Daniels and shrimp? Was he heaping it on, or could I trust this story? How long had this been going on and to the tune of what financial figure?

"If you had to guess, do you know how much a year your 'fringe benefits' amounted to?" I put forward, quietly trying to mask my doubt.

"Two hundred thousand or more," he offered coolly through a cloud of smoke.

"Did your parents know?" I ask, hoping to hide my incredulousness.

"Now they do. They didn't totally know, nobody totally knows, but they had a pretty good idea, and my mother said, 'It wasn't right and we should have stopped you.' I said, how were you gonna stop this?

"They treated me like shit at Ford. I was just another nigger in a white man's world."

Here he was, an extremely light-skinned, educated, African-American man laying claim to the N word while positioning himself as the victim. I felt almost suffocated by what I saw as his braggadocio.

Bullshit, I wanted to say, but I sat still, my stomach sinking, churning.

He went on spinning an equally exaggerated tale about acquiring a Rolex watch for Henry Ford's mistress at some ridiculous discount for doling out what he claimed was one of the largest purchasing department contracts in Ford history. As he went on, the tales got taller, and the exaggerations more outlandish. Big names were dropped with more regularity, mention of luxurious goods more frequent. Then he veered off to his youth and being sent to the prep school, Munson Academy, because he was so light skinned, with straight blond hair and light eyes. He could attend segregated schools, he said, because he passed.

Finally I stepped in to steer the conversation toward his relationship with my mother in Boston.

"Then one day I met a young lady who transferred to Boston University from University of Illinois whose name was Adrienne Pilibosian. I said, nobody's got a name Pilibosian! You gotta be kiddin'!"

"Did you know any Armenians?" I ask. But he had swerved off on another tangent, claiming to have loaned money while in Boston to Charlie Parker—"Bird" as he referred to him—to get his horn out of hock, there because he had gotten into smack. This was a remnant from an earlier conversation in which he claimed to have run the Newport Jazz Festival for a couple guys named Cecil and George Wein. Among other outrageous claims, he said he'd supplied musicians with drugs, gotten arrested for speeding in a car with Miles Davis, and had slept with Billie Holiday. Veering back, he began to recall his interest in my mother.

"She was interesting, she was not unattractive, she was bubbly. One thing led to another and we got involved. One thing led to another and she became pregnant. One thing led to another and she decided to— I think not knowing where I was really coming from and fearing her father and family—she went to Long Beach. When she told me she was pregnant I think one of the first things that went through my head, although I never said it, was we gotta get married. That's my responsibility 'cause that's the way I was raised."

"So what happened?" I lobbed quietly, innocently.

"I think she came up with the idea of—I probably concurred—of going to Los Angeles and having the baby, giving it up for adoption. And I went off! My mind is focused on, I gotta get money, you know?"

"To help her?"

"Yeah, to help her, myself, still thinking this is my responsibility, and there's a cost involved. I went out to Atlantic City, worked as a busboy, a bellhop."

"Adi was out in LA?"

"Yeah, and then sometime late summer, I think, I called her and told her this is crazy. I don't want you to give up the baby for adoption. I want you to have the baby and come here, we'll get married. We can make a go of it. I went back to Boston and got an apartment."

"Did you tell your parents?"

He looks serious, pensive now. "I really don't remember telling my parents," he states almost quizzically. "So she came back to Tavern Road and I got a job."

"Where were you working?"

"At Goren's Department Store running their printing presses. Then one day, I don't remember how many days after she came with you, we went down to the justice of the peace, city hall, and got married." The sharp bravado has softened and a melancholic mood prevails. "I wasn't naive enough then or now to say that I never really showed your mother true love or what I felt inside... and I still don't to a lot of people. And I know that did something to her. I know she was unhappy. So I said, OK, probably the best thing to do is to go to Virginia. I can finish an education, maybe she could too..."

"You thought about bringing her there?"

"I thought we could have a somewhat happier life. But the constitution of the Commonwealth of Virginia forbids, even to this day, they don't enforce it, but blacks and whites can't live under the same roof."

It was hard to believe that this outrageous statute still stood. It probably did at one time, but in 1996? Truth is, there was a Virginia law—the Racial Integrity Act—forbidding blacks and whites to marry (either in the state or another) or have sex together. That law, in the case of

The photographs he kept in his wallet after we left.

Loving vs. Virginia, was struck down in a 1967 Supreme Court decision. I let my doubts at the time slide as I posed my next question: "Was race ever an issue between the two of you?"

"I think it was from time to time. For example, her mother came out to visit and stayed in a hotel and only came by the house to see you when I was at work. I never met the woman. After you and your mother left, I sent electric trains, a winter coat, a hat... I never heard if they were received or not. I'd call and your grandmother would answer the phone. She was not too pleasant."

"Did you feel people looked at the two of you differently being a mixed race couple?"

"I did. I don't know if she did or not, but I was aware of it. I think sometimes whites maybe because of their, for lack of a better word, 'psychological power base,' they don't really give a shit. They feel they can do anything any time they want to. Being black and realizing that it's

out there, then seeing it from time to time... you're cognizant of it at all times. There's little nuances that whites do; a look, the way they look, how they look, what they say, or don't say..."

"Do you remember her sister and brother-in-law visiting?"

"Oh yeah. They came to the apartment. I can see them sitting on the couch. They were tolerant. The sister was sent out to check it out and the mother came later. Like I said, I never saw her though.

"I came home from work one day and a lot of shit was packed up. I walked in and you were ready to go. Then the shit hit the fan... Your mother felt that her father might not be agreeable to it and might not treat you right. She was concerned enough then that she canceled going for about two or three weeks."

"Did you ever speak with him, her father?"

"No, Jesus, you gotta be kidding!" he says to me, laughing incredulously. "Anyway, after a couple of weeks, he convinced her everything would be OK and it was on again, and you were gone.

"The thing that I remember..." he starts as the pain he is now unable to mask grabs hold of him, "she confronted me and said that she did not want her child to be raised in a situation that he would not be capable or able to get a job based on his abilities to live, based on what he could afford. Because being raised black neither one of those would be available to him.

"I looked at her and in my own mind I said, 'I can't really argue with this woman 'cause what she just said is a fact in this country.' I was shattered. I can't even argue in defense of keeping my own son because of racism in this country. The way she said—I honest to God can't remember exactly—but I couldn't argue, it was very true. Then she went through a thing where she wanted me to move to a small town in the Midwest and pass for white, give up my family totally, which meant they could have no contact with you because I'm going to try and pass, which I told her I didn't think I could do, nor did I want to.

"Anyway, you guys left. A truck came and picked up the toy chest Harry Leroy had made and hand painted, and whatever other things she wanted to take. I was out of it... kept working."

"Did you think I'd ever come back?"

"I don't know. I guess I'd say I didn't. I think maybe as time went on I lost hope."

For the moment his cool demeanor and street toughness have evaporated. We sat still for a moment, a momentary reprieve from his winding monologue. The classical music strains in the background sounded like a dramatic ending to a scene out of a Francis Ford Coppola movie. I was exhausted, having taken what seemed like a rollercoaster of a ride through his life and mind.

I thought about the difficulties in understanding how the races saw each other. How I was a product of both, raised as white, discovering I'm also black, now hoping, wishing, trying to discover how to embrace them both.

THE SOUTH

A fter the conversation with my father, I felt the quest I had embarked on five thousand miles earlier had come to an end— or at least to a point of convenient pause. It was time now to head back across the country. There was one last diversion, however. Just south of Virginia Beach and the warm coziness of my grandparents' home lived a couple of old girlfriends who I'd not seen since high school graduation, the very same sisters who, unbeknownst to them, gave me the courage to come out of my shell as a young boy. The sisters of my high school infatuation, Kim and Roz, the Smittle girls. The temptation to revisit a long lost obsession only a few hundred miles away was one I was unable to resist.

I found myself barreling down Interstate Highway 95 South heading toward Wilmington, North Carolina, and the home of my mother's best friend, Drus-

Druscilla and her husband with their two girls, Roz and Kim.

cilla, the very same woman who'd brought her daughters to that cabin on the shores of Wisconsin's Lake Winnebago when we were teens. After the death of her husband years prior, she'd moved just outside of Wilmington, down the road from Kim, who was now married with twins. I had had a secret crush on Kim throughout high school, but it was her younger sister Roz that I actually once dated in the year after that summer day in the rubber raft. Roz had also moved down south with her Brooklyn-bred husband and their kids, to be closer to her mother.

I'm not sure what I expected from my visit. A few laughs, some old stories, a dinner, perhaps a chance to experience yet more "southern hospitality." I guess it was curiosity, or better yet, a frame of reference on how far we'd all aged.

I found myself at Druscilla's doorstep in the late afternoon as the sun was beginning its descent, creating glorious hues of oranges and pinks across the pines and eucalyptus trees along the shore.

"Well, how y'all doin'?" Dru teased me with her southern worst.

"Awful purdy 'round these parts ma'am," I joked as I gave her a big hug.

"C'mon in. We'll get ya settled."

I stepped eagerly into her tree-shaded home. I saw she had already set out some fruit and paté on the coffee table.

"Wow! I didn't expect such treatment."

Oh, you know, that's the way we do it down here. A little bit of what we call southern hospitality."

"Nice."

"It's good to see you, Michael. I'm glad you came."

"Likewise," I replied as we settled down for drinks and appetizers in her sunken living room.

As the sun sank lower, shafts of light reflected through the trees created shifting patterns in the room. I was nervous about the impending reunion with her daughters, but felt a nice slow easiness as we sipped our drinks and chatted. Then a quick flashback passed as Druscilla looked over at me while adjusting her silver hair with black streaks, which made her look like Cruella de Vil. I remember sitting as a teen in her living room, awkwardly waiting for her daughters to emerge.

To make final preparations for dinner, she leads me into the kitchen. "Sit... sit down. I'll prepare. You sit."

"No argument there," I say as I sit at the dining table facing her kitchen. She begins grabbing bowls from the refrigerator and sets them on the kitchen counter. "So do you like it here?" I ask her.

"Sure I do. It's warm, it's pretty, my daughters are here with my grandchildren. What's not to like?"

"I guess." I agree, "It just seems so backward here... you know... kind of stuck in the past."

"Oh it is that! Hell, I still hear people talking about the Civil War like it happened last week... *and* spouting off like they won! They've been callin' me a liberal and a Yankee since I moved down here six years ago."

She sets breads, various bowls of chopped vegetables and dip on the table. I can't quite tell if this is dinner or a second round of appetizers. She then grabs herself a drink, refills mine, and sits across the table from me.

"Help yourself," she tells me.

I look across the table at the assorted array of greenery. It's as if I'd landed in a garden vegetable plot.

Smiling at the organic-ness of my surroundings, I say, "Looks great. I forgot you were a vegetarian."

"Are you a big meat eater?" she asks almost apologetically.

"Not really... this is fine," I cover, secretly wishing for a steak or at least a strip of bacon wedged under the lettuce.

I look up from my garden plate and notice the resemblance to her daughters in her smooth elegant features. What must they look like now? How have they aged? Would they look like her?

"Your family," she said, "what are they like?"

"Oh jeez... they're wonderful... it's wonderful. My eighty-year-old grandparents are the embodiment of love."

"I'm sure they missed you."

"No doubt about that."

We sit silent for a moment, the clicks of our forks on our plates the only noise intruding.

"Your mother was a brave young lady," she says finally. "It took a lot of courage to do what she did."

"I know," I say, almost choking as my throat constricts. It is getting dark. Druscilla gets up from the table and flips on a light.

"Would you care for anything else?"

"No, thank you... that was great."

"Well then," she says excitedly as she begins to clear up, "let's go see the girls!"

"Great. I can't wait."

I could really, but it was time to face the past. Time to move ahead. I helped her clear the table as I became increasingly nervous about this reunion. How would they look? What would we say after all these years? Exactly how much have I changed? That's what this was truly about, I decide... how much have *I* changed? They would be just a mirror.

It had been twenty years and I still had the picture in my mind of a young, nubile, long-haired brunette with startling eyes and a deep dark tan. I had such a schoolboy crush on Kim that I was mostly uncomfortable around her. I never had a chance. She was too beautiful, if that's possible. Here I was two decades later about to confront my dream-girl fear. Something inside told me it wouldn't be the same, but I needed to see her and find out if she still made me squirm.

We drove in Druscilla's bright red convertible down the curving roads lined with tall trees. We had the windows rolled down and the cool humid night air blew across our faces as we occasionally glanced at the full sky of stars arrayed above us. There was that familiar salt-water smell of the ocean and the occasional sound of waves pounding the shore. The air had a warm sticky feel to it, yet it was quite different from the humid air of the north.

As we drove further inland, the cool breezes waned and the swaying trees grew still. Crickets chirped their dissonant sounds and fireflies buzzed the woods we now passed through.

"Are we close?" I asked, nervously breaking the natural silence.

"Just up the road."

"Convenient," I said. I couldn't stop thinking of Kim dressed in diaphanous white, her soft brown hair like silk.

"There it is." Druscilla points across what appears to be a shimmering pond at a big brown-shingled house, its porch light illuminating the circle drive in front. I clenched my hands as we pull up to the porch littered with toys. Why have I come here again?

"Kim's not here," Dru says with a knowing glance.

"What?" I ask, confused by her revelation.

"She must be out."

"How do you know?"

"Her car's gone."

"Of course." I don't know if I felt relief or pain, but I was able to breathe again.

"I'm sure Lionel and the kids are home. Let's go in."

We navigate our way through the minefield of toys. The front door opens and there stands a bearded man of medium height. He has on loose-fitting clothing and a goofy grin on his disheveled face. I'm in shock. He's not at all what I had expected. How in the world did Kim end up with this southern hick?

"How y'all doin'?" he calls out to us from behind the screen door in one of those long musical southern drawls.

"Hello, Lionel," Druscilla purrs.

"Hi ya, Mom."

"This is Michael," she says. I'm paralyzed, mouth wide open as she grabs and pulls me up the steps toward the open door. I trip on a dump truck parked squarely in the middle of the third step.

"Howdy," he says to me, extending his hand. I offer mine in what seems like slow motion, realizing I'm failing to hide my stupefaction. "Welcome to Wilmington. I'm Kim's husband, Lionel."

"Nice to meet you," I lie, attempting a smile, shaking his hand as we step inside.

"How the hell 'r ya Dru?"

"Just fine, Lionel, where's my babies?"

"Sleepin'. Jus' put 'em down. Had a long day. Dog tired. How's yer trip?" He directs his attention to me and gives me the once-over. I avoid his gaze and scan the interior for clues. It's plain inside. No fancy furniture. No frilly art on the walls. I walk cautiously, careful not to trip over the littered floor of toys. It's very bright inside, as if every single light were on. I search the room quickly for photographs, perhaps a picture of Kim. There were none to be found. What kind of family doesn't have photographs?

"When'd'ya git in?" Lionel continues.

"A couple of hours ago. It's been fine, a great trip really," I answer distractedly.

"Where'd ya start from?"

"Virginia Beach."

"Hell, yeah, I bin there once. 'Bout six, seven hours in' it?"

"Something like that."

"Lionel, where's Kim?" Druscilla interjects.

"Out drinkin' with her sister, I suppose. Sumbody's birthday er sumthin'." It's as if he doesn't really care.

"Oh," Druscilla sighs disappointedly.

"Should be home by now."

"How was your day?" Dru asks almost out of obligation as she steps into the kitchen and pours herself a glass of water.

"Well, I'm glad ya asked. Great!" he bursts out, "Played eighteen today 'n it was a beautiful thing."

"Rough life," I joke with him.

"Gotta git it when ya kan. Best damn round I ever played. Shot in the low 80s."

"Can we see the babies?" The proud grandma interjects.

He leads us into the twins' room, which is dark except for the glow of light now spilling in from the room we've entered from. The room is bare except for a dresser against one wall and two cribs positioned in the middle of the near empty space. A girl with curly blonde hair and a boy of slightly larger size are sprawled out on their backs, with that heavy breathing snore of young children that seems so peaceful.

"This is Sky," says the proud grandma.

"And that's my boy, Lionel Jr.," Lionel Sr. smiles.

I suddenly feel so out-of-place, like a foreigner trapped on the wrong plane. I love kids, but here I am in the house of a guy who is married to my high school crush, in the bedroom of their two adorable kids. Druscilla strokes the girl on the head, gently pushing back the soft curls from her face. She is smiling warmly as she gazes down at the nodding baby.

"He's a big'un in't he?" Lionel pokes me as he grins.

"Oh yeah," I say out of obligation.

"I've already got him out in the yard swinging a four iron," he whispers with a glow of excitement across his face.

"Golfing?" I respond, incredulous.

"You bet cha."

"Go Tiger," I say as I pump my fist in Tiger Woods-like fashion. I find myself attempting to build a rapport with a guy I could really care less about. Druscilla starts to exit the room as Lionel turns to me and says, "Hey, did ya hear they gonna re-name Nike?"

"No," I say innocently, my sports-obsessed curiosity suddenly piqued at having perhaps missed this news flash in today's paper.

"Yeah," he says, "they gonna call it Niggy."

I thought I heard him wrong at first, but from the easy southern laugh which he was gently trying to suppress as not to wake the kids, I knew he meant what he said. I was part stunned, part amused. What the fuck just happened? How did we go from admiring two beautiful, peaceful, sleeping babies to a crass racist joke? Where did we detour, and what do I say? I can't simply let him lay that one out there without letting him know he's picked the wrong person to share his racist humor. I'd just come from the trip of a lifetime, a trip in search of my heritage, my African-American roots. Here was this white, good-ol'-boy southerner laughing in my face, having just shared with me what he thought was a funny racist joke.

"I don't think you want to go there," I say clumsily as we exit the room.

"Oh," he says, all knowing, "we got a liberal on our hands."

"No... no... I'm not a liberal." I deny it, although I certainly qualify as one. That wasn't the point.

"Yer a damn Yankee then!"

"No, Lionel, I'm not a Yankee," whatever the hell that northern reference has to do with anything. "I don't like labels."

"Hell, yer all alike," he says motioning to the now dumbstruck Druscilla who hasn't a clue as to what's just gone down in her babies' room. "Yer all liberals."

"No, I'm not," I continue to deny, "but if you really must know what I am"—I stare at him with an intensity he's obviously unprepared for. I can feel Druscilla across the room holding her breath, while Lionel looks as if he thinks I'm going to tell him a joke, or goof back with him—"I'm African American."

Druscilla, a look of horror on her face, stands rigid and confused across from us. Lionel is completely dumbstruck. He can see I'm dead serious but isn't quite sure how to respond. His mouth is wide open, jaw locked, eyes searching as he probes me up and down, looking for clues or a prompt for what to say. This is definitely a Kodak moment. Fuck you, you racist pig, I think. How's that for justice. Druscilla fidgets, not sure how to make peace here, while Lionel, astonished, stares at my light skin, confused, apparently still hoping for a quick punch line, as if I am joking. I wait it out, preferring to let Lionel sweat. Lionel finally laughs uncomfortably, looks over at Dru, then back to me and says, "What a day!"

"Nice to meet you, Lionel," I offer with a smile, as Druscilla and I head toward the door, a quick exit in mind.

"I'll let Kimberly know y'all stopped by."

"Yes, thanks," Druscilla adds, still stunned, "take care of my babies."

"Oh, you bet ya. Bye y'all."

We exit the house and the door closes swiftly behind us.

"What just happened in there?!" Dru asks as if blindsided.

I relate the sequence of events leading up to the revelation of my ancestry. She follows the story carefully, a look of disdain on her face as I relate Lionel's racist joke.

"God damn him! He's always doing something like that. It's a never-ending battle with these folks." We step toward her car as a bemused laugh suddenly rises up deep from within her.

"Well... I'm glad you find it humorous," I say testily.

She turns swiftly to explain: "No, don't you see? You are the first black man he has probably ever shaken hands with — and he didn't even know it."

There is a sense of delight on her face as she extends her hand to my cheek, smiles, then turns, making her way for the driver's side of her car. I stand and watch her as she gleefully absorbs this fact. I look up at the starlit sky, take a deep breath of the moist southern air, and smile widely. I reach for the handle then look back at the toy-strewn porch, the glow from the porch light illuminating a mass of cars, trucks, and dolls. The light suddenly blinks off. I open the door, smile at Druscilla as we share a moment under the trees, in the woods, out in the country. Dru starts the car, and we plunge into the night.

————————

I eventually did meet face to face with my boyhood dream girl. The next morning Druscilla and I joined Kim and her kids for breakfast. Kim still has the charm and beauty she once had, but two children and life with a drunk, racist, southern good-ol'-boy fisherman has tamed the overall glow. We laugh about old times and share present-day stories. She and her mother attempt to talk me into staying another day, but I decline. Kim seems to be relatively unmoved by my story of family/racial discovery, and I am no longer nervous, curious, or reflective on what might have been.

What I thought I would see in the reunion with an old flame has little to do with how well we've aged. The change I see has nothing to do with the physical. The change is inside me. It is how I perceive the world, life, humanity. As I interact with people who view me as white, I am also watching them, listening. Those who don't know of my discovery, my race, seem looser, freer, less restricted in how they speak. Those who do know tend to talk with a bit more caution from time to time, careful in how they phrase things, more introspective. The fact is that I really haven't changed, and yet I am different. I am multiracial, multicultural. I embrace many worlds, many cultures, many families. I feel all kinds of issues as if they are my own. I'm on both sides of the fence, looking in and out. Yet I am in disguise. I can pass in more than one world, my identity concealed. Incognito.

HEADING HOME

The journey westward bore little resemblance in my mind to the eastward-bound chatter-filled brain of doubt and confusion at the beginning of my biracial road odyssey. In its place was a feeling of conquest and relief.

As I traversed the southern states, riding on a kind of euphoria, I noticed little of the landscape. Before I knew it, I found myself once again in the otherworldly terrain of the southwest. New Mexico and Arizona this time around, the Grand Canyon, a majestic experience to cap off the trip of my life. I'd traveled thousands of miles, heard and seen my life reflected back to me by all kinds of people, family and friends, and was returning to the place I currently called home, the land of wonder and big stories, Hollywood. I had met crazy uncles, sweet aunts, and engaging cousins, spoke with siblings I struggled to understand, parents who struggled to raise me, a father I never knew, and grandparents who'd waited years for my return. Like stuff out of a movie, I'd tell myself, only it was real.

Struggling my entire life to piece together an identity I could not seem to grasp, I found myself—more of myself—on the roads, in the living rooms, and on a deck overlooking a lake. My identity is not so much an outward appearance but rather—as they are sometimes known to say in the rooms of a certain twelve-step program—an inside job.

By venturing out across the byways and into the hearts and homes of my family, I discovered that who I am is much more complicated than any simple label can define.

Yet perhaps as equally important as uncovering my biracial heritage was the discovery of a father, a family, and a rich history. Reflecting back on my journey I am also confronted by the different paths with which I chose to get here. Were all the girlfriends, failed relationships, alcohol and drug addiction, fights with parents, and choice of an unstable career simply the result of making bad decisions? Or could they have been the angst of a young child losing his father? The confusion of a boy not understanding how to relate to his family? Or the misplaced rebelliousness of a young man trying to figure out his identity?

What matters more now in the aftermath of my self-discovery is how I live my life and embrace who and what I am. I grew up thinking I was white, yet have now discovered the full truth. However, the truth is also that my experience growing up was not one that included minority racial undertones. I hadn't had the same experience as a darker-skinned person, but then there is no *one* "dark-skin experience." There are as many colors in the African-American community as there are experiences. Surely most, if not all, dark-skinned people in America (and many other places) have experienced some kind of racism. For them it is a system of disadvantage based on their race, while for the white community, it is a privilege most often unrecognized. The disadvantage is that the experience of racism can affect their professional lives, their social well-being, and their financial futures. Time and time again we are offered studies showing blacks well behind whites in earning power, more apt to be incarcerated, and more often rejected when it comes to housing and loans.

More often than not people of color, along with other minority ethnic groups, are viewed as a racial group, rather than as individuals. Those who can't pass for white learn to live with the common occurrence of being pulled over while driving black or being watched by sales clerks when shopping. Immigrants who come to this country with strange-sounding names, language barriers, different appearances, or unusual cultural practices often find themselves the target of hostility. It's not just a black/white thing; it permeates the whole of our richly diverse society.

But this is not always recognized nor understood by the white majority. What's amazing to me is how much in denial we are about these things. How the majority seems to fear that acceptance might somehow compromise their superior position in American society. There are countless numbers of people who will not or cannot fathom this reality. The fact that racism still exists and that people of color and other ethnicities feel left out of so much in the mainstream is a fact that if recognized would do wonders to our collective spirit. There is a richness in the diversity within the United States, a country in which the idea of the melting pot came to be celebrated, that many people have either never taken the time or had the curiosity to explore. Many people are only comfortable around people like themselves and deep down they fear what might happen if they opened themselves to the experience of others. Think about the large numbers of people who have the means to do so yet have never left this country to see another part of the world, another country, to meet its people and explore its culture.

I am not religious (nor antireligious, for that matter), but if this rich diversity is what is given us by God, or Buddha, or Allah, or simply the processes of human life operating over evolutionary time, how can we not want to embrace it all? Isn't that diversity in some way all of who we are? Much has been said about ours now being a global society, but hasn't it really always been that way? After all, as Americans, we're all from someplace else.

Since my journey, people ask me what it's like to have discovered I have black roots. How has my life changed? These questions, however, are loaded with different racial agendas depending on who's doing the asking. Black people don't ask me what it is like to be black, nor do they inquire of my passing whiteness, as passing is taboo in black America. There is, no matter what people say or even acknowledge, a great deal of diversity in the black community. No one leading black voice speaks for all black people.

White folks seem to expect me to have experienced shock, confusion, perhaps dismay mixed with anger and rejection. They are unable to hide their looks of disappointment and confusion when I tell them my life is simply fuller, richer, more complete. They want to know, have my relationships changed? Do I date black women? (Does it matter the color of the women I date?) Have my politics changed? Do I hang out in black nightclubs? What they fail to realize is that I am essentially the same person, the same human being. My color has not changed, my connections to people have not changed, I was the same before as I am now, only I'm out—that's right, I'm outted!

When I first discovered my black family, I became enamored with them. I visited my grandparents and relatives often, ate lots of soul food—although I had long been a frequent patron of Roscoe's House of Chicken and Waffles—and I was even engaged to a black woman for a short period of time. That, however, was a relationship disaster as I became thoroughly acquainted with what black men refer to as a gold digger. Yes, there are certainly cultural differences that most likely affect a portion of color-based dating. Yet as white America continues to embrace black culture and black America makes more inroads on acceptance in white America, those lines continue to shift and become blurred.

My sister remarked upon my discovery of a black father, "Damn, my brother's a brother!" And my mother worried that my rich Armenian roots would become buried under the embrace of my African-American heritage. I jumped on the black bandwagon, having been deprived for all those years of my total being. (On applications I checked the African-American box, as I figured "we" needed the numbers.) But after a while such swings have lessened in intensity. The ensuing years have given me a sense of culture, heritage, and belonging which up to this point in my life felt only half fulfilled by a rich Armenian tradition.

I don't expect everyone to understand my story, my journey to find myself, the confusion of my youth, the inability to connect with a father, the struggle to understand my place. If people still have so much trouble accepting other people's experiences different from theirs, then my story certainly will not resonate. Change, or even understanding it, is more than difficult; it is sometimes impossible.

Setting foot again in Los Angeles I found myself both exhausted and rejuvenated by the journey. I had discovered some remarkable things about myself, my family, my relationships with them.

Understanding the personal significance of the mountain I'd just climbed and piecing together its elements would take longer, as would figuring out what relevance it might have beyond myself. I knew — or thought I did — who I was, what I was, where I'd come from. What I didn't know at first was how to translate the richness of the odyssey into words, into my life. Knowing what I knew, how could I make sense of it all in order to convey it to others?

EPILOGUE

It took some time before I was finally able to flesh out the story of my journey, the odyssey whose description you hold in your hands. In the years following the road trip, I traveled back to Virginia Beach many times to delight in my grandparents' lives and stories. We shared many more of those fabulously cooked soul food delights, laughed over family photos, and together witnessed a biracial woman win a Best Actress Oscar Award. My father and I attempted to find more common ground upon which we could stand. There was art, and books and music, and sports, and more art discussed. Ethan would shuffle between my father—who had moved in with his parents following a quiet divorce from Sue—and his mother's in the outskirts of Virginia Beach. We'd gather every now and then, eat, talk, laugh, and promise to do it again. It was in this way we tried to forge our relationships together in the wake of so many missing years.

I do remain quite close to the family that raised me. Although Johnny remarried, my mom remained single, and my siblings and I navigate a sometimes awkward, sometimes deeply close relationship as we are spread across the globe. The age differences, geography, and diverse life experiences can sometimes make for challenging connections, yet we manage to take family trips to exotic places and laugh until we cry.

Meanwhile, I kept thinking I should tell my story. But how? To whom? And using what medium? Since my early school days I'd always been an actor and small-time writer for the stage. Long ago I started telling stories about my family to friends, then to strangers. I even worked a few into the leads I'd been asked to give at various twelve-step meetings and found the response to the story of my racial discovery quite encouraging. Soon I found myself a part of a storytelling group that met on a regular basis, and I began spinning yarns about the characters I'd met in my life while uncovering my extended family. I gradually began writing them down.

Then one day my sister Lora, of the tiny doll-like voice yet with the gift of creating beautiful and provocative works of art, suggested we should try and collaborate on something.

"What do you mean?" I queried.

"You know, art. We should find a way to make some kind of art together in someway or other."

"What exactly would that look like?"

"I don't know. Maybe you could read some of the stories you're writing and I could show some of the drawings I am working on?" she suggested innocently.

And that spring in her cooler than cool 4,000-square-foot artist's loft in the Bucktown section of Chicago, we gathered a group of friends and acquaintances for what we called a salon. Lora hung her latest groovy, mind-bending work on the walls, and people strolled, talked, and sipped wine. After an hour or so Lora walked over to where I was standing nervously, hands in pockets, talking with a friend.

"Are you ready, big boy?" she smiled an equally nervous smile, knowing the personal exposure that was about to occur.

"Oh God," I uttered, "I guess..."

"Let's do it, then," she replied. She encouraged folks to refill their drinks and gather around to hear some stories. The sixty or so who had made the excursion gathered around on couches, chairs, beds, even the floor, as I sat on a stool behind a music stand holding my script, an early version of these chapters. For an introduction, I sketched the nature of the odyssey, then stumbled recklessly into reading four or five chapters.

My confidence grew steadily over the course of the next forty minutes as people laughed, cried, and sat motionless until I came to a natural stopping point. Their enthusiastic applause greeted me with surprise as I sat drained from the emotional weight of what I was trying to express. Afterward, several people told me, "You should be doing this."

"I am," I told them, "I've been writing chapters for a book."

"No," they replied, "you should be performing this!"

As an actor I'd performed in a variety of shows and venues far and wide, but I'd never really been attracted to the idea of doing a one-man show. I assumed that's what they meant—performing my life story as a kind of one-man show on stage. I knew several performers whose genre is solo performance, but I enjoyed working with other actors. The idea of a one-man show about my own personal life seemed far too self-serving, self-indulgent.

And yet, at a second salon a few months later, different audience, I got the same response: "You should be doing this, performing this on stage!"

Thus I embarked on what would be another odyssey of sorts: a one-man solo performance on a cross-country tour that I've kept up now for over ten years. It began in Chicago on the most ominous of days, September 11, 2001, as I gathered a group of people to begin rehearsals for the "world" premier of the play, scheduled to be staged at the Bailiwick Theatre. The day was astonishing for both its tragic consequence across the globe and, personally, for the birth of what has turned out to be a performance project that has taken on a life of its own. Critical praise in Chicago propelled it to Kansas City in the fall of 2002 where it played in the Repertory Theatre to appreciative audiences. It was there I discovered during post-show talkbacks with several audiences that the piece had a way of opening doors for people to discuss an assortment of different personal and social issues: race, identity, divorce, adoption, family secrets, family histories, ethnic stereo-types, and so on. Audience members, both black and white, used it as a springboard for discussing with each other issues of race.

One night following a show during that run in Kansas City, I was informed by my stage manager there was an unidentified couple wait-ing to visit with me in the green room. Since I knew no one in the Kansas City area, my interest was piqued as to who this mysterious cou-ple might be. I quickly changed out of my performance clothes and made my way upstairs to the backstage waiting room. I was met there by a young couple, wife and husband, who appeared to be white. They had dressed for the theater wearing what might be their Sunday best and when I approached them, they nervously straightened themselves out as if to seem more presentable.

"Hello," I greeted them with a hand extended, "I understand you requested to meet with me. Michael, I'm pleased to meet you."

The wife smiling appreciatively stuck out her hand to meet mine.

"Darcy," she offered, "so pleased to meet you. Thank you so much for your time, and for the wonderful performance. This is my husband, Dominick...he wanted to meet you."

I turned to face her husband and saw in him what had gone unno-ticed in me most my life. My blackdar detected that he was unmistak-ably mixed and quite obviously deeply shaken as his eyes filled with water and his verbal skills failed to materialize. He attempted to talk, to say something, anything, then glanced at his wife for help as he strug-gled to keep the tears from flowing down his cheeks. She looked at him with the biggest heart imaginable, then offered me,

"He wants to tell you how much we both enjoyed the show. It was...it was...truly a remarkable story. We...he..." And then her verbal skills began to fail as well.

I did the only thing I could think of which was to reach for him and hug him with all the empathy I had, knowing full well he was me. I told his story.

We embraced in what can sometimes be that awkward manly hug and yet for some reason neither of us could let go. Finally backing away he looked at me, tears now streaming down his face, and offered what little he could manage to choke out.

"Thank you," he said, "thank you for telling your story." But I knew it was his as well.

For me, it was a lightbulb-goes-on moment. As I set out to perform the show across the country time and time again I was struck at how deeply moving the play became for audience members. Most strikingly however, I noticed how it allowed people to open up and dialogue about race and identity.

As a result, between 2005 and today, I have traveled the country performing the show for audiences at high schools, colleges, theaters, performing arts centers, festivals, corporations, government agencies and military installations, and then engaging people in post-performance dialogue about race and identity. I have learned a great deal, not only about my craft as an actor—after all, the school gym or auditorium can be a scary place to perform a one-man show in front of hundreds of attention-deprived middle & high school students—but a great deal about people's attitudes about race, stereotypes, and identity.

As I repeatedly perform the story of my life, I am continually amazed at how the story resonates with people of all ages and colors, from all walks of life. And because of this performance journey, the gift of being able to share my story, I have found there are many people like myself, young and old, still searching for who they are and how they fit in. The story of my life's journey has become not only a way to open a door for others, but a way for me to continue to explore, discover, and embrace all that is good—and bad—with that which surrounds us in American society and beyond. After all, our "identities"—who we are, how we present ourselves, and how we perceive each other—is absolutely fundamental to our experience as human beings.

SPECIAL THANKS

First and foremost my entire family:
Adrienne, Johnny, Christopher, Lora, Sid, all my grandparents,
aunts and uncles, cousins, and Gay....
All of 'em!

Jonathan Cobb for whom I owe a great deal of gratitude.
Dick Russell for whom I owe even more.
Mark Spector
A big thanks to Siobhan Drummond
Tom Greensfelder
The Forthill family
Jane Nichols-Sahlins & Bernie Sahlins
Alice Austen, LeVan Hawkins, Todd Logan, Gary Houston
Jo LeSoine, David Marciano, Carol Gifford, Rhonda Hampton
Danny Goldring, Bud Beyer, Michael Cullen, Peter Altman
Michael E. Myers
John Reinhardt
David Zak, Cecilie Keenan, Tommy Spiroff, Wallace Norman, Andi Dymond,
Constance Mortell, Etel Billig, Steve Scott, Jacqueline Beatka, Sue Betz,
Brian Perkinson, Lynn Baber, Matt Dudley, John Johnson, Jonathan Becker,
Kate Mulligan, Lyle Kanouse, Kilberg Reedy, Ronald E. Feiner, David Saltiel,
Maureen Murdock, Jake Cohen, Wanda Feldman, Randy Ryan,
Bass-Schuler Entertainment, Wolfman Productions, DHS Literary,
Richard Christensen, Lisa Beth Allen, Dr. Julian Earls, Dr. Eric Mizuno,
Don & Janemarie King, William & Janine Corrin, Sue Gifford & Marty Pollack
Larry Litzky
Ernie Lane, Cecil Averett, Chris Clepper, Don Bapst, Billy Carey, Mary Honour,
Mike Tutaj, Clover Morell, Marni Keenan, Sarah Rose Graber, Laura Smith Muir,
Coco Soodek, Scott Pink, Frank Karall
20th Century TV and Stereo Center

And to all the people who have written me over the years after seeing the play:
I am continually honored the story resonates with you. By sharing your
enthusiasm for the play you have kept me going year after year.

MICHAEL SIDNEY FOSBERG

Upon graduating with a BFA degree in theater from the University of Minnesota ('79), Michael cofounded the Small Change Original Theater in Minneapolis, where he wrote and directed tours of educational shows throughout Minnesota, Wisconsin, and North and South Dakota. Returning to Chicago in the early '80s he became involved with the Steppenwolf, Remains, Wisdom Bridge, and Goodman theaters, eventually cofounding the Huron Theater Ensemble. He ventured to Los Angeles in the late '80s and served as the director of education for the Living Library Theatre and as a teacher/director for South Coast Repertory's Young Actors Conservatory program. Moving back to Chicago in the late '90s, he was hired to write and direct much of the family entertainment at Navy Pier. In the summers, he can be found on the campus of Northwestern University, where he teaches acting and directs productions as a part of the National High School Institute "Cherubs" Theater Arts program.

Over the past twelve years he has been working to create a national dialogue on race and identity since launching his one-man autobiographical play *Incognito*. The author-actor-activist has performed his play throughout the United States at hundreds of arts venues & educational institutions, and his unique brand of diversity training has brought him before major corporations & government agencies throughout the country, including Alaska Airlines, Morgan Stanley, NASA, the Social Security Administration, the

National Training Center for the U.S. Army at Ft. Irwin, the FBI, Wells Fargo Bank, HCA Healthcare, The Mayo Clinic, and many others.

As a result of performing his own life story and the dialogue he facilitates with audiences across the country, he has frequently been featured in the media sharing his expertise on current race and identity issues. Michael has appeared on CNN, NPR, HLN, Public Radio International, Sirius-XM Radio, American Urban Radio Networks, *The Takeaway*, *The Tom Joyner Morning Show*, *The Tavis Smiley Show*, among many other outlets.

He is currently working on a screenplay version of this story, along with his latest book, tentatively titled, *Nobody Wants to Talk About It...ten years in the trenches talking about race, stereotypes, & identity*.

QUESTIONS AND TOPICS FOR DISCUSSION:

1. In "The Valley", Michael begins to question the concept of family. How important is it to see yourself reflected in those you grow up around? What impact does adoption—albeit in Michael's case by only his step-father—have on an adoptee's sense of self and family?

   In later chapters Michael talks about the awkwardness of sharing information about his biological father with his siblings. He is especially uncomfortable about this revelation with his stepfather, John Fosberg, the man who raised him. Should families discuss adoption more openly? What kind of information do you think should be shared? Or not shared? Michael's stepfather was shocked when he was told of Michael's biological father's race. This exposes the issue of family secrets and how they are or aren't shared. Do all families have secrets? Does your family have a secret?

   Later in the book, while visiting a farm in Kansas inhabited by a group of friends calling themselves a family, Michael begins to question the concept of how a family is formed. What is family? Can you create a family with those who are not blood related?

2. In the discovery of his biological father, Michael uncovers the fact that his father is black, African-American, colored, or...? What is the preferred term? Is there a universal acceptance of one term over another? With this discovery, Michael realizes that he is not simply "white" but also half "black". What would it feel like to discover you are not the person you thought you were? That you have a family, a history, and ethnicity you were unaware of. How would this discovery impact your life, the lives of those around you, your vision of yourself and society?

3. Michael's friend Tommy offers him some poignant advice on why he should forgive his mother for not telling him about his biological father. It has been said that forgiveness is the most difficult work we are ever asked to do, but the most rewarding. Can you describe a time or instance when that may have applied to you?

4. One of Michael's strong early family memories surrounding race happened during extended family dinners. His uncle was guilty of using the

"N" word, causing Michael confusion and discomfort. These episodes occurred during the 1960's, a time commonly associated with the Civil Rights Movement. Talk about that period, what it was like, what you personally remember, the language that was used back then, and the groundbreaking events that took place. Michael's uncle was Jewish, did this inform his world view? What kinds of things did Jew's experience during that time? Is it fair to compare the Jewish experience with that of Blacks?

5. Once Michael discovers his African-American roots and shares this with black friends, many claim to have known! He then begins to recall incidents in his life which could have provided clues to his black heritage. Many black families have a wide variety of shades within their blood. Can you tell the race or ethnicity of someone simply by looking at their features/skin? What is race? Is it a social construct? Did you know that scientists believe there are more differences within a race than between races?

6. The letter Michael receives from Sid's wife (A Holding Pattern) in which she expresses her unwillingness to accept Michael for having been brought up white, raises many issues around "passing". First of all, what is "passing", and why would anyone want to pass for something they are not? Michael discovers he has been "passing" his entire life and didn't know it…or was he? What is white privilege? (Page 143)

7. At the end of the chapter; Conviction (Page 148), as his own absentee father is lead off to prison, Michael questions the function of black men as fathers and the role they do or don't play in the lives of their children. Why is this phenomenon an American crisis? What role does a father play in their son's life?

8. Throughout later chapters in interviews with members of Michael's black family, it is revealed that race played a significant role in the dissolution of his parent's marriage. Do you think race still plays a significant role in biracial marriages? If so, what ways would it be the same, or different?

9. Michael's half-brother Ethan is Jewish and black, living in the South, surrounded by racist overtones. In what ways do we discriminate based on religion as well as race?

10. There is a good deal of information about Michael's Armenian family past and present. What did you know about the Armenian's prior to reading this? Does this somehow feel like a lost history? How are dif-

ferent immigrant family stories related? What are our current immigrant stories about?

11. Michael learns later about his mother's struggle with leaving his father in Boston through the letters his father kept. How different (or similar) might this struggle be today? In the late 1950's there were certainly biracial people, yet we either did not refer to them this way, or they did not self-identify as such. How has that changed today? Michael's cousin Harry Leroy suggests that as a black man married to a white woman, he "functions very comfortably in the black culture. But the black culture in places like Boston is less hospitable to Nancy (his wife) then the white culture is to me." Do you think there are differences in the way each community—black & white—accept or shun blacks or whites? Do you think there are regional differences? Are there differences caused within economic spheres? Would there be differences if the couple were a black woman and a white man?

12. With the price of higher education escalating out of reach for many, do you think Roy's (Michael's grandfather) assessment for the reason of Norfolk State University's low graduation rates is accurate? (Page 283)

13. How do you define yourself? Do you think identity is simple or complicated? Do you think that the way you see yourself is how other people see you? Do our identities change over time and if so, how?

FOR FURTHER STUDY:

BOOKS

To Kill a Mocking Bird, Harper Lee

Black Like Me, John Howard Griffin

The Help, Kathryn Stockett

The Immortal Life of Henrietta Lacks, Rebecca Skloot

The Color of Water, James McBride

The Warmth of Other Suns, Isabel Wilkerson

Invisible Man, Ralph Ellison

The Adventures of Huck Finn, Mark Twain

Puddin Head Wilson, Mark Twain

White Teeth, Zadie Smith

Midnight's Children, Salmon Rushdie

The Color Purple, Alice Walker

Americanah, Chimamanda Ngozi Adichie

Kingsblood Royal, Sinclair Lewis

On the Road, Jack Kerouac

Travels With Charley, John Steinbeck

Black, White and Jewish, Rebecca Walker

Long Walk to Freedom, Nelson Mandela

Black Genius, Dick Russell

The Autobiography of an Ex-Colored Man, James Weldon Johnson

Dreams from my Father, Barack Obama

Black Dog of Fate, Peter Balakian

Why are all the Black Kids Sitting Together in the Cafeteria, Beverly Daniel Tatum

A Hope in the Unseen, Ron Suskind

A Country of Strangers, David K. Shipler

Body & Soul, Frank Conroy

Beloved, Toni Morrison

John Henry Days, Colson Whitehead

PLAYS

A Raisin in The Sun, Lorraine Hansberry

Clybourne Park, Bruce Norris

Race, David Mamet

Luck of the Irish, Kirsten Greenidge

The plays of August Wilson

Driving Miss Daisy, Alfred Uhry

Indians, Arthur Kopit (also made into a movie by Robert Altman)

Superior Donuts, Tracy Letts

A Taste of Honey, Shelagh Delaney

MOVIES

Crash (2004)

Grand Canyon (1991)

American History X (1998)

The Laramie Project, (TV 2002, available on video)

Boys Don't Cry (1999)

Angels in America (2003 TV mini-series available on video)

The Crying Game (1992)

Guess Who's Coming to Dinner? (1967)

Higher Learning (1995)

Imitation of Life (two versions; 1934 & 1959)

Do the Right Thing (1989)

Bamboozled (2000)

Hairspray (2007)

Westside Story (1961)

Mississippi Masala (1991)

Mississippi Burning (1988)

Boycott (TV 2001 available on video)

Rosewood (1997)

Slumdog Millionaire (2008)

INCOGNITO
THE PLAY

Incognito, a theatrical presentation, has been presented at theaters, performing arts centers, middle schools, high schools, colleges and universities, military bases, and corporations across the country (and in the Bahamas). After each show, I have had the privilege to engage audiences of all colors, young and old, in candid dialogue about identity, race, stereotypes, family history, adoption, and finding a father. In some respects I have been considered a diversity speaker, although what I present is hardly a speech. My one-man play is intended to be both a dynamic dramatic presentation and a refreshingly personal but non-threatening approach to tackling these often divisive issues. The play allows audience members to gain insight on their own personal journeys, enabling them to open up in ways traditional methods often don't allow.

I offer two versions of the play: a 50-minute presentation which generally fits within school assembly parameters and utilizes a couple of props and a few sound cues, and a 75-minute version which can be staged minimally or with a full complement of set, props, sound, and projections, depending upon the venue's technical capabilities. The 75-minute version is generally only performed during a run at a theater.

If you would like more information about a presentation for your organization, email us: or write to us:

info@incognitotheplay.com   Incognito, Inc.
or visit our website: 6110 N. Francisco Ave.
www.incognitotheplay.com   Chicago, IL 60659

"Emotionally gripping, his presentation of his life journey provided our audience with a face-to-face encounter with the meaning of racial identity and challenged us all to examine our assumptions about our own identity in this multicultural world."
—Choate Rosemary Hall, Wallingford, CT

"Your story is a message that needs to be shared far and wide."
—Director of Education & Training, Mayo Clinic

"You have an amazing gift and definitely inspired the Wells Fargo team." —VP Diversity & Inclusion, Wells Fargo Bank

"By far the BEST session in several years of this conference."
—conf. attendee, The Multicultural Forum on Workplace Diversity

"The discussion after was very inspiring, motivating, and meaningful. I can't stress enough...the talk after was GREAT!"
—Student, Penn St. University, Great Valley